International Political Economy Series

Series Editor

Timothy M. Shaw, Emeritus Professor, University of Massachusetts
Boston, Boston, MA, USA;
University of London, London, UK

The global political economy is in flux as a series of cumulative crises impacts its organization and governance. The IPE series has tracked its development in both analysis and structure over the last three decades. It has always had a concentration on the global South. Now the South increasingly challenges the North as the centre of development, also reflected in a growing number of submissions and publications on indebted Eurozone economies in Southern Europe. An indispensable resource for scholars and researchers, the series examines a variety of capitalisms and connections by focusing on emerging economies, companies and sectors, debates and policies. It informs diverse policy communities as the established trans-Atlantic North declines and 'the rest', especially the BRICS, rise.

NOW INDEXED ON SCOPUS!

Rina Kashyap

The Political Economy of Security/Development in the Neoliberal Age

R2P and the UN

palgrave
macmillan

Rina Kashyap
Lady Shri Ram College for Women
University of Delhi
New Delhi, India

ISSN 2662-2483 ISSN 2662-2491 (electronic)
International Political Economy Series
ISBN 978-3-031-37278-0 ISBN 978-3-031-37279-7 (eBook)
https://doi.org/10.1007/978-3-031-37279-7

This Palgrave Macmillan imprint is published by the registered company Springer Nature Switzerland AG
The registered company address is: Gewerbestrasse 11, 6330 Cham, Switzerland

To My Parents

Acknowledgements

It is a privilege to reside in the ivory tower to engage in a life of the mind. Lest this advantage turn into a luxury of incubating lazy whimsical ideas, the admonishing ethical gaze reveals this privilege as being made possible by the social burden shouldered by fellow human beings. Randhir Singh's exhortation—the task of social sciences is *change* and this involves figuring out what are the right questions and if need be, changing the terms of debate—was always at the back of my mind in the entirety of this research quest. This book emerges from my doctoral project under the supervision of James Busumtwi-Sam who generously continued to make time to guide me even after his institutional obligation to me was long over. He obviously does not subscribe to the book's often-repeated neoliberal dictum of 'market as a site of truth veridiction.' James ensured that the pursuit be punctuated by critical interrogations of the realities of the global and local. His mentorship involved patient erasures of my frequent self-doubts, allowing me the freedom to unboundedly explore and stretch the boundaries of my research question. Thus, un-caged, the question's answer(s) could rightfully transgress the borders of the subfields in the International Relations/Political Science discipline(s). It is only in retrospect that I can appreciate the dexterity with which he guided me to lose myself without getting lost.

Intellectual enrichment also came from others. In Laurent Dobuzinskis, I encountered the most genial 'devil's advocate' questioning my premises. The encouraging nod to my 'right intuitions' by Rob B.J.

Walker, who encountered a version of this book as my doctoral external examiner, was crucial in this venture. His advice and challenge—to make my conclusion the premise of my *next* research—ensure that this subject will continue to unsettle me and be with me for some time to come.

I appreciate the encouragement received from Simon Fraser University's Political Science Department faculty—Tsuyoshi Kawasaki, Anil Hira, David Laycock, Marjorie Cohen, Aude-Claire Fourot, and Douglas Ross. Conversations with Bruce Baum (University of British Columbia) and Howard Zehr (Eastern Mennonite University) helped me think through the research problem. Thank you to Shantala Singh, Sherry Lloyd, Bryn Dharmaratne, Lynn Kool, and Eliza So—their 'administration' ensured that problems of quotidian logistics of university graduate life did not side-track me.

I recognize and deeply appreciate that some of the scholars/practitioners—Thomas Weiss, Ramesh Thakur, Andrea Bartoli, Simon Adams, Lisa Schirch, and Jayne Docherty went out of the way to accommodate the interview sessions in their tightly packed schedules. I am grateful to Jean Marie Guehenno for sidestepping the red-tape to host me as a Visiting Fellow at the Center for International Conflict Resolution, School of International and Public Affairs, Columbia University. He plucked an hour out of his brief one-day stopover in New York—before heading back for crisis resolution talks in another continent—to give me the interview. I was humbled by this gesture of generosity which was based solely on the perceived intent and promise of my research. Incidents like this embolden you to do your bit to upend modernity's bane of a 'society of strangers.'

Similarly, the GCR2P and ICR2P staff made time for the interviews even as they were engaged with the frenetic advocacy activity at the UN on the developing Syrian Crisis. My late friend and classmate, the ever effervescent, Kumar Jha Anuraj, and another friend at the UN who wishes to remain anonymous, facilitated my access to the UN and snowballed several interviews with UN officials for me. The OSAPG officials' commitment and belief in R2P were evident, they were frank and forthcoming about their work and directed me to their colleagues in other UN Departments—including UNDP, UNDPA, UNDPKO, OCHA, and UNOCC—engaged in the R2P mandate. I applaud their commitment. I thank all my interviewees for sharing their views on R2P with remarkable candour.

The grants and scholarships from Social Sciences and Humanities Research Council, (Joseph-Armand Bombardier CGS Doctoral Scholarship; Michael Smith Foreign Travel Study Supplement) and Simon Fraser University were crucial in facilitating my field trips and in helping me devote some exclusive time to research.

I am grateful to my colleagues—Pamela Batra and Anita Bagai—for generously sharing my administrative workload during the writing phase. Renu Behl guided me through my anxieties and doubts about impending submission dates and the frequent writer's block. Discussions with Neera Chandoke and her sharp observations, premised on the intersection of political theory and international relations, were invaluable in the manuscript's revisions. Thanks also to Hardip Rawat for his expeditious processing of the leave application paperwork and to Kamla Rawat at the LSR Library for helping me access books including those not on the shelf.

Accompanying me on this journey are a host of other teachers, colleagues, friends, and family. There are friends—Anjali Bhatia (persuasive out of box observations), Anna Barrera, Ravindra Karnena, and Ivan Jankovich—who were stimulating interlocutors on the subject. Aseema Sinha and Asma Hashmi read portions of the manuscript in its many draft avatars, I am grateful for their comments. Aseema Sinha introduced me to her contacts at the World Bank. Atul Chaturvedi made available his personal collection of books. Julie MacArthur and Smita Sahgal were my 'go to persons' for advice on a scholar's rites of passage. Friends—Lisa O'Hara, Lynne Cruz, Margaret Johnson, Saloni Prabhakar, and Anish Sharma—whose hearths and homes were my comfort zones in New York, New Westminster, Burnaby, and Washington DC respectively. Then there are friends whose spirited cheers made the finishing line appear within a not so difficult reach—Anja Novak, Nancy Teeple, and Daniel D. Guedes de Andrade, Rajiv Sharma, Tejinder Kaur Juneja, Jayshree Yamunan, Serder Kaya, Nilofar Sakhi, Fadi El Hajjar, Samina Shahid, Denis Dogah and Bouchra Kachoub, Shweta Singh, Paranjoy Bordoloi, Ruchi Bhargava, Bunny Chawla, and Nevart Khatchadourian. And when the cursor on the screen stubbornly blinked for days at a stationary point, a friend's advice about the art of the (re)start of the introduction spurred me on the fast track.

The last one year and a half has been one of personal challenges that could have sealed the fate of this project if it were not for the support of both Timothy Shaw and Anca Pusca at Palgrave Macmillan. Timothy

Shaw guided me to the latest developments on the subject matter, his wit and humour ensured that this book enterprise be a happy one. I am grateful and appreciative of Anca Pusca's faith in this project, her immense patience and support as I missed the submission dates more than a couple of times.

I am grateful to Meenakshi Gopinath who as principal of Lady Shri Ram College played a crucial role in my getting a sabbatical from teaching to pursue this research. Enormous amount of student debt (of the non-financial type) is owed to her for guiding me in my very first research paper *Communalism* and teaching me to look for hidden linkages.

Rahil Kashyap was always a smile away. My late aunt, Janak Dang, had made herself available 24/7 and provided emotional anchorage. Neelima Sharma, Nama Kashyap Boury, Sudhir Boury, and Anamra Kashyap Boury—have been my taken for granted fellow travellers and empathetic worriers. This student's progress would not have been possible without her first teachers—papa and ma. My father (Virender Kumar Kashyap) encouraged and respected my questions which emerged from the base built by my mother (Pushpa Kashyap). In these years she has stood by me, given me strength and faith—in ways only a mother can—in my ability to take this project to its conclusion.

Contents

Acronyms

APR2P	Asia Pacific Centre on Responsibility to Protect
AU	African Union
CGG	Commission on Global Governance
CHS	Commission on Human Security
CSS	Critical Security Studies
DAD	Development Assistance Committee
DCD	Development Co-Operation Directorate
ECOWAS	Economic Community of West African States
FFF	Freedom from Fear
FFW	Freedom from Want
FOA	Framework of Analysis
GCR2P	Global Centre for Responsibility to Protect
HDR	Human Development Report
HS	Human Security
HSU	Human Security Unit
ICC	International Criminal Court
ICDSI	Independent Commission on Disarmament and Security Issues
ICIDI	The Independent Commission on International Development
ICISS	International Commission on Intervention and State Sovereignty
ICRtoP	International Coalition for Responsibility to Protect
IDP	Internally Displaced People
IFI	International Financial Institutions
ILC	International Law Commission

ILO	International Labour Organization
IMF	International Monetary Fund
IR	International Relations
ISIS	Islamic State of Iraq and Syria
MINURCAT	United Nations Mission in the Central African Republic and Chad
MINUSCA	United Nations Multidimensional Integrated Stabilization Mission in the Central African Republic
MINUSMA	United Nations Multidimensional Integrated Stabilization Mission in Mali
MINUSTAH	United Nations Stabilization Mission in Haiti
MONUC	United Nations Organization Mission in the Democratic Republic of the Congo
MONUSCA	United Nations Organization Stabilization Mission in the Democratic Republic of the Congo
NIEO	New International Order
OHCHR	Office of the United Nations High Commissioner for Human Rights
ONUB	United Nations Operation in Burundi
OSAPG	Office of the Special Adviser on Prevention of Genocide
P5	Permanent Five (at the UN Security Council)
R2P or RtoP	Responsibility to Protect
RwP	Responsibility While Protecting
SAPG	Special Adviser on Prevention of Genocide
SAR2P	Special Adviser on Responsibility to Protect
UN	United Nations
UNAMID	African Union-United Nations Hybrid Operation in Darfur
UNAOC	United Nations Alliance of Civilizations
UNCTAD	United Nations Conference on Trade and Development
UNDESA	Department of Economic and Social Affairs
UNDOCO	United Nations Department Operations Coordination Office
UNDP	United Nations Development Programme
UNDPA or DPA	United Nations Department of Political Affairs
UNDPKO or DPKO	United Nations Department of Peacekeeping Operations
UNEP	United Nations Environment Programme
UNESCO	United Nations Economic and Social Council
UNFPA	United Nations Population Fund[1]

[1] The acronym UNFPA originally denoted United Nation's Fund for Population Activities.

UNGA or GA	United Nations General Assembly
UNGC	United Nations Global Compact
UNHCR	United Nations High Commissioner for Refugees
UNHRC or HRC	United Nations Human Rights Council
UNICEF	United Nations Children's Fund[2]
UNIFIL	United Nations Interim Force in Lebanon
UNISFA	United Nations Organization Interim Security Force for Abyei
UNITAR	United Nations Institute for Training and Research
UNMIL	United Nations Mission in Liberia
UNMIS	United Nations Mission in the Sudan
UNMISET	United Nations Mission of Support in East Timor
UNMISS	United Nations Mission in the Republic of South Sudan
UNMIT	United Nations Integrated Mission in Timor-Leste
UNOCC or OCC	United Nations Operations and Crisis Centre
UNOCHA or OCHA	United Nations Office for the Coordination of Humanitarian Affairs
UNOCI	United Nations Operation in Cote D'Ivoire
UNODC	United Nations Office on Drugs and Crime
UNOGPR2P	United Nations Office on Genocide Prevention and the Responsibility to Protect
UNOMSIL	United Nations Observer Mission in Sierra Leone
UNPBC	United Nations Peacebuilding Commission
UNPBSO	United Nations Peacebuilding Support Office
UNPKO	United Nations Peacekeeping Operations
UNSC or SC	United Nations Security Council
UNSG or SG	United Nations Secretary-General
UNSMIS	United Nations Supervision Mission in Syria
UNTAET	United Nations Transitional Administration in East Timor
USG	Under-Secretary-General
WCED	The World Commission on Environment and Development
WFM-IGP	World Federalist Movement - Institute for Global Policy
WWII	World War II

[2] The acronym UNICEF originall denoted United Nation's International Children's Fund.

CHAPTER 1

Introduction

Genocide in its modern articulations is the non-admissible culmination of our times. So, is 'responsibility to protect' (R2P)—an admissible institutionalized measure to prevent atrocity crimes—a discursive articulation of the 'banality' of modern genocide?

The concept of R2P as a response to situations of violent conflict and insecurity was first formally articulated by the International Commission on Intervention and State Sovereignty (ICISS Report) (2001), and subsequently endorsed by the United Nations General Assembly (UNGA) through the World Summit Outcome Document (WSOD) 2005. Since then, the UN has been the context of several activities related to R2P.[1] The political and security significance of these developments is indicated by the proliferating academic and policy literature on R2P.[2] R2P's

[1] See A/RES/63/308; A/RES/60/1; A/63/677; S/2007/721; A/64/864.

[2] See Banda (2007), Bellamy (2008, 2009), Breau (2006), Bruennee and Toope (2006), Cooper and Kohler (2009), Etzioni (2006), Herro (2015), Hoffmann and Nollkaemper (2012a, b), Luck (2008), Reinold (2013), Thakur (2004, 2005, 2006, 2020), Thakur and Maley (2015), Warner (2003), Weiss and Hubert (2001), Wheeler (2005), and World Federalist Movement-International Policy Group (2003). Routledge has a 22 book series—4 of which are to be published in 2023—edited by Alex Bellamy, Sara E. Davies, and Monica Serrano, on Global Politics and the Responsibility to Protect (see http://www.routledge.com/books/series/GPRP/).

R. Kashyap, *The Political Economy of Security/Development in the Neoliberal Age*, International Political Economy Series,
https://doi.org/10.1007/978-3-031-37279-7_1

endorsement by the UN General Assembly (UNGA)—that serves as a source of international legitimacy (see Claude 1984; Weiss and Daws 2007) signalled R2P's entry into the UN. Six years later the UN Security Council sanctioned military operation in Libya in the name of R2P (S/RES/1973/2011). R2P advocates celebrate this mandate for the first coercive operation under R2P as evidence of its rapid maturation into a norm (2001–2011) (Evans 2012; Lotze 2014; Thakur 2011); indeed, the R2P norm is now part of the vocabulary of diplomacy, policy, and practice (Labonte 2016: 145). Even the rueing over the failure of the international community to apply R2P for atrocity prevention in Myanmar (Mennecke and Stensurd 2021: 111–130) is indicative of the hope and expectations that are still riding on R2P in our crisis—financial, climate, and political—punctuated times.

This book expands the conversation on R2P by locating it in the historical context of changes in the liberal/neoliberal[3] security/development dispositif—institutions, practices, regulations, laws, scientific statements, philosophical, moral propositions, etc.—which have informed the UN system's policies and programs since its inception. The institutional and operational manifestations of R2P as a security *and* development response when compared with that of other recent UN-supported commissions on similar issues show that R2P has received strong advocacy within the UN and that it fits into the latter's conceptualization of security and development.

The location of R2P in the UN's liberal/neoliberal security/development dispositif is evidence of the fact that global economy imperatives, operating on the principle of the free market, shape the role of the UN in the international arena (and in the respective domestic sphere of its member states). The liberal and neoliberal modes of the UN are best understood as points on a liberal continuum that differ only in terms of their recommendations regarding the *degree* and *type* of intervention by international institutions and the state. Despite its premise of a restrictive role for non-market entities in the market, neoliberal economic policy has necessitated a greater role for the state and international institutions (such as the UN); that *greater role* has meant enhancement of responsibility of these institutions in some areas even as they are in retreat from

[3] In addition to Michel Foucault's Birth of Biopolitics, the term neoliberal (and neoliberalism) in this book draws from the global political economy literature (see Cox 1987; Craig and Porter 2006; Gill 1995; Harvey 2007; Peck 2010; Plehwe et al. 2006).

others. The concept of 'responsibility' in R2P is an example of the same imperative.

R2P's stated aim—to ensure the protection of people from atrocity crime—that is, to prevent the loss of human life from *physical* violence, there must be a provision of security, specifically physical security. This book moves away from the dominant literature's view of R2P—as a security measure—to argue instead that it is a security/development measure. This is the *first* point. The circularity of the relationship between security and development, dynamics more adequately captured by the term security/development rather than security-development nexus.[4]

In R2P's conceptualization development refers to ad hoc and discrete economic social policies such as 'targeted economic development assistance,' 'improving education' and creating a robust civil society (Bellamy 2015: 47). The argument of R2P as a security/development measure, on the other hand, is that the need for R2P like measures is a *consequence of certain kind of development practices*. The political unrest (and othering) that neoliberal economic policies yield heightens ethnic and religious tensions leading to different minorities in different parts of the country being scapegoated for the economic hardships generated by market forces (see Fischer 2020; Gudavarthy and Vijay 2020). The consequences create congenial conditions for violence, scapegoating, and atrocity crimes. To end atrocity crime requires changing that development paradigm (and practice). The political dilemma of choosing between saving human lives and particular development path is resolved via a compromise in which atrocity crime is *contained*—in terms of numbers, duration, and geographical spread—within the existing development framework via protection measures such as R2P.

What is this development? The word *development* here is a question of political economy—a liberal/neoliberal political economy—I use the terms (embedded)liberal[5] and neoliberal political economy, since contemporary scholarship prefers these nomenclatures over that of the *outdated term*, capitalism. The free market is central to both embedded liberalism and neoliberalism, though both differ in terms of degrees in their quest for the 'aspired purity' of the market. The *second* point is that in the

[4] The relationship between security and development is not peculiar to the neoliberal age, it can be traced to the era of colonialism (see Duffield 2006).

[5] In the book the word liberal when used in the coinage *liberal/neoliberal* denotes embedded liberalism.

neoliberal age, R2P is a debris collector of the responsibilities left behind by the receded embedded liberalism.

Since R2P embodies measures that are in conjunction with the liberal/neoliberal security/development ethos, it is not surprising that R2P has got so quickly incorporated in the UN. This incorporation is merely a discursive rearticulation not a discursive shift in the UN's liberal/neoliberal security/development dispositif. This is the book's *third point*.

Context of R2P

UN's promotion of R2P since 2005 entails a number of institutional and operational initiatives which indicate R2Ps incorporation into the UN. These include the appointment of the Special Adviser on the R2P (SAR2P) and the addition of the R2P portfolio into the Office of the Special Adviser for the Prevention of Genocide (OSAPG) at the UN. Further, in 2012 the UN Secretary-General (UNSG) directed the SAR2P to 'lead a system-wide assessment' of how tools available under the UN Charter 'specifically Chapters VI, VIII and VIIII' can be employed for atrocity crime prevention (Ban Ki-moon 2012). R2P advocates are quick to claim certain international interventions as instances of R2P success stories, examples include the UN response to the violence following the 2008 elections in Kenya (Sharma 2016) and the 2011 elections in Cote D'Ivoire (Savas-Cazala 2022), and the Security Council authorized 2011 military intervention in Libya (Thakur and Maley 2015: 3).[6] R2P advocates took the lead to condemn the civilian killings in the Syrian Civil War—after the Arab Spring in 2011—and pressed for an international response. The continuation of atrocity crimes in 'Central African Republic, the Democratic Republic of the Congo, the Democratic People's Republic of Korea, Iraq, Libya, Nigeria, South Sudan, the Sudan, the Syrian Arab Republic and Yemen' underline the need and therefore, relevance of R2P (A/69/981-S/2015/500/para1). The relevance of R2P has only grown in our crisis afflicted times, let's take two examples: (a). the deteriorating situation of climate change (and its consequences of water and food shortages, migration and loss of traditional livelihoods, particularly in the Global South); (b) the onset of

[6] International engagements in Guinea and Kyrgyzstan that prevented the recurrence of atrocity crimes too are claimed as examples of R2P success (A/69/981-S/2015/500/para8).

the pandemic era presaged by COVID-19. Such conditions exacerbate atrocity crimes as they increase pre-existing structural inequalities to the detriment of the already vulnerable communities, thus the *urgent need* of R2P.[7]

R2P is not without its detractors such as Noam Chomsky (2009) who place R2P in the long lineage of imperial interventions. The criticism gained credence with those who believed that the military intervention in Libya was a ruse for 'regime change' (Campbell 2013; Findlay 2011; Kuperman 2013; Ralph and Gallagher 2015; Thakur 2013; Wouters et al. 2012). Others argue that in the context of the unchanged reality of the politics of the Permanent Five (P5) at the UN Security Council and the persistence of national interest considerations, R2P is structurally disabled to auger a 'new era' (Hehir 2013b: 158; also see Bellamy 2009; Weiss 2011).

A body of work—some empirical, some normative—seeks to save R2P from the above pessimistic dismissal. More recently, there is a concerted focus on the private sector's responsibility in constructing peace (Forrer and Seyle 2016; Ruggie 2008; Seyle and Aloye 2015). This push for the private sector to play a proactive and constructive role in prevention of atrocity crimes uses the trope of pragmatism and morality. Since the site of atrocity crime would be similar to the Hobbesian *state of war of all against all* where there is *no art, no culture, no industry*,[8] it would make sense for the private sector to invest in measures that ensure political stability—a prerequisite for market stability. There are case studies detailing how certain Global North states work towards ensuring that revenue of extractive industries not be used to finance conflict (Shankleman 2016). And if this rationale can be enmeshed with the upscaling of corporate social responsibility as a contributor to the R2P agenda, then such *best practices* of the business world would be a great source of legitimacy. Chapter 4 of the book refers to this matter briefly to point out how the UN and R2P advocates work towards expanding the circle of stakeholders in R2P by including various non-state actors. John Ruggie's reports—'UN Global Compact' and 'UN Guiding Principles on Business and Human Rights,' as the *UN Assistant Secretary-General for Strategic Planning* and the *UN*

[7] https://www.cfg.polis.cam.ac.uk/commentary/there-responsibility-protect-world-pandemics.

[8] See Hobbes (1985: 185–186).

Secretary-General's Special Representative for Business and Human Rights are important contributions in this regard. Both reports put forward a concept of social responsibility (a la embedded liberalism) and seek to cushion the harsh consequences of the neoliberal market. The optics of corporate social responsibility (CSR) is of immense significance for the business community to legitimate its profits, but we must acknowledge that there are in this field genuine bleeding hearts and well-intentioned individuals (and actions) and thus always the possibility of some CSR practice contributing constructively in atrocity prevention. However, we may note that the argument of security/development embeds it in the global political economy which is a *system* governed by its own logic, it cannot be simply defined as a *collection* of individual businesses and entrepreneurs; in this case the whole is greater than the sum of its parts.

R2P's capturing the imagination of the policy, political, and academic worlds raises some questions. Does the 'noise' inside and outside the UN signal the adoption of an R2P framework that is a radical break from the past? What does it mean to have an R2P framework? Does it displace old modes of thinking and ways of responding to mass killings? How did genocide, crimes against humanity, ethnic cleansing, and war crimes come to be considered grave enough to legitimately question a nation-state's claim to sovereignty—a normative principle of international law, one that also *orders* the international? All these queries further lead to an intriguing puzzle as to how the UN, a microcosm of the international system, came to promote an idea that appears to challenge a principle—sovereignty—which it is mandated to protect. While literature on R2P discusses these issues, there is one question that escapes its close scrutiny: What does the fulfilment, in *full (not partial or ad hoc) measure* of the responsibilities of prevention and rebuilding which inform R2P's three pillars[9] entail? The varying degrees of prevention and rebuilding responsibilities of different actors (states, regional and international organizations including non-governmental organizations) if executed wholly and not partially pose a radical challenge to the international *economic* order; there is an implied requirement of the recasting of the international

[9] The Secretary-General in his 2009 annual report on R2P identified the three pillars as: Pillar one describes the protection responsibilities of the State, Pillar two refers to the international assistance and capacity building responsibility of international community while pillar three is the timely and decisive response of the UN Member States (A/63/677/2009).

political economy, thus making R2P a challenge to the very ordering principle of the global political and economic system. R2P, then, would be a discursive shift.

Objectives of the Book

The choice of UN as a site to understand the above is dictated by the fact that R2P has officially been adopted and subsequently promoted by it. Understanding the evolution and impact of R2P within the UN system can be done by asking three questions: (a) In what ways has R2P been incorporated into the UN?; (b) Does this incorporation represent a significant change in the way the UN has approached the relationship between security and development?; (c) What are the normative and political implications of R2Ps incorporation for the UN's approach to security and development? The search for answers must begin by the acknowledgement that historically the UN's vision about security and development, including the relationship between the two, has been informed (*and limited*) by particular versions of liberalism. Following this awareness we must undertake three tasks, *first* identify and map empirically R2P's material (institutional and operational), ideational, and normative incorporation at the UN. *Second*, to understand *how* this incorporation of R2P came to be, and whether it represents a significant change in the UN's security and development approach. The *third* task, following the above concerns, is to assess critically what the observed incorporation of R2P denotes for the actors and issues of this international domain(s) of security and development.

Most locate R2P's origin in the 'official birth certificates,' either in the ICISS Report (2001) or the World Summit Outcome Document (WSOD) 2005. To accept this putative origin is to reduce R2P to an idea—ignoring its materiality—and attribute it to the genius of a few individuals (e.g., the ICISS Commissioners). Indeed, the ICISS, the WSOD, and subsequent UN documents that endorsed R2P must themselves be historicized. The genesis puzzle of R2P gets a shade more complex as its close scrutiny reveals R2P's consonance with the underpinnings and ethos of the neoliberal global political economy.

The ICISS was set up to resolve the 'international community's' dilemma of how to respond to situations of egregious violation of human rights in a sovereign state. The memory of the UN's (and the international community's) inaction to the genocide in Rwanda (1994) and

NATO's unilateral humanitarian intervention in Kosovo (1999) provided the backdrop to the ICISS. In addition, this literature on R2P traces the *intellectual roots* of the ICISS to Francis M. Deng's (Deng et al. 1996) conceptualization of 'sovereignty as responsibility' and Kofi Annan's (1999) articulation of 'two concepts of sovereignty' that underlined the transcendence of human rights over sovereignty (see Bellamy 2008: 617; Weiss 2007: 89). The UN's 'politics of peace' today is premised on the belief that peace within states is a prerequisite for interstate peace (Barnett 2010: 46). Thus, the debate on R2P's goals is between those who believe that R2P is a humanitarian-militaristic intervention and others who perceive it as encompassing a range of measures (military and non-military) aimed at prevention and protection (Bellamy 2009: 33). The latter includes measures such as capacity building of the host state, and diplomatic and humanitarian measures to protect the population from atrocity crimes. R2P is regarded as one of the 'UN ideas that changed the world' (Jolly et al. 2009: 18) and is credited with changing the moral optic of the traditional humanitarian-intervention debate by replacing the argument of 'right to intervene' with that of 'responsibility to protect.' This projection of R2P, as a novel way of *thinking*, has drawn the constructivists' interest in R2P as a norm (see Glanville 2016).

Historicizing R2P in the liberal/neoliberal discourse and practices of security/development in the post-Second World War period rescues R2P from its misleading reduction to simply an ideational and normatively driven response to situations of violent conflict and insecurity. Anne Orford argued early on that R2P is a codification of already existing UN practices, therefore, contra Ban Ki-Moon who exhorts the international community to transform R2P 'from promise to practice' she observes that the concept transforms 'practice into promise' (2011: 2). While this book echoes the view that the template of R2P's three pillars lays claim to the entire UN security/development dispositif, it goes further to argue that this appropriation (by R2P) of the UN's repertoire of tools is necessary to meet the imperatives of the global political economy—wherein the logic of neoliberal development policies—*in* and *of* the Global North and *in* the Global South—create a permanent demand for security measures to maintain law and order.

While in this book the lineage of R2P is traced to the founding moments of the United Nations (and its Charter), R.B.J. Walker[10] points out that the liberal security/development problematique can be traced further back to the works of Thomas Hobbes, Immanuel Kant, and Max Weber. Indeed, the link between security and development was well established by the mid-nineteenth century and more or less canonical by the time of Max Weber's formulation of what eventually became the 'realist' tradition in international relations. Though I agree with this argument, a discussion of *this* genealogy is beyond the scope of the book.

International relations literature describes the security and development linkage as 'security-development *nexus*,'[11]—this book frames the linkage as 'security/development *dispositif*'. The term, nexus, denotes the coming together of two or more discrete fields while dispositif points to the seamlessness of the ostensibly separate fields. Employing the concept of dispositif—that is both generative and framing as it brings together both the discursive and material (i.e., discourse as practice)—R2P is located within a larger discursive power/knowledge structure, and its connections to broader historical and contemporary aspects of the global political economy are identified. Next, within this framework of the security/development dispositif, Foucauldian notions of *governmentality* (1991) and *biopolitics* (2008) are employed to 'make sense' of the observed patterns of R2P's incorporation into the UN. Revealing R2P as a technique of neoliberal governmentality in the UN's security/development dispositif leads to the discernment of the *materiality* of the R2P *idea*, thereby, filling a major gap in the literature, which emphasizes R2P as a norm (see Badescue and Weiss 2010; Labonte 2016). R2P in its incipient formulation and in its continuing evolution has had a conceptual flexibility that nestles it in both collective security and human security—the dominant security/development discourse(s) of the UN. This malleability puts the R2P norm status in a nebulous—not necessarily a disadvantaged—realm where different advocacy voices claim their

[10] R.B.J. Walker in an interview with me in June 2016.

[11] For literature on the security-development nexus, see DCD/DAD (2004), Duffield (2001a, b, 2006, 2007, 2010), Duffield et al. (2001), Spear and Williams (2012), and Stern and Ojendal (2010).

respective distinctive *moon sighting*[12] leading to the R2P norm being variously identified as old, new, single, or collective (Labonte 2016: 134). Thus the privileging in the UN of the ICISS report over previous security (and development) commissions' reports (see Chapter 3).

Central Argument

This book makes three core arguments to answer the above questions.

First, that to date, *R2P's incorporation into the UN has been uneven.* For example, while the Secretary-General and SAR2P promote R2P, the Office for the Coordination of Humanitarian Affairs (OCHA) refrains from associating with the R2P doctrine. The dilemma that R2P poses for the UN is exemplified in the UNGA's response(s), on the one hand it facilitated R2P's entry into the UN via WSOD (2005), yet majority of its Global South Member States are suspicious of the third pillar's military component; R2P encounters both *acceptance* and *resistance*.

Support for R2P is not uniform across the major UN departments—while some support it, others are resistant to or dismissive of it. There are apprehensions that R2P is essentially a 'Trojan horse' of the powerful states to legitimize intervention in the affairs of the weak (Bellamy 2006: 32). R2P's premise of 'sovereignty as responsibility' is pregnant with *conceptual* challenges to certain key established norms of international law and principles of the UN Charter, namely, sovereignty and territorial integrity of states. In the eyes of the critics, it is this possible conceptual 'turning over its head' of the very premise of the Westphalian system that makes the R2P terrain a slippery slope. Such an argument is amenable to the contention that resistance to the *new* R2P idea is symptomatic of the UN's inertia as a historical institution trapped by the logic of path-dependency.

The resistance to R2P is also a result of the inevitable turf battles and power struggles that accompany the introduction of what appears to be new ideas/initiatives and creation of new offices and roles—such

[12] Celebration of Islamic religious occasions such as Eid are contingent on moon sighting. In some countries such as Pakistan moon sighting becomes an occasion of confusion and controversy as religious leaders from different regions claim different moon sightings. https://indianexpress.com/article/religion/pakistan-launches-its-first-ever-moon-sighting-website-5752117/.

as that of the SAR2P. If R2P *knowledge* gains legitimacy as a security paradigm then it has power consequences for the construction of the categories of the protectors, the protected, and the enemies. Not only is knowledge (the construction of meaning) a form of power but power is always implicated in questions such as when and whom of its application. This *potential* power of defining identities, interests, agenda setting, and prioritizing goals makes the existing security and development departments of the UN wary of R2P. For example, OCHA visibly distances itself from R2P to protect its own 'pure' humanitarian work from being 'contaminated' by R2P's interventionist rhetoric. To understand the simultaneity of the advocacy of R2P and the resistance to it, the focus should widen beyond the individual entities of R2P advocates and opponents—in terms of departments, Member States, epistemic community, and norm entrepreneurs—to contextualize their dialectics in the broader liberal/neoliberal security/development dispositif and analyse whether these dialectics have altered the landscape of this dispositif.

The *second* argument is that the uneven incorporation of R2P represents a 'discursive rearticulation' rather than a 'discursive shift,' that is to say that there is no profound substantive change. Discursive rearticulation suggests relative continuity with *the earlier* line of thinking. A *discursive formation* comes into being whenever texts, institutions, and practices refer to the same object, same style, strategies and have a common institutional and political pattern supported by a *regime of truth* (Foucault 1972: 73). In our times (including the R2P time) this regime of truth is the liberal/neoliberal governmentality. So, it is analytically limiting to view R2P as a discrete document and practice, R2P must be contextualized in the broader liberal/neoliberal security/ development dispositif of which the UN itself is a part. Besides the UN this dispositif includes political and economic international and regional organizations such as UN agencies (World Bank, International Monetary Fund, and the International Labour Organization), World Trade Organization, World Intellectual Property Organization, Regional Development Banks, International Criminal Court, OXFAM, European Union, Association of Southeast Asian Nations (ASEAN), think tanks, academia and non-governmental organizations, and domestic security/ development agencies of both the developed and developing states.[13]

[13] The developed and the developing states do not enjoy parity in terms of their respective roles and benefits in the dispositif. The former clearly are dominant and the

The liberal/neoliberal security/development dispositif has a global sweep and its exigencies frame the competition or the power play (and resistance) between these organizations. Although the book's focus is limited to the primary UN organs and departments, it is done so on the premise that the existing UN security/development dispositif is itself a part of the existing broader liberal/neoliberal security/development dispositif.[14] This explains how the OSAPG has made other international/regional and civil society organizations its outreach partners.

Although a new coinage in the lexicon of international affairs, R2P's underlying philosophy is neither transformational nor a major departure from the course of existing international laws and conventions (Welsh 2013: 373). R2P's affinity with the principles of the UN Charter and related paraphernalia of international organizations and international law facilitate R2P's incorporation within the UN.[15] R2P advocates point to its association with the human security discourse within the UN (Murray 2013). The ICISS Report regards human security as one of the 'fundamental objectives of modern international institutions' (2001: 1.28). R2P's goals to prevent, protect, and rebuild[16] echo the twin human security goals of 'freedom from fear' (FFF) and 'freedom from want' (FFW). The broad concept of human security aims to meet both goals while the narrower version focuses only on freedom from fear. Recall here that the

primary beneficiaries, but significantly the latter's resistance is mainly aimed at either dislodging the developed states dominant position or squeezing itself into that space of dominance. Decolonization saw developing countries for a while questioning the premise of this liberal/neoliberal dispositif; the Non-Aligned Movement and the demand for a New International Economic Order are two such examples.

[14] The terms—liberal/neoliberal security/development dispositif, UN security/development dispositif, and the UN liberal/neoliberal security/development dispositif—are used interchangeably. I use the terms liberal governmentality, neoliberal governmentality, and liberal/neoliberal governmentality interchangeably, unless otherwise specified. A related note is that the neoliberal security/development policies and programmes are identified or critiqued under the generic rubric of liberal peacebuilding project in the existing literature on security and development issues.

[15] For example, the list of the four crimes under R2P is similar to the list of crimes identified in both the 1998 Rome Statute and the 2001 Constitutive Act of the African Union (Welsh 2013: 374).

[16] These ICISS Report goals are reflected in 2005 WSOD's paragraph139, whereby the international community commits itself to help states build capacity to protect populations from atrocity crimes. This aspect was further elaborated in the subsequent Secretary-General annual reports on R2P.

terminology of these 'freedoms' popularized via the concept of human security was used way back by the US President Franklin D. Roosevelt in his 1941 State of the Union Address. The UN system was tasked to meet these goals of FFW and FFW via the collective security doctrine and the embedded liberalism framework respectively. Since the goal of FFW falls outside the mandate of the collective security doctrine, with the dislodging of embedded liberalism by neoliberalism, collective security had to make *not vacate* room for human security.

Certainly, there are strategic and political imperatives of the liberal/neoliberal order that necessitated the recourse to human security. In the 'neoliberal narrative'[17] embedded liberalism's and its domestic counterpart's—the welfare state—policies of economic intervention to create employment and address issues of social injustice enfeebled a country's 'moral fibre', 'eroded personal responsibility and the over-riding duty of the poor to work' and ignored Friedrich Hayek's dictum that '"common good" either did not exist or could not be calculated.' Structural adjustment programme (SAP) was a neoliberal response to the economic crisis of the 1970s–1980s whereby, the UN Specialized Agencies—the World Bank and the IMF—did not just reinforce the rationale for free market forces and free trade but made the offer of aid, debt relief, and foreign investment in the Global South contingent on policies of 'good governance', e.g., elections, 'multi-party politics' and 'rule of law' (Hall 2015: 15–16). The secession of the state from the economy and social sectors along with the SAP conditionalities resulted in even harsher economic hardships for the Global South populations even as multinational corporations made 'profit over people' (see Chomsky 1999; Rapley 2004; Touraine 2001). The decade of the eighties was also the beginning of the post-Cold War order which came with new political and strategic challenges with political uncertainty compounding in no small measure by the vanishing of the Cold War bipolarity certitudes—duly lamented by Kenneth Waltz (1993) and John Mearsheimer (1990)—prompting Western states to identify new threats even as they redefined their strategic interests (Busumtwi-Sam 2002). Despite being the promotors of neoliberal economic policy, the developed states too were not immune from its

[17] The current historical period, described as a neoliberal era, is understood to have begun in the late 1970s with the demise of the welfare state at the domestic level and embedded liberalism in the international arena (see Abdelal and Ruggie 2009; Harvey 2007; Ruggie 1982, 2008; Saad-Filho and Johnston 2004).

impact, they too experienced a crisis of consensus and legitimacy in their domestic sphere (Chandler 2003; Ignatieff 1997; McCormack 2010). One consequence was the adoption of an 'interventionist ethical foreign policy,' in the hope that it would be a potent tool to create 'a sense of political purpose and mission' (Chandler 2003: 299) by protecting human rights and 'saving strangers' (Wheeler 2000).[18] An often-overlooked fact is that neoliberalism is not just market economics but also a complex of cultural and political values and practices (see Giroux 2004). R2P is thus guided by a mix of economic/political imperatives—wherein it serves as an example, to borrow a term from David Held and Anthony McGrew (2003), of a *global riot control police*—and ostensible *noble* intentions—of saving populations from atrocity crimes; thus, R2P is this and that!

The antagonistic positing of collective security and human security is false. Human security does not displace or erase collective security as the UN security paradigm, indeed human security requires collective security responses to meet its goal of freedom from fear. Collective security requires human security in the neoliberal economy to take charge of overseeing and collecting the *debris of responsibilities* left behind by the retreat of embedded liberalism. Collective security and human security are complementary. Human security[19] is embedded along with collective security in the UN security/development dispositif; R2P nests in both human security and collective security. This explains why there is both scepticism over and support for R2P within the UN. Those wary of R2P view it as military intervention, an instance of a robust application of collective security—which itself is hostage to the Permanent Five's strategic interests. The advocates of R2P see it as a bid to promote human rights and human security.

R2P's incorporation at the UN, though uneven, is possible because it is very much within the framework of the UN Charter (and related documents like the Rome Statute 1998 and Constitutive Act of the African Union 2001) (see Heiher 2013a, b; Welsh 2013). The UN Secretary-General repeatedly underscores the point that R2P is a continuation of principles of conventional and customary international humanitarian law, international human rights law, and international criminal law (A/

[18] 'The post-Cold War search for new ideals and common bonds in an era of failed ideologies appears to have contributed to a growing appreciation of human rights as a set of values' (Francesca Klug in Chandler 2003: 229).

[19] The concept of human security is discussed at length in Chapters 2 and 3.

63/677/2009). Even the ostensibly radical recasting of one of the key features of international relations—sovereignty—as responsibility—which serves as a major premise of R2P—does not disrupt the international order. R2P remains within the framework of sovereignty albeit one reconstituted by powerful states through their 'hegemonic law making activities' (Reinold 2013: i).

While the purpose is to understand and demonstrate how R2P is a discursive rearticulation (not discursive shift) of the liberal/neoliberal security/development dispositif, this analysis briefly roves the realm of speculation (in Chapter 6) to explore how R2P could be a discursive shift. R2P would be a discursive shift if the responsibilities of prevention and rebuilding are realized on the ground in ways that yield more *meaningful* short- and long-term results than those seen in Afghanistan which was run over by the Taliban with the withdrawal of American troops in 2021. This would strengthen pillars 1 (the protection responsibilities of the state) and 2 (international assistance and capacity-building), thus making pillar 3 (timely and decisive response) redundant. In such a case R2P with its three pillars would recast some of the key normative/ideational themes of R2P i.e., responsibility, sovereignty, morality, and protection. This discursive shift would entail key institutional/operational changes at the UN, such as the creation of an Economic Security Council that could address the structural root causes of atrocity crimes. The membership of this Council would be a rotating one amongst states with the lowest GDP.

Three, the above claim of the embeddedness of R2P at the UN is further bolstered by the fact that the key themes[20] of R2P—legality, sovereignty, protection, morality, and responsibility—are in consonance with the ethos of the UN's liberal/neoliberal security/development dispositif. R2P is nested in the broader biopolitical 'environment shaping' risk management and disciplinary technologies characteristic of neoliberal globalization within which the UN functions; the UN does not challenge this globalization.

The inter-related[21] concepts of governmentality, biopolitics, and dispositif are insightful exegesis on the phenomenon of neoliberalism and provide the ontological and epistemological basis to analyse R2P

[20] See Chapter 6.

[21] Governmentality and biopolitics are inter-related concepts although some treat the two terms as synonyms (Kelly 2010: 3).

as a measure of the liberal/neoliberal security/development dispositif of the UN. Foucault explains governmentality, the art or rationality of government as.

> Ensemble of institutions, procedures, analyses, and reflections, calculations, and tactics that allow the exercise of this very specific, albeit very complex, power that has the population as its target, political economy as its major form of knowledge, and apparatuses of security as its essential technical instrument. (2007: 108)

The target of governmentality is population because the latter emerged as a problem in the eighteenth century and it continues to be so. Biopolitics is the attempt 'to rationalize the problems posed to governmental practice by phenomena characteristic of a set of living beings forming a population: health, hygiene, birthrate, life expectancy, race…' (Foucault 2008: 317). Biopolitics consists of policies and practices that aim to shape a target population's behaviour. Biopolitical measures are taken by governments as well as other actors to identify and control the trends, tendencies, and processes that unfold within a target population and which influence that population's productivity, vitality, social structures, and overall behaviour (Foucault 1990: 140). Development as conceptualized by the World Bank aims to change the activities and even the way of thinking of people, therefore receipt of development aid by a country is made contingent on the conduct and behaviour of its population (Duffield 2001a: 312); 'good governance' is an alias of 'good conduct.' Neoliberal governmentality employs biopolitical measures as one of its principal governance technologies (policies, practices, strategies, etc.), informed by particular governance rationalities (theories, ideologies, etc.). Biopolitical measures are technologies operationalized on a quotidian basis and deal with both the normal—such as birthrate—and the exceptional occurrences such as the pandemic. The second decade of the twenty-first century ended with the beginning of COVID-19 of literally global proportions, the consequent lockdowns and vaccination drives being dramatic measures to ensure the population's life and health.

R2P qualifies as a technique of governmentality since it involves: (1) The identification of conflict-ridden, civil war striven, 'failed states,' politically unstable, poor third world states as objects of knowledge; (2) The construction of vulnerable individuals/groups, communities, states i.e., victims (the protected) as subjects of power; (3) Using the responsibility to prevent, react, and rebuild as technologies of power (governance) to be exercised by select states, regional organizations, and international organizations as security providers (the protectors). R2P thus has the power to *name names*: it labels certain international situations as crisis and creates categories of the protector and the protected. The pulpit from where R2P is being advocated lends its articulation further legitimacy. This pulpit is no ordinary platform, as the UN—which on account of the universal membership of nation-states, enjoys a *unique* authority to speak on behalf of the global community of states; also, UN *specialized* agencies possess the authority to speak as experts. The ICISS report emphasized this view and catalogued the UN's comparative advantages vis-à-vis other international organizations as including: 'universal membership, political legitimacy, administrative impartiality, technical expertise, convening and mobilizing power, and dedication of its staff' (2001: 6.26). This bestows legitimacy to the UN *acts* of governmentality, the conduct of conduct, that include diagnoses, identification, and classification of populations/ states as ill (failed) or at risk of being so ('failed' or 'failing') in need of cure/aid. The UN medicinal arsenal are a host of development and security measures including the *bitter pill* of Security Council certified aerial attacks or ground troops; this is the twinning of collective security and human security tools and goals.

While the concept of governmentality establishes the link between security and development in the domains of both theory and practice, biopolitics too offers insights on R2P goals of protection of populations from genocide, war crimes, crimes against humanity, and ethnic cleansing. Foucault reveals the imperative of thanatopolitics—i.e., the politics of death—as the distinctive feature of modern-time genocides as an inevitable accompaniment of biopolitics.[22] Foucault drew attention to one of the 'puzzling antinomies of our political reason' whereby mechanisms of destruction and care coexist in political structures (2000: 405). Under biopolitics there is the 'simultaneous possibility of protecting life and of the holocaust' (Foucault in Dreyfus and Rabinow 1983: 138). The lenses of biopolitics and governmentality enable the viewing and understanding of the singular R2P as part of the liberal/neoliberal security/ development apparatus i.e., dispositif. Foucault defines *dispositif* as a

[22] In the writings of Giorgio Agamben (1998) and Michael Hardt and Antonio Negri (2000) biopolitics is mainly about thanatopolitics.

> heterogeneous ensemble consisting of discourses, institutions, architectural forms, regulatory decisions, laws, administrative measures, scientific statements, philosophical, moral and philanthropic propositions- in short, the said as much as the unsaid. Such are the elements of the apparatus. The apparatus itself is the system of relations that can be established between these elements. Secondly, what I am trying to identify in this apparatus is precisely the connection that can exist between these heterogeneous elements. Thus, a particular discourse can figure at one time as the programme of an institution, and at another time it can function as a means of justifying or masking a practice which itself remains silent...Thirdly, I understand by the term 'apparatus' a sort of...formation which has as its major function at a given historical moment that of responding to an *urgent need*. (1980: 194–195)

There is a veritable cottage industry of research centres and civil society organizations dedicated to the promotion of R2P (Hehir 2013a: 6). Foucauldian problematization via dispositif enables a broad scan of the R2P problematique that goes beyond the formal functions of the Office of the Special Representative on the Prevention of Genocide (OSAPG) (where the office of the Special Representative on R2P is located) and other related UN organs, agencies, and departments. Dispositif makes visible the connecting threads between the UN and the *outside* entities—this book discusses three of them—the *Global Centre for Responsibility to Protect* (GCR2P), the *International Coalition for the Responsibility to Protect* (ICR2P) (both located in New York, USA), and the *Asia Pacific Centre for the Responsibility to Protect* (APR2P) (located in Brisbane, Australia). The mission of these three international non-governmental organizations/centres is the promotion of R2P and they provide significant intellectual input (expertise and knowledge creation) in the conceptual development of R2P. The advocacy work of GCR2P and ICR2P involves regular lobbying with UN officials and state missions on the issue of R2P. The Secretary-General, too, underlined the role of the private sector and civil society in making possible the operationalization of the third pillar of R2P (see A/63/677/2009/para59). The WSOD (2005) reduced R2P to three paragraphs and these three INGOs are important sites for R2P's exposition. Important questions in this regard are: whether the ICISS report is being retrieved?; are new meanings being inserted and the 'old' being subverted? is a particular meaning of R2P being accented? The ascendancy of R2P within the UN also gains traction from the work being done on the issue outside the UN; multiple entities are engaged in the enterprise of knowledge generation on R2P.

As a concept, dispositif has greater analytical depth and purchase over that of epistemic communities/policy communities/discursive coalitions (Keck and Sikkink 1998; Krause Hansen et al. 2002; Mbabazi et al. 2005; Stone and Maxwell 2005) which views *experts* engaged in knowledge generation as discrete entities and pressure groups. The concept of dispositif takes the discussion of the knowledge generation enterprise further by drawing attention to two points—(a) the embeddedness of an epistemic community within a broader dispositif and the linkages between these knowledge experts and other elements of the apparatus (dispositif); (b) the creation of 'forms of subjectification' such as the construction of categories of protector and protected (Deleuze 1992: 164). Dispositif reveals the power implications of the construction of these categories and practices of protection in the R2P discourse.

R2P[23] privileges a certain meaning of responsibility echoing the neoliberal governmentality's technology of responsibilization. The neoliberal tenet—free market as an embodiment of rationality—regards market as a site of truth veridiction including the veridiction of governmental practice, that is the practices of government must be in accordance with the rationality of the market (Foucault 2008: 30–35). Both neoliberal governmentality and R2P recast the traditional or Westphalian notion of state sovereignty. Both introduce *new* but *similarly* accented notions of responsibility: in governmentality, the state's new acts of commission (responsibility for the optimization of the prosperity of the population i.e., biopolitics) are accompanied by ostensible[24] acts of omission (i.e., the carving of the economy as a sphere independent of state interference). The neoliberal notion of responsibility transfers greater responsibility to the individual citizen for 'social risks such as illness, unemployment, poverty etc.' (Lemke 2002: 59). Similarly, R2P's redefinition of state sovereignty introduces a new concept of responsibility for both the state

[23] I do not suggest that the idea of responsibility is new since this concept has a long history not only in liberal thought but also animates different religions and cultures across time and space. What is significant for me is the accent on particular meaning(s) of responsibility that has come to the fore today.

[24] In practice, the neoliberal state plays an active role in insulating the market from threats emerging from the political domain, particularly from democracy and social justice movements.

and its citizens while recasting the responsibility and accountability of the global governmentality institutions i.e., the UN, World Bank and, IMF.[25] With the end of embedded liberalism (Ruggie 1982) international institutions reduced their former responsibilities and exhorted the individual state(s) to assume greater responsibility for its own welfare and development. This individualization of responsibility of the state is transacted by transferring its responsibility to the citizens. R2P's purpose(s) of protection and the ensuing categories of the protector and the protected are the consequences of this transaction of responsibility. The neoliberal individuated notion of responsibility frames the current UN security/development dispositif and creates a corresponding notion of protection.

The Concept of Responsibility: The ICISS Report and the WSOD

The continuum of responsibility, as defined in the ICISS report, consists of responsibility to: prevent, protect, and rebuild. A further taxonomy in the report identifies a hierarchy of actors—host state, regional organization, and international organization—who must share the burden of these responsibilities. Paragraphs 138–139 of the SOD reiterate the responsibilities of the state and the international community to protect populations from atrocity crimes (A/RES/601/2005). Subsequently, the concept of responsibility of these pithy paragraphs was elaborated as 'the three pillars of responsibility' by the Secretary-General in his 2009 Report on Implementing the Responsibility to Protect (A/63/677/2009). The *content* of these pillars is similar to the ICISS's report's three responsibilities (prevention, protection, and rebuilding), which encompassed the broad human security agenda of freedom from fear and want. As stated earlier most of the literature on R2P examines the issue of responsibility primarily in the context of the terms of reference set by the ICISS report: responsibility of the host state and responsibility of the international community. In other words, the discussion ends up focusing on questions of role allocation of actors (states, international organizations), and logistics and feasibility of the operation to protect. This focus on the *present or current moment* de-historicizes the crisis, and forecloses any discussion

25 Larner and Walters (2004) work is one of the earliest ones on the upscaling of governmentality to the global level. Also see Legg (2012).

of structural causation that created conditions whereby populations need protection. Responsibility is a historical question as the subject's—population, group/community, or the individual—competence and potential to respond to problems are determined by the political, social, and economic structures in which the subject is embedded.[26] Measures of 'responsibility to prevent' and 'responsibility to rebuild' built on the premises of such erasures or discounting of facts are likely to fail, and so also other post-conflict peacebuilding efforts. In this process the transformative potential of human security is diluted as the focus remains on the *reactive* purpose to realize the lost 'freedom from fear' instead of mainstreaming the *preventive* and *rebuilding* goals of 'freedom from want' (Black 2006; Schittecatte 2006). Not surprisingly, issues of international economic inequality, unfair trade regimes, and lack of autonomy of poor states under the World Bank and IMF programs are not on this agenda (McCormack 2011: 105).

The above flaws invite suspicion that R2P is a pretext to smuggle in old ideas of just war whereby the west can impose unilateral moral judgements onto weaker states (Franceschet 2006). R2P, then, is labelled as a realist response that reinforces, rather than challenges, existing policy frameworks. The first two pillars and the non-coercive measures of pillar three are seen as window dressing aimed at setting the stage for the 'timely and decisive action' of military intervention. In this light R2P appears as exaggerating new post-Cold War security threats and locating them in the developing world, so as to enable the exercise of biopower by the west (Chandler 2008). Thus, the argument that human security prioritizes people rather than states is more accurately understood in terms of effective states prioritizing populations living within ineffective ones (Duffield 2006). The concern for the 'population at risk' (ICISS 2001) renders the individual body accessible to—and thus a subject of—state security. This is a repeat of the national security's structuring logic (Berman 2007), making possible the co-option of human security by political elites. Also, the responsibility for the international community, in effect (despite the responsibility to prevent), starts only from a 'present moment' i.e., the

[26] Chad Lavin's critique—via the works of Karl Marx, Michel Foucault, and Judith Butler—of the liberal privileging of individual responsibility without regard to structures is useful in this regard. See Lavin, Chad (2008) *The Politics of Responsibility* University of Illinois Press.

onset of the crisis. This dehistoricizing of a conflict situation only reconfirms the 1960s modernization theory's thesis that third-world regimes are crisis-prone because of their inherent *political backwardness*.

Responsibility: Two Meanings

The conceptualization of responsibilities in terms of the actors in R2P can be understood as a conflation of two meanings—responsibility as duty/obligation and responsibility as accountability i.e., bearing the consequences of one's actions.[27] Different conceptualizations of responsibility reside on different ontological planes. As they differ on the questions of—responsibility of what or of whom? Whose responsibility? How is the responsibility to be operationalized? The responsibility discourse normalizes a particular reality and identifies and isolates some phenomena and actors as problems that must be rectified; most often the solution to the problem emerges from the very process and discourse that has created the problem. The deployment of the word to focus on certain kinds of events/problems/crisis/people/regions resonates with the political, cultural, and economic imperatives and values of the North. R2P's articulation of 'responsibility as duty' makes it incumbent on the members of the international community to fulfil their obligation to protect the vulnerable people. The second meaning is derived from the principles of individuation that undergird the free market whereby the buyer and seller, by virtue of their autonomy to make choices must bear consequences of their decisions; note that political liberalism rests on 'everyday conceptions of persons as the basic units of thought, deliberation, and responsibility' (Rawls in Lavin 2008: x). Like the liberals, the neoliberals' conceptualization of responsibility is rooted in the notion of individual autonomy.[28] Under neoliberalism one has to accept or submit to that bundle of rights necessary for capital accumulation. These rights include

[27] The meaning of responsibility in international law is liability. Lorealea Michaelis and Genevieve Fuji Johnson make a distinction between responsibility and political obligation on the ground that there is the presumption of a degree of agency in the former (2013: 4).

[28] William Connolly has termed as 'ontopolitical' Rawls' conceptualization of responsibility. 'Connolly's cast reveals the circularity at work in Rawlsian liberalism: though Rawls roots liberal autonomy in a political commitment to individual responsibility, this responsibility is itself rooted in an unstated commitment to individual autonomy' (Lavin 2008: x).

individual responsibility and liability (Harvey 2007: 181). This second meaning is particularly relevant in the context of the neoliberal ethos that permeates notions of economic development in the UN system. Responsibility as accountability is demanded of states (primarily in the Global South) where there are egregious violations of human rights.

Responsibility: Governmentality's Insights

Despite the proliferating literature on the subject (Arneson 2011, 2008; Auhagen and Bierhoff 2001; Darling-Smith 2007; Fleurbaey 2008; Raffoul 2010; Scheffler 1992) there is an absence of a critical engagement with the concept of responsibility. Most studies tend to focus on 'particular types of situations (discrete events) at the cost of others (impersonal and enduring conditions of deprivation)' whereby they are not equipped to assign responsibility to recalcitrant social conditions like poverty (Lavin 2008: vii). However, the concept of responsibility receives critical treatment in the hands of Foucault (1980), Butler (2004), Young (2003, 2004), and Lavin (2008). Each one offers a different insight in her respective critique of the neoliberal conceptualization of responsibility. Young (2003, 2004) argues that the liberal 'blame model' of responsibility is inadequate to deal with complicated issues of social injustice. Young's social connection model of political responsibility underlines our responsibility for 'redressing harms' that result from our 'participation in social processes that systematically produce these harms' (Michaelis and Johnson 2013: 9). Writing in the context of 9/11, Judith Butler criticizes the limitations of an ontopolitical sensibility that favours individual causality and immediate criminal punishment (Lavin 2008: xiii).[29] Linking the arguments of Marxism and postmodernism, Lavin dubs the theory of individual autonomy as politically and ontologically dubious and sets out to expose the 'porosity of the boundaries between subject and object, structure and agent, private and public' (2008: ix–xi).

[29] Butler criticizes the reductive discourse of individual responsibility that paradoxically translates the postliberal *explanation* (of 9/11 causes as being varied and going back to Middle East politics) as '*exonerations*.' She, therefore, says that 'responsibility must be rethought without the dubious narratives of heroes and villains conjuring events out of thin air. This rethinking distributes rather than disperses responsibility, emphasizing not individual martyrs and their causal action but rather the ability to respond that is afforded to socially constituted agents' (Lavin 2008: xiii).

That conceptualization of responsibility is a political act framing political agenda(s) and informing the relationship between citizens and the state is nowhere better analysed than in Michel Foucault's concept of governmentality (2007, 2008). Foucault points out how neoliberal governmentality creates and justifies the responsible citizen as one who assumes as her own, the responsibilities which once belonged to the welfare state. However, at the same time the neoliberal state retains for itself some responsibility for the population—including that of development of new practices and types of intervention, for example, social medicine and public hygiene which involve problems of demography—it does so while respecting certain forms of freedom as freedom is the condition of governing well. It means that it is necessary to laissez faire i.e., manage and no longer control through rules and regulations (Foucault 2007: 350–354). Self-monitoring as an additional surveillance tactic for the state draws its legitimacy from the presumption of conditions that make possible a free individual—the idea of which is itself embedded in the Hobbesian and Lockean conceptualization of human nature as selfish and rational (Macpherson 2011). Unlike paradigms such as that of altruism and communitarianism, the epistemological leap of liberal/neoliberal notion of individual responsibility frames it as a prerequisite and consequence of freedom and free will. Classical liberalism along with its close cousin, libertarianism, endorses negative liberty as the only valid form of liberty, thus in the liberal/neoliberal template the mere absence of state regulations creates freedom and not merely conditions for freedom. HS's second goal of freedom from want would be identified as positive liberty which itself would be regarded as a noble ideal suited more in the realm of justice but unqualified for the portals of liberty. It is this principle that legitimizes moral fatigue of liberal peacebuilding's humanitarianism—the American withdrawal from Afghanistan and Iraq. The limits of liberal humanitarianism are easily reached sooner than later because that act/practice if based on the instinct of charity is an exception, a move out of the normal as the normal one is to take responsibility of the self. In the charity template one is spurred by the goodness of one's heart to take responsibility for others. In the liberal frame this goodness is an exception, it is legitimate only if it is quick and of a short duration so that both the 'do gooder' and the recipient of the good can resume their respective responsibilities of looking after themselves. The short temporary nature of the charity is important so as to not create a society of parasites or stall the free play of the free will. The discrete acts of charity can work, give fillip, bear fruition if only a little push, a little cheer was required by an otherwise empowered person. But what happens when structures are the cause for the non-fulfilment of FFW? While neoliberalism may not even consider as legitimate the expectation that state or society assumes responsibility to meet the goal of FFW, liberalism can respond in only half measures and only temporarily so to meet this goal.

However, this casting of responsibility as individual freedom, though a fundamental premise of the liberal and neoliberal ideology, is not a panacea for the problems endemic to neoliberal policies. Liberal ideology and institutions (e.g., representative government, competitive markets, and belief in individual efficacy) provide particular possibilities for agency, however, as markets and states become less responsible to the demands of consumers and citizens, the limits of liberal responsibility become increasingly difficult to deny (Lavin 2008: 136). This critical lens of responsibility brings forth both the neoliberal ethos underpinning R2P and the limits of R2P as a response to situations of humanitarian crisis. The liberal/neoliberal governmentality's imperative to 'make live and let die' (Foucault 1997: 237) helps us understand the UN's authorization of military action to protect 'population at risk' in Libya and its refrain in a similar situation in Syria. This concern to protect the 'population at risk' builds on the argument of the risk consequences associated with the 'failed states' discourse[30] (Chauvet and Collier 2008; Ghani and Lockhart 2008; Krasner 2004) that has emerged as an important element of the liberal/neoliberal security/development dispositif.[31] During the 1990s, the proposition that poor countries have a higher risk of falling into conflict than rich ones (because the resulting social exclusion can be exploited by *violent* and *criminal* leaders in the former) coalesced into a consensus. If sustainable development brought the issue of collective self-reproduction centre-stage, the rediscovery of internal war during the 1990s problematized the nature of the state in the developing world: weak and failing states existing in zones of crisis can be captured

[30] This is discussed briefly in Chapter 2.

[31] Note that the concept of risk has long been associated with the entrepreneurial spirit, and therefore, celebrated as a free market principle (Keynes 2004; Bernstein 1996) and today contemporary security practices are also being increasingly described through the category of risk (Aradau et al. 2008; O'Malley 2004; Kessler 2010; Tsoukala 2010). In both the fields of market and security, the aim is not the avoidance of threats or deterrence but the management of risks (Kessler 2010: 17).

by unsuitable rulers. The perception of these rulers as the illegitimate enemies of development, together with concerns that disaffected people are liable to be drawn to them, establishes an interventionist dynamic (Duffield 2006). This is the premise of R2P's notion of sovereignty as responsibility whereby risk is a technology for governing harms. Security, in liberal government, has both a positive sense of facilitating the creative and productive liberty of the population and a negative sense of preserving the population's safety from violence and depredation (O'Malley 2004).

By noting R2P's foregrounding of the notion of 'sovereignty as responsibility' one can understand some aspects of the current international scenario: the developed North 'permits' and 'encourages' 'freedom' (read sovereignty) of the Global South states, the latter are to use this freedom to self-discipline (Abrahamsen 2004). They are given the learning tools by international experts (from international organizations such as the UN and its specialized agencies, the World Bank and the IMF) that teach them the rules of how to behave (good governance) so as to allow for the smooth functioning of the global free market. When they do not behave properly (efficiently govern), that is, fail in their responsibility, the North forced by the moral optic of R2P assumes that responsibility and intervenes. R2P feeds into a discourse that pathologizes the weak or less developed states 'rendering intervention by powerful states and international institutions less clear and accountable' (McCormack 2011: 9); thus, R2P remains embedded in the discourse of humanitarian intervention (Watson 2011: 4).

Neoliberal policies being pushed by international institutions force the Global South states to bypass the various 'stages of development' (Rostow 1960) and adopt a market economy. This fast forwarding entails, contra the liberal/neoliberal governmentality, 'over-regulation' by the states in the South and adoption of repressive policies towards their own population. However, events such as the *Arab Spring* demonstrate that in this *age of democracy* the denial of political rights and freedom does not find acquiescence among the citizens of the states in the Global South. The kind of development resulting from the contradictions of neoliberal market and the consequent political instability in the states of the South makes them conflict-prone, whereby, it is difficult for them to 'behave.' Therefore, the situation in these countries is more often than not primed for an 'R2P' type intervention. Intervention in emergency situations is a convenient response of the North. Delivery of emergency assistance assuages the conscience of advantaged groups in the North as they address 'symptoms of vast global inequality without addressing underlying structural causes, or in some cases by extending the very economic practices that contribute to poverty and human vulnerability' (Watson 2011: 16). The human security agenda is thus revealed as the unrivalled moment of liberal expansionism, which proceeds on the basis of alleviating suffering in zones of political instability and crisis (Evans 2010: 419). Human security enables the North to continue its dictation of the South, indeed 'the rules of the game' of human security are made by the 'state centric, Northern, masculinized liberal system' (Christie 2010: 187).

Overview of the Book

The argument of the book—R2P's incorporation at the UN is possible by the fact that R2P is a liberal/neoliberal security/development measure in consonance with the UN's security/development dispositif—is made through seven chapters. This chapter *Introduction* establishes the context in which R2P acquired currency. Chapter 2 *Understanding R2P as a Security/Development Measure: Security and Development in the Discipline of International Relations and in the UN Security/Development Dispositif* is a genealogical review of the discourse on security/development in the discipline of IR and its simultaneous trajectory in the UN. It argues that the UN's security/development paradigm, since its inception, has been informed by liberal approaches: (a) embedded liberalism (from 1945 to the late 1970s); (b) neoliberalism (from the late 1970s to the present).

The empirical mapping of the R2P field is done across two chapters wherein the primary sources of data are documents from the UN archives[32] and the reports of key international commissions on security and development. Chapter 3 *Historical Context of R2P* traces the genealogy of R2P to the UN Charter and reports of key international commissions on issues of security/development and brings forth the continuity between the UN's security/development doctrines from collective security to human security. It discusses the key features of

[32] Other international organizations like African Union have incorporated R2P but UNGA because of its 'universal' membership of international states enjoys an 'unmatched' legitimacy (World Bank, IMF—weighted voting—continue to be dominated by US and Western Europe, while the UN despite the special powers of the P5 at the Security Council has a General Assembly where all states enjoy equal legal status).

the 2001 ICISS Report and the R2P-related paragraphs of the 2005 World Summit Outcome Document. Chapter 4 *The Material and the Ideational Dimensions of R2P in the UN's Security/Development Dispositif* illustrates the nature and dimensions of R2P's status within and *outside* the UN institutional structure. The category of the *outside*, that is the non-UN entity includes three INGOs and think tanks—International Coalition for Responsibility to Protect (ICR2P), Global Centre for Responsibility to Protect (GCR2P), and Asia Pacific Centre on Responsibility to Protect (APR2P) which work closely with UN officials to promote R2P at the UN and other international, regional, and national fora.

The analysis—in Chapters 5 and 6—of the above empirical mapping is supplemented with interviews of UN officials and the personnel of INGOs/think tanks and academics, who have either in the past been associated with R2P through the ICISS Report or have current research interest on the subject. While the former provides the practitioner's insight (including the 'turf battles' within the UN where some of the departments consider R2P as duplication of work or appropriation of their mandate), the latter provide a critique which focuses on both the limitations of R2P as it exists and the potential of a 'tweaked' R2P to make a constructive difference. Chapter 5 *Understanding the Map: Locating R2P in the UN's Security/Development Dispositif* explores the institutional, normative, and ideational dimensions of R2P that have emerged from its *official* conceptual refinement as articulated in UNGA and UNSC resolutions and the UNSG's annual reports on R2P. The presence of both critics and advocates of R2P at the UN results into its *uneven* incorporation in the organization. Chapter 6 *Understanding the Map: R2P as Discursive Rearticulation within the Liberal/Neoliberal Security/ Development Dispositif* analyses the unevenness as simply a reflection of the very nature of the UN's security/development dispositif. The nature of incorporation of R2P at the UN demonstrates that R2P is not a *discursive shift* but a *discursive rearticulation* within the UN's security/ development dispositif.

Chapter 7 *R2P: The Journey So Far* summarizes the book and suggests possible future directions for research. It forays into exploring the possibilities of R2P overcoming the constraints of its embeddedness so that its responsibility/protection mandate is realized in critical and just measures, and concludes that this requires addressing structural causes of the four atrocity crimes.

References

Abdelal, Rawi and John G. Ruggie. 2009. The Principles of Embedded Liberalism: Social Legitimacy and Global Capitalism. In *New Perspectives on Regulation*, ed. David Moss and John Cisternino. Cambridge, MA: The Tobin Project, One Mifflin Place.

Abrahamsen, Rita. 2004. The Partnerships in Global Governance. *Third World Quarterly* 25 (8): 1453–1467.

Agamben, Giorgio. 1998. *Homo Sacer: Sovereign Power and Bare Life*, trans. Daniel Heller-Roazen. Stanford: Stanford University Press.

Annan, Kofi. 1999. Two Concepts of Sovereignty. *The Economist*, September 18, pp. 49–50.

Aradau, Claudia, Luis-Lobo Guerrero, and Rens Van Munster. 2008. Security, Technologies of Risk, and the Political: Guest Editors' Introduction. *Security Dialogue* 39 (2–3): 147–154.

Arneson, Richard. 2008. Rawls, Responsibility, and Distributive Justice. In *Justice, Political Liberalism, and Utilitarianism: Themes from Harsanyi and Rawls*, ed. Marc Fleurbaey, Maurice Salles, and John A. Weymark. Cambridge: Cambridge University Press.

Arneson, Richard. 2011. Luck Egalitarianism: A Primer. In *Responsibility and Distributive Justice*, ed. Carl Knight and Zofia Stemplowska. Oxford: Oxford University Press.

Auhagen, Ann Elisabeth, and Hans-Werner Bierhoff, eds. 2001. *Responsibility: The Many Faces of a Social Phenomenon*. London: Routledge.

Badescue, Cristina, and Thomas Weiss. 2010. Misrepresenting R2P and Advancing Norms: An Alternative Spiral? *International Studies Perspectives* 19 (2): 111–128.

Ban Ki-moon. 2012. *Statement' Secretary-General's Address to Stanley Foundation Conference on Responsibility to Protect*. New York, January 18. http://www.un.org/sg/STATEMENTS/index.asp?nid=5813.

Banda, Maria. 2007. The Responsibility to Protect: Moving the Agenda Forward. Paper for the UN Association of Canada.

Barnett, Michael N. 2010. *The International Humanitarian Order*. New York: Routledge.

Bellamy, Alex J. 2006. The Responsibility to Protect or Trojan Horse? The Crisis in Darfur and Humanitarian Intervention after Iraq. *Ethics and International Affairs* 19 (2): 31–54.

Bellamy, Alex J. 2008. The Responsibility to Protect and the Problem of Military Intervention. *International Affairs* 84 (4): 615–639.

Bellamy, Alex J. 2009. Realizing the Responsibility to Protect. *International Studies Perspectives* 10 (2): 111–128.

Bellamy, Alex. 2015. The Three Pillars of the Responsibility to Protect. *Pensamiento Propio* 41 (20): 35–64.

Berman, Jacqueline. 2007. The Vital Core: From Bare Life to the Biopolitics of Human Security. In *Protecting Human Security in a Post 9/11 World: Critical and Global Insights*, ed. Giorgio Shani, Makoto Sato, and Mustapha Kamal Pasha. New York: Palgrave MacMillan.
Bernstein, Peter. 1996. *Against the Gods: The Remarkable Story of Risk*. New York: Wiley.
Black, David R. 2006. Mapping the Interplay of Human Security Practice and Debates: The Canadian Experience. In *A Decade of Human Security: Global Governance and New Multilateralisms*, ed. Sandra J. Maclean, David R. Black, and Timothy M. Shaw. Aldershot and Burlington, VT: Ashgate.
Breau, Susan C. 2006. The Impact of Responsibility to Protect on Peacekeeping. *Journal of Conflict and Security Law* 11 (3): 429–464.
Bruennee, Jutta, and Stephan J. Toope. 2006. Norms, Institutions, and UN Reform: The Responsibility to Protect. *Behind the Headlines* 63 (3): 1–20.
Busumtwi-Sam, James. 2002. Development and Human Security: Whose Security and From What? *International Journal* Spring: 239–258.
Butler, Judith. 2004. *Precarious Life*. New York: Verso.
Campbell, Horace. 2013. *NATO's Failure in Libya: Lessons for Africa*. Pretoria: Africa Institute of South Africa.
Chandler, David. 2003. Rhetoric Without Responsibility: The Attraction of 'Ethical' Foreign Policy. *The British Journal of Politics and International Relations* 5 (3): 295–316.
Chandler, David. 2008. The Dog That Did Not Bark. *Security Dialogue* 39 (4): 427–438.
Chauvet, Lisa, and Paul Collier. 2008. What Are the Preconditions for Turnarounds in Failing States? *Conflict Management and Peace Science* 25 (4): 332–348.
Chomsky, Noam. 1999. *Profit Over People—Neoliberalism and Global Order*. New York: Seven Stories Press.
Chomsky, Noam. 2009. The Responsibility to Protect. Lecture Delivered at the UNGA, July 223.
Christie, Ryerson. 2010. Critical Voices and Human Security: To Endure, or to Engage or to Critique? *Security Dialogue* 41 (2): 169–190.
Claude, Inis L., Jr. 1984. *Swords into Plowshares: The Problems and Progress of International Organization*. New York: Random House.
Cooper, Richard H., and Juliette Voinov Kohler, eds. 2009. *Responsibility to Protect: The Global Moral Compact for the 21st Century*. New York: Palgrave Macmillan.
Cox, Robert W. 1987. *Production, Power, and World Order: Social Forces in the Making of History*. New York: Columbia University.
Craig, David, and Doug Porter. 2006. *Development Beyond Neoliberalism? Governance, Poverty Reduction, and Political Economy*. New York: Routledge.

Darling-Smith, Barbara, ed. 2007. *Responsibility*. Lanham: Lexington Books.

DCD/DAC. 2004. The Security and Development: Challenges for Aid. In *Organisation for Economic Cooperation and Development, Development Assistance Committee High Level Meeting*, April 15–16 (DCD/DAC(2004)9/REV2). http://www.peacepalacelibrary.nl/ebooks/files/31785359.pdf. Accessed on 24 Oct 2014.

Deleuze, Gilles. 1992. What Is a Dispositif? In *Michel Foucault Philosopher: Essays Translated from the French and German*, ed. Timothy J. Armstrong. New York: Routledge.

Deng, Francis, Sadikiel Kimaro, Terrence Lyons, Donald Rothchild, and William I. Zartman. 1996. *Sovereignty as Responsibility: Conflict Management in Africa*. Washington, DC: Brookings Institute.

Dreyfus, Hubert L., and Paul Rabinow. 1983. *Michel Foucault: Beyond Structuralism and Herneneutics*. New York: Routledge.

Duffield, Mark, Joanna Macrae, and Devon Curtis. 2001. Editorial: Politics and Humanitarian Aid. *Disasters, Special Issue: Politics and Humanitarian Aid* 25 (4): 269–274.

Duffield, Mark. 2001a. Governing the Borderlands: Decoding the Power of Aid. *Disasters* 25 (4): 308–320.

Duffield, Mark. 2001b. *Global Governance and the New Wars: The Merging of Security and Development*. London: Zed Books.

Duffield, Mark. 2006. Linking Development and Security in an Age of Terror. In *New Interfaces Between Security and Development: Changing Concepts and Approaches*, ed. Stephan Klingebiel. Bonn: German Development Institute.

Duffield, Mark. 2007. *Development, Security and Unending War: Governing the World of Peoples*. Cambridge: Polity Press.

Duffield, Mark. 2010. The Liberal Way of Development and the Development-Security Impasse: Exploring the Global Life-Chance Divide. *Security Dialogue* 41 (1): 53–76.

Etzioni, Amitai. 2006. Sovereignty as Responsibility. *Orbis* 50 (1): 71–85.

Evans, Brad. 2010. Foucault's Legacy: Security, War and Violence in the 21st Century. *Security Dialogue* 41 (4): 413–433.

Evans, Gareth. 2012. Responsibility While Protecting. *Project Syndicate*, January 27. www.project-syndicate.org/commentary/responsibility-while-protecting.

Findlay, Martha Hall. 2011. *Can R2P Survive Libya and Syria?* Canadian Defence and Foreign Affairs Institute.

Fischer, Andrew M. 2020. The Dark Sides of Social Policy: From Neoliberalism to Resurgent Right-Wing Populism. *Development and Change* 51 (2): 371–397.

Fleurbaey, Marc. 2008. *Fairness, Responsibility, and Welfare*. Oxford: Oxford University Press.

Forrer, John, and Conor Seyle, eds. 2016. *The Role of Business in Responsibility to Protect*. London: Cambridge University Press.
Foucault, Michel. 1972. *The Archaeology of Knowledge and the Discourses of Language*. New York: Pantheon.
Foucault, Michel. 1980. *Power/Knowledge: Selected Interviews and Other Writings 1972–1977*, ed. Colin Gordon. New York: Pantheon Books.
Foucault, Michel. 1990. *The History of Sexuality: An Introduction*, vol. I. New York: Vintage Books.
Foucault, Michel. 1991. Governmentality. In *Foucault Effect*, ed. Graham Burchell, Colin Gordon, and Peter Miller. Chicago: University of Chicago Press.
Foucault, Michel. 1997. *Society Must Be Defended: Lectures at the College de France, 1975–76*. New York: Picador.
Foucault, Michel. 2000. The Political Technology of Individuals. In *Essential Works of Foucault*, ed. James D. Faubion, pp. 403–418. New York: New Press.
Foucault, Michel. 2007. *Security, Territory, Population: Lectures at the College De France 1977–78*. New York: Palgrave.
Foucault, Michel. 2008. *The Birth of Biopolitics: Lectures at the College de France, 1978–79*. New York: Palgrave Macmillan.
Franceschet, Antonio. 2006. Global Legalism and Human Security. In *A Decade of Human Security: Global Governance and New Multilateralisms*, ed. Sandra J. Maclean, David R. Black, and Timothy M. Shaw. Aldershot and Burlington, VT: Ashgate.
Ghani, Ashraf, and Clare Lockhart. 2008. *Fixing Failed States: A Framework for Building a Fractured World*. New York: Oxford University Press.
Gill, Stephen. 1995. The Global Panoptican? The Neoliberal State, Economic Life, and Democratic Surveillance. *Alternatives* 20 (1): 1–49.
Giroux, Henry A. 2004. *The Terror of Neoliberalism: Authoritarianism and the Eclipse of Democracy*. Herndon: Paradigm Publishers.
Glanville, Luke. 2016. Does R2P Matter? Interpreting the Impact of a Norm. *Cooperation and Conflict* 52 (2): 184–199.
Gudavarthy, Ajay, and G. Vijay. 2020. Social Policy and Political Mobilization in India: Producing Hierarchical Fraternity and Polarized Differences. *Development and Change* 51 (2): 463–484.
Hall, Stuart. 2015. The Neoliberal Revolution. In *The Neoliberal Crisis: A Soundings Collection*, ed. Sally Davison and Katherine Harris. London: Lawrence & Wishart. Project MUSE. Web. 11 Nov 2015. https://muse.jhu.edu/.
Hardt, Michael, and Antonio Negri. 2000. *Empire*. Cambridge, MA: Harvard University Press.
Harvey, David. 2007. *A Brief History of Neoliberalism*. New York: Oxford University Press.

Hehir, Aidan. 2013a. *Humanitarian Intervention: An Introduction*. Houndsmills Basingstoke, Hampshire: Palgrave Macmillan.
Hehir, Aidan. 2013b. The Permanence of Inconsistency: Libya, the Security Council, and the Responsibility to Protect. *International Security* 38 (1): 137–159.
Held, David, and Anthony McGrew. 2003. The Great Globalization Debate: An Introduction. In *The Global Transformations Reader: An Introduction to the Globalization Debate*, ed. David Held and Anthony McGrew. Cambridge: Polity Press.
Herro, Annie. 2015. *UN Emergency Peace Service and the Responsibility to Protect*. Abingdon, Oxon: Routledge.
Hobbes, Thomas. 1985. *Leviathan*. London: Penguin Books.
Hoffmann, Julia, and Andre Nollkaemper. 2012a. Introduction. In *Responsibility to Protect: From Principle to Practice*, ed. Julia Hoffmann and Andre Nollkaemper. Amsterdam: Pallas Publication.
Hoffmann, Julia, and Andre Nollkaemper. 2012b. Concluding Observations. In *Responsibility to Protect: From Principle to Practice*, ed. Julia Hoffmann and Andre Nollkaemper. Amsterdam: Pallas Publication.
Ignatieff, Michael. 1997. *The Warrior's Honor: Ethnic War and the Modern Conscience*. New York: Metropolitan Books.
International Commission on Intervention and State Sovereignty. 2001. *The Responsibility to Protect*. Ottawa: International Development Research Centre.
Jolly, Richard, Louis Emmerij, and Thomas G. Weiss. 2009. *UN Ideas That Changed the World*. Bloomington: Indiana University Press.
Keck, Margaret, and Kathryn Sikkink. 1998. *Activists Beyond Borders: Advocacy Networks in International Politics*. Ithaca: Cornell University Press.
Kelly, Mark G. 2010. International Biopolitics: Foucault, Globalization and Imperialism. *Theoria* 57 (123): 1–26.
Kessler, Oliver. 2010. Risk. In *The Routledge Handbook of New Security Studies*, ed. Peter Burgess. New York: Routledge.
Keynes, John M. 2004. *The End of Laissez-Faire: The Economic Consequences of the Peace*. Amherst, New York: Prometheus Books.
Krasner, Stephen D. 2004. Sharing Sovereignty: New Institutions for Collapsed and Failing States. *International Security* 29 (2): 85–120.
Krause Hansen, Hans, Dorte Salskov-Iversen, and Sven Bislev. 2002. Transnational Discourse Communities: Globalizing Public Management. In *Understanding the Global Polity*, ed. R. Higgott and M. Ougaard. London: Routledge.
Kuperman, Alan J. 2013. A Model Humanitarian Intervention? Reassessing NATO's Libya Campaign. *International Security* 38 (1): 105–136.

Labonte, Melissa. 2016 (2014). R2P's Status as a Norm. In *The Oxford Handbook of Responsibility to Protect*, ed. Alex J. Bellamy and Tim Dunne, 133–150. Oxford: Oxford University Press.
Larner, Wendy, and William Walters. 2004. Introduction: Global Governmentality. In *Global Governmentality: Governing International Spaces*, ed. Wendy Larner and William Walters. London: Routledge.
Lavin, Chad. 2008. *The Politics of Responsibility*. Urbana: University of Illinois Press.
Legg, Stephen. 2012. 'The Life of Individuals as Well as of Nations:' International Law and the League of Nations' Anti-Trafficking Governmentalities. *Leiden Journal of International Law* 25: 647–664.
Lemke, Thomas. 2002. Foucault, Governmentality, and Critique. *Rethinking Marxism: A Journal of Economics, Culture & Society* 14 (3): 49–64.
Lotze, Walter. 2014. The African Union and the Protection of Civilians: Can Africa Protect its Most Vulnerable Populations? In *Handbook of Africa's International Relations*, ed. Tim Murithi. New York: Routledge.
Luck, Edward C. 2008. The Responsible Sovereign and the Responsibility to Protect. In *Annual Review of United Nations Affairs 2006/2007*, ed. Karl P. Sauvant and Joachim W. Muller. Oxford: Oxford University Press.
Macpherson, C.B. 2011. *The Political Theory of Possessive Individualism: Hobbes to Locke*. Oxford: Ontario.
Mbabazi, Pamela, Sandra Maclean, and Timothy Shaw. 2005. Research for Reconstruction in Africa: Challenges for Policy Communities and Coalitions. In *Global Knowledge Networks and International Development: Bridges Across Boundaries*, ed. Diane Stone and Simon Maxwell. London: Routledge.
McCormack, Tara. 2010. *Critique, Security and Power: The Political Limits to Emancipatory Approaches*. New York: Routledge.
McCormack, Tara. 2011. The Limits to Emancipation in the Human Security Framework. In *Critical Perspectives on Human Security: Rethinking Emancipation and Power in International Relations*, ed. David Chandler and Nik Hynek. New York: Routledge.
Mearsheimer, John. 1990. Back to the Future: Instability in Europe after the Cold War: International Institutions. *International Security* 19 (3): 5–49.
Mennecke, Martin, and Ellen E. Stensurd. 2021. The Failure of the International Community to Apply R2P and Atrocity Prevention in Myanmar. *Global Responsibility to Protect* 2 (3): 111–130.
Michaelis, Lorealea, and Genevieve Fuji Johnson. 2013. Political Responsibility Refocused. In *Political Responsibility Refocused: Thinking Justice after Iris Marion Young*, ed. Genevieve Fuji Johnson and Loralea Michaelis. Toronto: University of Toronto.
Murray, Robert W. 2013. Humanitarianism, Responsibility or Rationality? Evaluating Intervention as State Strategy. In *Libya: The Responsibility to Protect*

and the Future of Humanitarian Intervention, ed. Aidan Hehir and Robert W. Murray. New York: Palgrave Macmillan.

O'Malley, Pat. 2004. *Risk, Uncertainty and Government*. London: Glasshouse Press.

Orford, Anne. 2011. *International Authority and the Responsibility to Protect*. Cambridge: Cambridge University Press.

Peck, Jamie. 2010. *Constructions of Neoliberal Reason*. Oxford: Oxford University Press.

Plehwe, Dieter, Bernard J.A. Walpen, and Gisela Neunhoffer. 2006. *Neolberal Hegemony: A Global Critique*. London: Routledge.

Raffoul, Francois. 2010. *The Origins of Responsibility*. Bloomington: Indiana University Press.

Ralph, Jason, and Adrian Gallagher. 2015. Legitimacy Faultlines in International Society: The Responsibility to Prosecute After Libya. *Review of International Studies* 41 (3): 553–573.

Rapley, John. 2004. *Globalization and Inequality: Neoliberalism's Downward Spiral*. Boulder, CO: Lynne Rienner.

Reinold, Theresa. 2013. *Sovereignty and the Responsibility to Protect: The Power of Norms and the Norms of the Powerful*. New York: Routlegde.

Rostow, Walt Whitman. 1960. *The Stages of Economic Growth: A Non-Communist Manifesto*. Cambridge: Cambridge University Press.

Ruggie, John G. 1982. International Regimes, Transactions, and Change: Embedded Liberalism in the Postwar Economic Order. *International Organization* 36 (2): 379–415.

Ruggie, John G. 2008. Taking Embedded Liberalism Global: The Corporate Connection. In *Embedding Global Markets: An Enduring Challenge*, ed. John Gerard Ruggie. Burlington: Ashgate.

Saad-Filho, Alfredo, and Deborah Johnston, eds. 2004. *Neoliberalism: A Critical Reader*. London: Pluto Press.

Savas-Cazala, Menet. 2022. Cote D'Ivoire: A Timely and Decisive R2P Action? In *The Responsibility to Protect Twenty Years On*, ed. P. Gozen Ercan, 107–131. Cham: Palgrave Macmillan.

Scheffler, Samuel. 1992. Responsibility, Reactive Attitudes, and Liberalism in Philosophy and Politics. *Philosophy and Public Affairs* 21 (4): 299–323.

Schittecatte, Catherine. 2006. Toward a More Inclusive Global Governance and Enhanced Human Security. In *A Decade of Human Security: Global Governance and New Multilateralisms*, ed. Sandra J. Maclean, David R. Black, and Timothy M. Shaw. Aldershot and Burlington, VT: Ashgate.

Seyle, C., and E. Aloyo. 2015. The Role of Business in the Responsibility to Protect. In *The Responsibility to Protect and the Third Pillar*, ed. D. Fiott and J. Koops. London: Palgrave Macmillan.

Shankleman, Jill. 2016. R2P and the Extractive Industries. In *The Role of Business in Responsibility to Protect*, ed. John Forrer and Conor Seyle. London: Cambridge University Press.
Sharma, Serena. 2016. *The Responsibility to Protect and the International Criminal Court: Protection and Prosecution in Kenya*. New York: Routledge.
Spear, Joanna, and Paul D. Williams, eds. 2012. *Security and Development in Global Politics: A Critical Comparison*. Washington, DC: Georgetown University Press.
Stern, Maria, and Joakim Ojendal. 2010. Mapping the Security–Development Nexus: Conflict, Complexity, Cacophony, Convergence? *Security Dialogue* 41 (1): 5–30.
Stone, Diane, and Simon Maxwell, eds. 2005. *In Global Knowledge Networks and International Development: Bridges Across Boundaries*. London: Routledge.
Thakur, Ramesh. 2004. Iraq and the Responsibility to Protect. *Behind the Headlines* 62: 1–16.
Thakur, Ramesh. 2005. A Shared Responsibility for a More Secure World. *Global Governance* 11 (3): 281–289.
Thakur, Ramesh. 2006. *The United Nations, Peace and Security: From Collective Security to Responsibility to Protect*. Cambridge: Cambridge University Press.
Thakur, Ramesh. 2011. UN Breathes New Life into "Responsibility to Protect. *Toronto Star*, March 21. www.thestar.com/opinion/editorialopinion/2011/03/21/un_breathes_life_intoresponsibility_to_protect.html.
Thakur, Ramesh. 2013. R2P After Libya and Syria: Engaging Emerging Powers. *The Washington Quarterly* 36 (2): 61–76.
Thakur, Ramesh. 2020. *Reviewing the Responsibility to Protect: Origins, Implementation and Controversies*. Abingdon: Routledge.
Thakur, Ramesh and William Maley. 2015. Introduction: Theorising the Responsibility to Protect. In *Theorising the Responsibility to Protect*, ed. Ramesh Thakur and William Maley. Cambridge: Cambridge University Press.
Touraine, Alain. 2001. *Beyond Neoliberalism*. Cambridge: Polity.
Tsoukala, Anastassia. 2010. Risk-Focused Security Policies and Human Rights: The Impossible Symbiosis. In *Mapping Transatlantic Security Relations: The EU, Canada and the War on Terror*, ed. Mark Salter. London: Routledge.
United Nations General Assembly. 2005. *2005 World Summit Outcome*. UN Doc. A/RES/60/1, October 24.
United Nations General Assembly. 2009. *The Responsibility to Protect*. UN Doc. A/RES/63/308, October 7.
United Nations Secretary-General. 2009. *Implementing the Responsibility to Protect*. Report of the Secretary-General. UN Doc. A/63/677/2009, January 12.

United Nations Secretary-General. 2010. *Early Warning, Assessment and the Responsibility to Protect*. Report of the Secretary-General. UN Doc. A/64/864/2010, July 14.

United Nations Secretary-General. 2015. *A Vital and Enduring Commitment: Implementing the Responsibility to Protect*. Report of the Secretary-General. UN Doc. A/69/981-S/2015/500, July 13.

United Nations Security Council. 2007. *UN Doc. S/2007/721*, December 7.

Waltz, Kenneth Neal. 1993. The Emerging Structure of International Politics. *International Security* 18 (2): 44–79.

Warner, Daniel. 2003. The Responsibility to Protect and Irresponsible, Cynical Engagement. *Millennium—Journal of International Studies* 32 (1): 109–121.

Watson, Scott. 2011. The 'Human' as Referent Object? Humanitarianism as Securitization. *Security Dialogue* 42 (1): 3–20.

Weiss, Thomas G. 2007. *Humanitarian Intervention: Ideas in Action*. Cambridge, MA: Polity Press.

Weiss, Thomas G. 2011. RtoP Alive and Well After Libya. *Ethics & International Affairs* 25 (3): 287–292.

Weiss, Thomas G., and Don Hubert. 2001. *The Responsibility to Protect: Research, Bibliography, Background*. Ottawa: IDRC.

Weiss, Thomas G., and Sam Daws, eds. 2007. *The Oxford Handbook of the United Nations*. New York: Oxford University Press.

Welsh, Jennifer. 2013. Norm Contestation and the Responsibility to Protect. *Global Responsibility to Protect* 5 (4): 365–396.

Wheeler, Nicholas J. 2000. *Saving Strangers: Humanitarian Intervention in International Society*. New York: Oxford University Press.

Wheeler, Nicholas J. 2005. The Emerging Norm of Collective Responsibility to Protect after R2P and HLP. Paper presented at the BISA Conference, University of Warwick, December 20–22.

World Federalist Movement-International Policy Group. 2003. Civil Society Perspectives on the Responsibility to Protect, Final Report, April 30.

Wouters, Jan, Philip De Man, and Marie Vincent. 2012. The Responsibility to Protect and Regional Organizations. In *Responsibility to Protect: From Principle to Practice*, ed. Julia Hoffmann and Andre Nollkaemper. Amsterdam: Pallas Publication.

Young, Iris Marion. 2003. From Guilt to Solidarity: Sweatshops and Political Responsibility. *Dissent* 50 (2): 39–44.

Young, Iris Marion. 2004. Responsibility and Global Labor Justice. *Journal of Political Philosophy* 12 (4): 365–388.

CHAPTER 2

Understanding R2P as a Security/Development Measure: Security and Development in the Discipline of International Relations and in the UN Security/Development Dispositif

Introduction

Analysing R2P is an occasion to encounter intimacy between concepts—(a) liberalism/neoliberalism; (b) security/development[1]—followed by the discovery of a *kinship* amongst them, and concluding with an invention of a clustered term *liberal/neoliberal security/development dispositif*. This task of analysis involves examining these concepts in the context of the interaction between the realms of academics (disciplines), policy-making, and practice. The UN is a world of policy and practice that has also at various points enlisted the services of individuals from academia. Academic disciplines, in their ideal type mode, must begin with an acknowledgment and examination of *reality*—such as social, political, or economic—and then follow it up with an evaluation that endorses or

[1] In this chapter the relationship between security and development is described using two terms—security/development and security-development. Security/development is my preferred term as it is in consonance with my analytical argument. I use of the term security-development, only when paraphrasing quotations that employ the term.

R. Kashyap, *The Political Economy of Security/Development in the Neoliberal Age*, International Political Economy Series,
https://doi.org/10.1007/978-3-031-37279-7_2

criticizes. While the world of policy and practice is about *what is to be done* and *doing it* respectively, academics including philosophers from the yore have taken on self-appointed advisory roles—examples include Plato's *Republic*, Kautilya's *Arthshastra*, Machiavelli's *Prince*, and Kant's *Towards Perpetual Peace: A Philosophical Project*—and suggested to a ruler or a people a way out of an identified social or political problem or crisis. International Relations scholarship has both informed and reflected the policy world of international politics including that of the UN. For example, the list of academics involved in the formulation and operationalization of R2P includes Thomas Weiss, Ramesh Thakur, Edward Luck, Jennifer Welsh, and Karen Smith.[2] Economists, Mahbub ul Haq and Amartya Sen, made prominent contributions towards the articulation of the concepts of human development and human security at the UN. An International Relations scholar, John Ruggie, on his two short-term stints at the UN authored two reports the *UN Global Compact* and the *UN Guiding Principles on Business and Human Rights*. There is a proliferation of research literature in think tanks and universities on the issue of the 'security-development nexus' (Stern and Ojendal 2010: 6), such research in Europe, Canada, and the United States is mostly state-funded (Williams 2012: 22). The policy/practice world is a site of praxis for the conceptual advancement of security/development.[3] Academic writing on security/development has mostly articulated the changes on the ground i.e., it has played catch up with the policy world (Williams 2012). The veritable growth of the 'official "report industry"' (Stern and Ojendal

[2] Thomas Weiss is Presidential Professor of Political Science, City University of New York. He served as Research Director at the ICISS. Ramesh Thakur is Professor, Australian National University College of Asia and Pacific. He was a member of the ICISS. Edward Luck, Professor of International Relations is currently Dean, Joan B. Kroc School of Peace Studies, University of San Diego. He served as the SAR2P (February 2008–July 2013). Jennifer Welsh is Professor and Chair of International Relations, European University Institute, Florence. In July 2013, she was appointed as SAR2P. Karen Smith, Lecturer in International Relations at Leiden University, was SAR2P (2019–2021).

[3] The writings of Mark Duffield, former Oxfam Country Representative in Sudan and adviser to several government departments and international NGOs, are an example of the same. See http://dbms.ilrt.bris.ac.uk/spais/people/person/mark-r-duffield/.

2010: 6) is a result of the work of international organizations,[4] international non-governmental organizations,[5] and national governments.[6] Indeed, the UN's Outreach Division of the Department of Public Information conducts the United Nations Academic Programme aimed at building association between the United Nations and 'institutions of higher learning throughout the world.'[7]

This chapter is divided into five sections. Section 2.1 unpacks the term—liberal/neoliberal security-development dispositif via the discussion of liberalism/neoliberalism. It locates the issues of security and development at the UN in embedded liberalism and asserts that the UN has from its inception regarded the two as inter-related. Although the discipline of IR did not ignore issues of development (and economy), it *prioritized* security as the primary concern of states in international anarchy. Section 2.2 discusses the crisis and retreat of embedded liberalism following the collapse of the original Bretton Woods compromise (Ruggie 1982) and the critique of the welfare state by the New Right in the developed world, which led to the formulation of neoliberal economic policies. Neoliberal IR scholars responded to the new reality by rationalizing the neoliberal avatars of the UN and its specialized agencies—World Bank and the IMF—and emphasizing institutionalism as a guarantor of international co-operation. While approaches that expanded the concept of security to take into account development concerns were *accommodated*, the neo avatars of realism and liberalism reigned as dominant approaches in IR. In Sect. 2.3, I discuss how in the 1990s the catalogue of international problems came to include the *new problems* of intrastate conflicts, failed states, and human insecurity. The UN responded to these challenges through the policies of human security, which was

[4] Such as the UN, World Bank, IMF, European Union (e.g., *The European Security Strategy* adopted by the European Council in 2004, reviewed and confirmed in 2008), OECD (e.g., 'The Security and Development: Challenges for Aid' (OECD), *Development Assistance Committee High-Level Meeting*, April 15–16 (DCD/DAC(2004)9/REV2), available at http://www.peacepalacelibrary.nl/ebooks/files/31785359.pdf. Accessed on 24 October 2014), and African Union (e.g., *Solemn Declaration on a Common African Defence and Security Policy* [2004]).

[5] Such as OXFAM and Save the Children.

[6] Examples: *The National Security Strategy of the United States of America* (2006, 2010), *The National Security Strategy of the United Kingdom: Security in an Interdependent World* (2008).

[7] See https://academicimpact.un.org/content/about-unai.

announced as a new security paradigm. Section 2.4 is a brief summation of the critical literature in IR and analyses human security and similar liberal peacebuilding measures like R2P as efforts to stem this disorder and crisis, which is of neoliberal making. More recently, these scholars have employed the Foucauldian lenses of biopolitics and governmentality to make this point. Section 2.5 reiterates the significance of examining the UN security/development dispositif in the context of parallel developments in the academic world. It points out that contrary to the hype of a new paradigm label thrust on human security—in which R2P was sought to be embedded—its adoption by the UN has not led to any radical shifts in the latter's security/development dispositif.

Liberalism/Neoliberalism

Liberalism at the UN assumed two avatars: (a) embedded liberalism (1945–late 1970s); (b) neoliberalism (1980s to the present). R2P was introduced at the UN in the neoliberal phase. Despite their differences, embedded liberalism and neoliberalism inhabit points on a liberal continuum because of their subscription to the philosophy and practice of the free market.[8] The adjective free in the free market, as we know, refers to market being free of the state, i.e., the state and the economy are regarded as distinct spheres, and normatively so. While the role of the welfare state in embedded liberalism (Ruggie 1982) is part of the liberal lore, its 'crucial,' albeit diluted, presence in a neoliberal economy is hushed up (of course not by its critics); the state performs the important function of 'insulation of markets' and saving it from the 'disruptive effects of democracy' (Slobidian 2018: 4–11). A liberal continuum

[8] Therefore, liberalism is prefixed with *neo* and not *new* as the former denotes continuity and/or reinvigoration of an idea, whereas a novel or fresh idea, on the other hand, is best described as new. Manuel B. Aalberts views neoliberalism as 'more than traditional liberalism and it is not capitalism by another name. It is a specific movement *within* capitalism that relies on some but not all of the old principles of economic liberalism' (2013: 1053). Rich literature on the subject reveals the self-contradiction of neoliberalism, while neoliberal ideology decries state regulation, the reality of neoliberal practice sees the state intervening to facilitate giant corporations in market transactions (1054). Also, neoliberalism is in a state of constant evolution and diversification. The streams within neoliberalism exist with 'critical differences' between them: 'for example, between American, British and European "social market" versions; Southeast Asian state-supported growth and Chinese "state capitalism"; Russia's oligarchic/kleptomanic state and monetarist "experiments" in Latin America' (fa: 16). Italics mine.

is a testimony to its adeptness at appropriating challenges even when it involves adaptation and change; indeed, its survival or rather flourishing, is possible because it works hard to make itself relevant and render alternatives, if not unthinkable, then at least appear impractical.

Embedded liberalism refers to the post-Second World War international economic order, also described as the Bretton Woods system. Inspired by Keynesian domestic economics, laying claim to Polanyian dictum to not separate economic theory from social policy, embedded liberalism aimed at avoiding the repeat of the 1930s Great Depression—the economic crisis, widely credited as a major cause of the Second World War—thereby ensuring peace, democracy and order. The Bretton Woods institutions'—the IMF and the World Bank—trade and monetary regimes aimed to construct an international economic order operating on the principle of 'market rationality' (Ruggie 1982: 381) that would ensure stability. The simultaneous pursuit of the two required the application of Keynesian wisdom to the domestic economy and its upscaling to the international, albeit not uniformly (to all countries) but with variations—the criteria dictated by political and strategic considerations of the US that had emerged as one of the superpowers in the post-Second World War order. The World Bank followed the template set by the economic component of US foreign policy. The US Marshall Plan made available aid for post-war economic reconstruction of Western European countries and went hand in hand with the Truman Doctrine that pledged military and economic aid to countries under threat from internal or external forces (see Busumtwi-Sam 2004). By 1960 the circle of aid recipients was expanded to include the third world, a task actively taken by the World Bank's International Development Association that provided resources for poor countries that lacked creditworthiness.[9]

The premise of the neoliberal economic and political ideology is that an economy framed by institutions of private property, free market, and free trade is most suited to liberate the human entrepreneurial spirit; indeed, it is proposed as an appropriate guide to all human action. The state is conceptualized with minimal functions primarily to maintain law and order to preserve this economic framework. The global turn towards neoliberalism in the late 1970s involved 'deregulation, privatization, and withdrawal of the state from many areas of social provision' (Harvey 2–3).

[9] See https://www.worldbank.org/en/archive/history.

This subscription to the faith in the wisdom of the free hand of the market as a panacea for human well-being at first glance may appear as a recall to the theory of classical liberal economists—Adam Smith and David Ricardo. However, it is much closer to that of twentieth-century libertarians—Friedrich Hayek's and Milton Friedman's version of the free market. The latter's neoliberalism includes a 'public pedagogy and political ideology' which is 'far more ruthless' and makes possible a society and culture that sustains a 'barbaric notion of authoritarianism,' democracy itself becomes captive to 'the rapacious laws of the market economy', it is a 'virulent and brutal form of market capitalism' (Giroux 2004: xxii–xxiii). So, while it is relatively easy to tell apart embedded liberalism from neoliberalism, the latter's distinctiveness from classical economic liberalism is not so obvious. This distinctiveness, however, must be noted to contextualize and understand the violence, populist politics, and protest politics or what Pierre Rosanvallon (2008) called 'counter-democracy' that punctuate our neoliberal age. Adam Smith's (2010) theoretical installation of 'moral sentiments' in the free market was perhaps a prescient suggestion to gatekeep the 'barbarism'[10] that Rosa Luxemburg would draw attention to two centuries later. Michel Foucault's identification of neoliberal governmentality's promotion of market as a 'site of truth veridiction' (2008)—to which all other domains, social and political, must conform—and positing its apparently positive biopolitics with the inevitability of (and obviously negative) thanatopolitics is similar to Luxemburg's unembellished articulation of the *not so noble* truth of the market economy. Foucault underlines that while classical liberalism was premised on laissez faire, neoliberalism[11] is marked by an 'exercise of political power' modelled on the 'principles of a market economy' which 'index a general art of government' (2008: 131).

[10] 'Socialism or barbarism', a slogan made famous by Rosa Luxemburg in the midst of the First World War. Also see Luxemburg (2010).

[11] Francois Ewald guards against the misreading of *The Birth of Biopolitics* as Foucault's endorsement of neoliberalism. The distinction between the two liberalisms is sharply made in Europe, the American version informs the popular understanding of neoliberalism while 'welfare state protection, and social safety net' is associated with German liberalism (2015). http://blogs.law.columbia.edu/foucault1313/2016/01/24/ewaldneoliberalism/, Accessed on 10 May 2023.

Foucault (2008) analyses liberalism through the concept of governmentality—the art of governing.[12] The singularity of biopolitics as a feature of neoliberal governmentality lies in its accompaniment—thanatopolitics, that is, politics of death—an inevitable consequence of neoliberal governmentality. The paradox of the neoliberal market, in a politically conscious, democracy expectant times is that thanatopolitics is the necessity of biopolitics to lubricate the machinery of the neoliberal market by ensuring the presence and provision of healthy human resources and eager consumers. However, even health and eagerness are no guarantees to escape the fate of thanatos, since the neoliberal market, irrespective of its degrees of prosperity, cannot accommodate all. The neoliberal market is premised on the inevitability, or rather a normative inevitability of inequality. Its prosperity: (a) cannot be equally available to all; (b) cannot be available at all for some. Since there is not good and *enough* prosperity for all in society, some will be out of range of the sovereign's *make live* dictum (biopolitics), the structural logic will ensure that the non-prosperous die (the *let die* dictum) (thanatopolitics). These deaths could be a result of acts of commission (R2P's atrocity crimes) or non-commission (the fact of poverty). Atrocity crimes involve two ontological moves, *one,* the demotion of population from that of the species of human beings and *two,* its segmentation into categories such as ethnicity, nationality, and, religious. The individual narratives of thanatopolitics and atrocity crimes could be different, they may involve scapegoating, vote bank politics, perceived appeasement of minority groups, and reclamation of lost national glory. The act of killing could be via gas chambers, machetes, lynching, etc.—this modern barbarism, Foucault cautions, must not be confused with medieval barbarism; it is modern precisely because its reasons are imperatives of our times, imperatives of neoliberal governmentality.

These versions of liberalism frame the economy (and therefore, notions of development) and are accompanied by their respective versions of security; security and development are thus intimately related to each other. The continuity between embedded liberalism and neoliberalism indicates the similarity and continuity in their respective conceptualizations of security. R2P is a measure of both security and development.

[12] Foucault's analysis of liberal governmentality in the *The Birth of Biopolitics* includes: English liberalism (eighteenth century), German ordoliberalism (twentieth century), French neoliberalism (twentieth century), and American neoliberalism (twentieth century).

Security/Development

The logic of neoliberal security/development policies necessitates endorsement of human security articulations which collect and redistribute some select debris of security/development responsibilities—left behind by the receded embedded liberalism—between the state, private sector, and civil society, which may work individually or in collaboration. The burgeoning of public–private partnerships in the neoliberal era is an example of a new collaborative division of labour. Indeed, these partnerships are an 'advanced form of liberal power... that help produce modern, self-disciplined citizens and states by enlisting them as responsible agents in their own development' (Abrahamsen 2004: 1453; Also see Hodge et al. 2010; Hodge and Greve 2005; Jooste and Scott 2012; Loxley 2010, 2012).

The ICISS Report justified R2P by invoking two human security goals—freedom from want and freedom from fear. Accusations of R2P as a mask for imperial designs of military intervention are made primarily in the context of R2P's pursuit of the second human security goal. However, the Secretary-General's annual reports on R2P underline several development-related measures of the UN as R2P's instruments (under R2P pillars one and two).

R2P is a security/development measure, best understood through the Foucauldian lenses of biopolitics and governmentality, which reveal its liberal/neoliberal underpinnings. This chapter is a genealogical review of the security/development discourse in the discipline of IR and its trajectory in the UN.

R2P is celebrated as a new idea in the context of the 'ideational' turn (that began in the 1980s) in International Relations (IR) scholarship and the policy world (see Thakur et al. 2005; Gofas and Hay 2010).[13] I locate R2P in the UN's liberal/neoliberal security/development dispositif. Though the UN's mandate since its inception accorded importance to both security and development, the *link* between the two was not always *clearly* articulated and acknowledged until 1994 when the concept of

[13] The ideational turn brought attention to theoretical approaches (particularly that of constructivism) other than those of realism and liberalism (and their respective neo avatars) in the discipline of IR.

human security (HS) and its twin goals of freedom from fear (FFF) and freedom from want (FFW) were put forward.[14]

R2P is a prominent manifestation of HS (see Murray 2013). The ICISS Report advocated the simultaneous pursuit of the goals of FFF and FFW, but the World Summit Outcome Document (2005) limited R2P's agenda to FFF only. The dilution of the R2P goal to FFF i.e., a narrow conception of HS—a security goal, ***unadulterated*** by development concerns—was viewed as a pragmatic move to operationalize R2P (Bellamy 2009; Evans and Sahnoun 2002; Weiss 2001). This attenuated R2P agenda put aside the broad conception of HS (FFF and FFW), that combines both security and development concerns. However, R2P, through the prevention and rebuilding agenda (that informs the three R2P pillars) outlined by the Secretary-General's annual reports on R2P, made a ***return*** to the broad agenda of human security.

This difference in opinions on the proper goals of R2P is symptomatic of the discipline of IR's traditional treatment of security and development as separate issues (Buzan 2000). The worlds of scholarship and policy/practice influence but do not mirror each other, the exact reflection of the diversity in the domain of scholarship would make the policy realm chaotic. However, dissident voices in scholarship often find a place in the dominant strand's adaptive or co-optative mode. Liberalism has been particularly adept in this act (Foucault 2008), not surprisingly, those who endorse the security/development relationship, term it as a liberal peacebuilding project (Paris 2010) while the critics see the liberal underpinnings of this nexus as the primary hurdle to emancipation. Security/development is not so much a relationship of mimesis but one characterized by the circularity of dynamics similar to those of the power/knowledge relationship (Foucault 1980).[15]

Taking into account the ideological congruity of liberal/neoliberal ideas between the dominant strands of scholarship and the policy world on this subject, this research proposes that the ICISS Report (2001) and the World Summit Outcome Document (2005) are not singular events

[14] Note that this UN-*supported* ICISS report seeks to embed R2P in the UN's human security discourse which itself is a part of the broader security/development dispositif of the UN (also see Duffield 2006: 23).

[15] Foucault theorizes knowledge as always being an exercise of power and power as a function of knowledge. The two share an intimate relationship that qualifies them to the conjoined status of a singular entity (See Foucault 1980, 1990).

but articulations that conform to the UN's existing security/development ideas and practices. This is shown by tracing R2P's genealogy to the UN Charter's philosophy and the UN-supported commissions (since the late 1970s) on the issues of security/development. The concepts of biopolitics and governmentality, *upscaled*[16] to the international level, reveal R2P as a measure of the UN's liberal/neoliberal security/development dispositif.

The above genealogical assignment is supplemented by a similar exploration of the concepts of security and development in the discipline of International Relations (IR) in order to establish the latter's correspondence to the UN's evolving security/development paradigm. Two clarifications must be made before proceeding further. *First,* this book concentrates on the *discipline* of IR since the UN is an international organization and is the advocate of R2P. Although references wherever relevant are made to organizations other than the UN, it is the latter as a field of policy/practice that is the focus of this study.

Second, interrogating the epistemological categorization of security and development as distinct domains, must begin by an acknowledgement that, security and development are essentially contested concepts that are based on different ontologies and refer to different realities (Chandler 2008; International Peace Academy 2006 in Stern and Ojendal 2010: 6; Uvin 2008). Concepts are descriptive and *prescriptive* in nature, as discursive constructions they create reality that they seem to mirror, and serve certain interests (Stern and Ojendal 2010: 7); we may recall here a similar but more famed observation 'Theory is always *for* someone and *for* some purpose' (Cox 1996: 87). The concepts of security and development have undergone individual stretching and broadening[17] even leading to accusations of poaching on each other's territories. This perceived transgression of boundaries also leads to security/development being viewed as a nexus that is characterized by either securitization of development or developmentalization of security. Nevertheless, the predominant concern of the discipline continues to be security even as development issues have made inroads via the sub-discipline of political economy. Despite this recognition, development still has a subordinate status in IR and

[16] The application of the concepts (biopolitics and governmentality) to developing countries is also criticized on the grounds that these ideas were developed by Foucault to understand the domestic society of the 'developed' world (Duffield 2006: 13).

[17] This broadening gives security/development an interdisciplinary character; scholars writing on the subject borrow from economics, psychology, and biosciences.

realist/neorealist writings refer to it only as a dimension or issue that can be a possible problem for national or international security. Also, the non-realization of development promises of equity and social justice is portrayed as mere postponement and justified via the liberal/neoliberal 'trickle-down theory'—benefits of economic growth in a free market reach the marginalized in the long run.[18] Such claims have come under scrutiny, particularly in the critical security studies literature that problematizes the concepts of security and development, and critiques this linkage as a liberal peacebuilding project. Michel Foucault's concept of governmentality underscores this link as characterized by a deep and enduring circularity—security/development that serves the neoliberal economy.[19] Following Foucault, I treat the two concepts as part of a singular complex i.e., the liberal/neoliberal governmentality, therefore, the validity of the term liberal/neoliberal security/development.

The trajectory of the security/development dispositif within the United Nations has not entailed a radical shift, but only a shift in emphasis. While the UN Charter recognizes the relationship between the two goals i.e., of security and development, security is seen as a hard issue demanding immediate response and manifestation compared to the soft issue of development which can make do with a relatively delayed response since its materialization anyways requires a long period of gestation, it can be achieved only gradually and incrementally. The organization's concept of security as collective security (UN Charter, Chapter VII) was accompanied by a development agenda of embedded liberalism pursued within the framework of the Bretton Woods system. With the collapse of the Bretton Woods system in the 1970s, the development paradigm shifted to neoliberalism. The development agenda of the World Bank and the IMF for the third-world countries was informed by structural adjustment policies (SAP), the so-called 'Washington Consensus' (Williamson 1990) initiated in the wake of the 1982 developing countries' debt crisis. SAP failed to stem the economic crisis in the third world: 'If the original objective was "adjustment with growth", there is not much evidence that structural adjustment lending generated either adjustment

[18] Samir Amin (1974, 1976, 1977) describes such phenomena as 'growth without development': while economic growth measures success in terms of numbers and statistics, development is a holistic approach that takes into account the social and political indicators of economic development.

[19] See Chapters 6 and 7.

or growth' (Easterly 2005: 20; also see Abbott et al. 2010; Dreher 2006; Herbst 1990; Rodrik 2007; Serra and Stiglitz 2008). The 1990s violent intrastate conflict took place against this historical backdrop, that is, it was the economic crisis and not some congenital ethnic hatred that fuelled these conflicts. The new concept i.e., of human security was put forward in 1994 as a remedy for these 'new ills' and 'new wars' (see Kaldor 2012).

Having established a connection between human security and neoliberalism, we should steer clear of the misleading conclusion of a strict fidelity between collective security and human security with embedded liberalism and neoliberalism respectively. This assertion is made on the basis of three points: (a) Human security is about both security and development; (b) Collective security persists within the UN, challenges and criticisms to it notwithstanding; (c) The difference between embedded liberalism and neoliberalism is only in terms of degrees, since both seek to preserve the free market and project it as a panacea. The discarded responsibilities or the *debris of responsibilities* of embedded liberalism in the era of neoliberalism have been redistributed via human security to not just states and international organizations like the UN but also to a wide array of civil society actors. Therefore, a key concern of my research is the examination of R2P's concept of responsibility to see whether it conforms to the meanings that undergird the liberal/neoliberal notion of responsibility. While the concept of human security is widely regarded as the brainchild of the 1994 United Nations Development Programme (UNDP) report, the World Bank's euphemistic acknowledgement of the same was done through its endorsement of *human development* in the 1980 WDR. Also, significant in this regard is the 2011 WDR highlighting the interlinkages between conflict, security, and development, and amongst other things recommending initiatives such as the *Ibrahim Prize for Leadership* whereby the North recognizes and encourages *responsible* leadership in conflict-ridden states (WDR 2011: 37).

The UN Security/Development Dispositif and Embedded Liberalism

The goals of security and development have been on the UN's agenda ever since its inception (UN Charter, Article 1). These aims of security and development were to be achieved within the framework of embedded liberalism and collective security. The inextricable link between security and development is implied in the *Preamble* of the UN Charter that aims to achieve 'international peace and security' and avoid 'the scourge of war', requires the UN to 'promote respect for international law,' 'reaffirm faith in fundamental human rights', and achieve 'social progress and better standards of life.' 'Armed force' is to be used in the 'common interest' and 'international machinery' is to be employed for the 'promotion of the economic and social advancement of all peoples.'[20] Also evident here is the transposition of ends and means, that is, security and development are both goals and instruments to achieve the same. These means and ends were defined within the framework of a post-war international economic order of embedded liberalism (Ruggie 1982: 382–383) and collective security, which were institutionalized in the UN, World Bank, and IMF.

Embedded liberalism was the result of the 'grand social bargain' which brokered the agreement of different social groups to open markets on the promise that the social adjustment costs of this market would be controlled and distributed within society (Ruggie 2008: 231). The era of laissez faire liberalism, 'the self-regulating market', of the 19th and early twentieth centuries that dis-embedded the market from social relations had, as Karl Polanyi (1957) observed, come to an end. The post-war era saw the welfare state model become the *ideal type* for most countries in the first and third worlds; Keynesian economics ensured that the markets were reined in by the state. Marshall Plan (1948) (within the context of the Truman Doctrine) for the reconstruction of Western Europe best exemplified embedded liberalism's multilateralism endorsed and operationalized by the UN, the IMF, and the World Bank. This Keynesian recipe entailed 'interventionist policy on the allocations of resources, price stability, the level of savings, the choice of investments, and a policy of full employment' (Foucault 2008: 80). Avoiding the exacerbation of the social and economic inequalities—the inevitable consequence of free markets– was a political imperative for the liberal states led by US and UK to prevent the successful emergence of the communist model in war-ravaged economies and *imagination* of Western Europe. Foucault views liberal governmentality in the post-Second World War period as being tasked with the three objectives—to reconstruct the war economy into a peace economy, 'planned economy model of the Marshall Plan', and the 'social objectives that were considered politically indispensable in order

[20] See http://www.un.org/en/documents/charter/preamble.shtml.

to avoid renewal of fascism and Nazism in Europe' (2008: 80). Development was a form of social engineering whereby it became a conduct (by the World Bank, IMF and the UN) of conduct (of the war-ravaged economies and the soon to emerge post-colonial societies). A mention must be made here of the 'prophetic liberal utopianism of modernization theory' (Gilman 2003: 77, fn 38) that gave the academic stamp of legitimacy to these plans of social engineering. The modernization thesis (Rostow 1960, 1963, 1971) proposed a linear model of five stages of economic modernization as rites of passage for traditional societies to develop. The local modernized elite and international experts were to provide leadership to pilot the country towards development.

IR—The Privileging of Security and the Relative Neglect of Economy

Modernization theory resonated with the views of key political scientists of the time (see Lipset 1960; Pye 1966) but was not embraced by IR scholars for whom the issue of security, not that of development, was primary. This was in keeping with the disciplines according to a near axiomatic status to the realist/neorealist concepts of human nature as rational and selfish (Morganthau 1967) and the casting of the international domain as anarchy (Milner 1993; Waltz 1959, 1979). The dominance of realist/neorealist approaches ensured the discipline's focus on strategic military concerns of the sovereign state. The immediate post-1945 era witnessed events and situations that were unsettling to say the least—the Cold War (including the proxy wars and arms race between the superpowers) and continuation of struggles for independence in colonies in Africa (e.g., Algeria, Rwanda, Somalia, Egypt, Libya), Asia (e.g., India, Burma, Ceylon, Cambodia, Singapore, Timor-Leste), and South America (Grenada, Bahamas, Jamaica, Guyana); this guaranteed IR's and its sub-field of security studies' preoccupation with 'statism, strategizing, and stability' (Booth 2005: 12). Though early prominent IR works—*Politics Among Nations: The Struggle for Power and Peace* (Morganthau 1967) and *Twenty Years' Crisis: An Introduction to the Study of International Relations* (Carr 1962)—discuss the economic dimension of national power under the 'taxonomies of power,' economic issues remained peripheral to the discipline (Ozkan 2012: 199). Marxist/neo-Marxist scholarship's critique of the relationship between economics and politics remained on the margins of IR.

Evidently, IR theory did not banish economics from within its folds but gave it a status secondary to that of security. IR's engagement on economic issues took place mostly via liberalism. Liberal institutionalism—functionalists (Mitrany 1975) and neofunctionalists (Haas 1958, 1964)—were preoccupied with how socio-economic and technical cooperation among states could produce peace, 'integration' and 'cooperation among states'—the UN specialized agencies and the formation of what became the European Union are the practical manifestations of these liberal functionalist concerns. In the late 1970s, this liberal concern turned to 'interdependence' (Keohane and Nye 1976, 1977; Baldwin 1980), and in the 1980s, to 'regimes' (Oye 1986). In this *limited* sense, liberalism in IR did engage with the issue of the relationship between economics and politics within and among developed nations, but the fate of developing nations was not part of this concern. Also, liberalism's notion of economic dependence (asymmetric interdependence) differed from the notion of 'dependency' developed by the dependency and world system theories to describe the relationship between developed and developing countries (Caporaso & Levine 1992). Subsequently, realist scholarship began to also explicitly address development issues in the 1980s (Krasner 1983).

Embedded Liberalism Challenged

A trenchant critique of this privileging of security and the neglect of development concerns came via a critique of the modernization theory by the dependency school (Amin 1976; Chilcote 1982; Frank 1966, 1967) and the world systems approach (Wallerstein, 1974, 1979, 1980). These scholars posited an ontological challenge to the dominant IR scholarship's *wisdom* that security interests trump economic ones in international anarchy. By arguing that underdevelopment in the periphery (third world/post-colonial states) is a result of its colonial/neocolonial relationship with the centre (the first world), these approaches revealed the capitalist underpinnings of the world economy as being inherently exploitative of the third world. They also exposed how relations of economic dependency undermined the political sovereignty of these countries. Without freeing themselves from this economic bondage with the first world, the post-colonial states could be neither secure nor developed. Not coincidentally the decade of the seventies was marked by the countries of the third world demanding *the revision of the Bretton Woods*

System and agitated for a New International Economic Order (NIEO) (A/RES/S-6/3201). The collapse of the Bretton Woods system in the early 1970s was the catalyst for the emergence of the sub-discipline of International Political Economy (IPE) within IR (Caporaso 1981; Cox 1987, 1996, 2002; Gilpin 1987, 2001; Helleiner 1994; Rodrik 1999; Strange 1984, 1986, 1998). *Driven by scholarship*[21] *and political agitation this moment was pregnant with possibilities to reframe: (a) the primary concern of IR as not security but political economy; (b) economy as being informed by the development concerns of and from the third world.* The 1970s Bretton Woods crisis led to the emergence of neoliberalism in the 1980s.

Embedded liberalism was challenged by the developing countries and also criticized by some states in the developed world albeit on very different grounds. The latter viewed embedded liberalism as the international counterpart of the welfare state that encouraged the citizens' parasitic dependence on the state's resources creating a 'crisis of overload and ungovernability' (Hay 2007: 53; also see Heilbroner 1985). This critique was popularly personified in the philosophy and politics of the New Right in the 1980s whose luminaries included US President Ronald Reagan and UK Prime Minister Margaret Thatcher (Auerbach 2007: 33–34). They proffered the free market as a solution whereby the liberated entrepreneurial spirit of individuals would benefit the individual and society. These mantras of privatization and liberalization of the economy were adopted by the World Bank and the IMF in response to the 1980s global economic crisis. Indeed, this crisis provided the context for the shift in the 'sites of North–South program production from the UN, UNCTAD, and the Non-Aligned Movement to the more conservative international financial institutions' i.e., the World Bank and the IMF (Livingstone 1992: 323). The dawn of neoliberalism coincided with the 'demise of the Third World Project' so the World Bank and IMF were duly 'scrubbed clean of old Keynesians and developmentalists' (Prashad 2012: 6–7).

[21] 'Development and underdevelopment are two sides of the same coin' (Frank 1967), 'the phenomenon of growth without development' (Amin 1976) became popular maxims for the critics of liberal political economy.

IR—The Expansion of Security as a Presage to Security/Development

The UN General Assembly resolution on the NIEO was only a symbolic victory against the Bretton Woods system as the latter soon morphed from embedded liberalism to neoliberalism. IR co-opted the scholarly dissent by relegating these challenges to the sub-discipline of international political economy (the junior partner in the enterprise of IR).[22] Besides the Gramscian scholarship, world systems approach, and dependency schools the literature in IPE also includes writings from neorealist (Gilpin 1987, 2001; Krasner 1983) and neoliberal (Keohane 1984, 2002; Keohane and Nye 1976, 1977; Keohane 2002, Russet and O'Neal 2001) scholars. They put forward the developed world's perspective on economic issues and ignored the interests (and perspectives on development) of the developing world; also, though the link between economy and security was acknowledged, it was security that got prioritized.[23] The neoliberals' primary question—'how is co-operation possible in anarchy?'—is very much within the neorealist framework and driven by the concern for security/stability/order in international anarchy. Despite the neorealist and neoliberal scholarship in IPE, security studies and IPE remain 'antagonistic enterprises' in IR (Buzan 2000: 15). As a sub-discipline within IR, security studies—flanked by neorealist/neoliberal approaches—have the status of the *first amongst equals.*

A context to bring development concerns to the fore was subsequently provided by post-positivist scholarship's[24] ontological and epistemological challenge to neorealism's/neoliberalism's premise of IR as a discrete area of action and discourse. This led to the 'most profound, ethically

[22] Also, the intra-paradigm debate between neorealists and neoliberals (christened the 'third great debate' of IR) hijacked some of the attention from the new approaches and by implication marked them as interlopers or outliers to the discipline.

[23] The IR scholarship is dominated by neorealism and neoliberalism writings by primarily American scholars. This 'American IR' hegemony is gradually being challenged from European and Asian perspectives (Waever 1998: 688).

[24] Post-positivists include feminists (Enloe 1989; Peterson and Runyan 2010; Tickner 1992, 2001; Tickner and Sjoberg 2011; Elshtain 2003); poststructuralists (Ashley 1984); critical theorists (Linklater 1990, 2007), neo-Gramscians (Cox 1987, 1996, 2002; Gill 1993), and a political theorist of the modern international (Walker 1993, 2010a, 2010b). They critiqued positivist epistemology subscribed by neorealism (Gilpin 1987, 2001; Krasner 1983; Waltz 1959, 1979) and neoliberalism (Keohane 1984, 2002; Keohane and Nye 1976, 1977; Russett and O'Neal 2001) and in the process breached the boundary between the domestic and the international.

promising, move in the redefinition of security' (Burke 2010: 93). A congenial environment for the *broadening* and *deepening* of the security agenda was created whereby development concerns found both a normative and critical link with those of security. This was done by recasting or re-envisioning security.[25]

The *solid, material,* and *unchanging* nature of security as put forward by the neorealists/neoliberals was challenged by the constructivists' emphasis on the role of ideas and culture, a point pithily encapsulated in the title of the 1992 Alexander Wendt's article *Anarchy is What the States Make of It: The Social Construction of Power Politics*. By stressing the role of ideas and values in determining state interests and identities (Phillips 2000: 5), constructivism drew attention to the contingency and mutability of the so-called facts of international politics—anarchy, war, enemy states, and allies.[26] The revelation of security as a constructed concept is the premise of the Copenhagen School's securitization theory. This formulation was a major conceptual breakthrough in the field of security studies (Williams 2012: 14). Securitization examined:

> The social processes by which issues get securitized (i.e., socially accepted definitions of threat) and also desecuritized (as in the ending of the Cold War, when many Soviet political initiatives unraveled the previous construction of threat even though military conditions changed little). (Buzan 2000: 3)

This *broadened* security agenda identified five sectors—military, environment, economy, society, and politics—as targets of securitization. However, it was criticized for not making a 'decisive break from traditional security thinking' as the securitization theory remained vulnerable to 'colonization by neorealist analysis and policy recommendation' (Sheehan 2005: 4). In terms of the security/development relationship, at best its contribution can be summed up as securitization of development.

[25] Indeed, re-envisioning became an important term in academia and policymaking, and was used to discuss a host of concepts—sovereignty, environment, education, etc.

[26] Writings that made important contributions in privileging culture along with the domestic to understand the terrain of the international include Checkel (1997, 1998), Gourevitch (1978, 1996), Katzenstein (1996), Keohane and Milner (1996), Lapid and Kratochwil (1996), and Risse-Kappen (1995).

This flaw is addressed by critical security studies[27] (CSS) by *deepening* the broadened concept of security. Deepening involves: (a) an ontology that embraces referents beyond the state, to include individuals and humanity; (b) an epistemology that engages 'with the real in world politics' and 'rejects naturalist approaches to knowledge'; (c) an orientation towards 'praxis'...that is 'explicitly emancipatory' (Booth 2005: 14). CSS overturns the traditional hierarchy between security and development. By introducing emancipation as a goal for security, it makes security contingent on the realization of a deepened (and multifaceted) concept of development. This line of argument also resonates with another view of security that gained currency in the 1990s—human security. Welcomed as a paradigm shift, human security became the significant other of the state/militaristic security (Glasius 2008; Kaldor 2007; Tadjbakhsh and Chenoy 2007). The traditional concept of state security appeared to be in decline in this era of 'extended security' whereby security was being stretched 'vertically' and 'horizontally' (Rothschild 1995). While vertical extension was seen in the increase in the number of *entities*—'nations', 'groups,' 'individuals,' 'international system', 'biosphere'—that need to be protected or secured, horizontal extension was evident in the range of issues that were now 'securitized'—military, political, economic, social, environmental, and human rights. Thus the 'political responsibility' for invigilating these concepts of security was diffused in all directions so as to include international institutions, regional governments, NGOs, public opinion and the press, and the 'abstract forces of nature or of the market' (Rothschild 1995: 55). New issues and actors (Booth 2005; Burgess 2010a; Buzan 1991a, 1991b; Buzan 1998; Dillon 1996; Duffield 2001; Duffield and Waddel 2006; Kaldor 2000) emerged in the post-Cold War security landscape. Issues of identity and culture became crucial to security studies (Burgess 2010b: 2). But amongst all these new articulations of 'extended security' it was human security that caught the imagination of the policy world and academia (see Tarnogorski 2013: 1). It was also this

[27] The 'label' CSS was first employed by Keith Krause and Michael C. Williams in their edited book *Critical Security Studies: Concepts and Cases which* emerged out of a conference *Strategies in Conflict: Critical Approaches to Security Studies* held at York University Toronto in 1994. They include the Copenhagen School, Aberystwyth or the Welsh School, constructivism, and poststructuralism as part of CSS. Ken Booth (Welsh School) makes exclusive claims to the theory of CSS and seeks to gatekeep the entry of the 'four pretenders: feminism, Copenhagen School, constructivism, and poststructuralism' (Mutimer 2010: 94).

embrace by the policy world that led to human security's quick domestication and loss of critical potential and radical promise (see Christie 2010).

The UN Security/Development Dispositif as an Exigent Response to Human Insecurity and 'Failed States' in the Era of Neoliberalism

The adoption of the human security agenda by the UN was an iteration of the links between security and some aspect of development made by the various UN sponsored commissions that punctuated the decade of the 1980s. This iteration picked up momentum in the 1990s with *An Agenda for Peace* 1992 (Boutros-Ghali 1995)[28] and the *Human Development Report* 1994.

Human security was acclaimed as a paradigm shift that displaced traditional notions of state security, and gave the UN new lens to see beyond the concept of collective security. Though the simultaneity of the goals of security and development has informed the UN agenda since its inception, their framing by the concept of human security gave this linkage a certain urgency and *potency* to meet the challenges of violence and insecurity occurring in various parts of the world in the late twentieth century. For example, the decade of the 1990s witnessed an unprecedented rise in the numbers of refugees and internally displaced people (IDP).[29]

Much of the burgeoning security/development literature[30] around this time identified the phenomenon of 'failed state'[31] as a major source of insecurity that endangered its own people and also those beyond its borders and 'the world at large' (Feltman 2013; Also see Ghani and Lockhart 2008; Helman and Ratner 1993; Howard 2014; Tschirgi et al. 2010; Carment et al. 2010). A failed state—administratively crippled and mired in political chaos—is ill-fated to be in perpetual economic crisis as

[28] http://www.un-documents.net/a47r120a.htm.

[29] Sudanese diplomat, Francis Deng, was appointed as the Representative of the UN Secretary-General on Internally Displaced People (IDP) in 1992. He put forward the concept of sovereignty as responsibility to design a response to the problem of IDP; subsequently, sovereignty as responsibility became the premise of responsibility to protect.

[30] See Spear and Williams (2012) and Stern and Ojendal (2010).

[31] Failed state, a Weberian term, is employed by Helman and Ratner in their article *Saving Failed States* (1992–1993).

its problems of poverty, food scarcity, and hunger get compounded by those of law and order (see Lockhart 2005).

In this neoliberal era the United Nations system has a complex task at hand—old problems persist even as new ones emerge. Having said this, it would be misleading to simply catalogue the security/development problems of the neoliberal era as old and new; *old* problems of poverty and underdevelopment persist but become more challenging for two broad reasons. *First*, new techniques[32] and non-income criteria—like gender, education, health, environment, functional capabilities, and social inclusion—of poverty measurement change the *form* and meaning of poverty (see Meyer and Sullivan 2012: 112–113).[33] This multi-dimensional conceptualization of poverty raises expectations from and expands the development agenda of the UN.[34] And, of course, UN delivery system gets overburdened in the case of failed states. *Second*, the problems of poverty, development, and insecurity acquire urgency for the UN, as their very existence is a statement on the UN's non-compliance with its Charter's promise made nearly seventy years ago. The problem of poverty is exacerbated by the exclusionary prosperity of the neoliberal age wherein the income inequality between and within states has increased (Harvey 2006a; Picketty 2014; Stiglitz 2002). The possibility of global political instability resulting from this gap has led countries in the Global North to recognize poverty as a political problem (see Stein 2008: 9).

The spate of counter-movements[35] in the closing decades of the twentieth century are articulations that cast poverty and economic inequality as

[32] Currently, the World Bank uses three measures of poverty—incidence of poverty (headcount index), depth of poverty (poverty gap), and poverty severity (squared poverty gap) (http://web.worldbank.org/WBSITE/EXTERNAL/TOPICS/EXTPOVERTY/EXTPA/0,,contentMDK:20242881~menuPK:435055~pagePK:148956~piPK:216618~theSitePK:430367,00.html).

[33] Also see http://web.worldbank.org/WBSITE/EXTERNAL/TOPICS/EXTPOVERTY/EXTPA/0,,contentMDK:20202198~menuPK:435055~pagePK:148956~piPK:216618~theSitePK:430367,00.html.

[34] This expanded development agenda also originates in the fact that human rights were gradually stretched by the UN from the first generation to the second and third generation of rights. See *International Covenant on Economic, Social, and Cultural Rights (1976), Rio Declaration on Environment and Development (1992), Draft Declaration of Indigenous People's Rights (1994).*

[35] Examples—the ecological resistance movements (Taylor 1995), the 1999 Battle of Seattle, and World Social Forums (since 2001). We must also note that counter-movements may themselves be vulnerable to neoliberal co-option (see Munck 2006).

'politically illegitimate' conditions and not the inevitable inconveniences (consequences) that must be borne by the poor (people and countries). These movements are seen as responses to 'neoliberalism's dynamic of accumulation by dispossession' (Carroll 2010: 173)[36] and also as examples of Karl Polanyi's 'double movement' wherein the market forces are opposed by social forces aiming at 'social protection' (Warner and Clifton 2014: 45). The *right to not be poor* and the promise of prosperity for all can no longer be *easily* postponed by national governments or the leading international organizations—the UN, World Bank, and the IMF. Political protests on economic issues acquire political traction in an age where citizens, according to Pierre Rosanvallon, use the mechanisms of 'oversight' (to monitor political rulers) and 'prevention' (to mobilize resistance to specific policies) to deepen democracy.[37] This demonstration of the 'surveillance power of society' is in a sense the inversion of the panopticon gaze (Rosanvallon 2008: 32). It is this possibility and mode of resistance that Foucault applauded in his support for the initiatives of Amnesty International, Terre des Hommes, and Medecins du Monde 'that have created this new right—that of private individuals to effectively intervene in the sphere of international policy and strategy' (1994: 475). Impatient citizens as individuals and as members of organizations from various parts of the world hold both national governments and international organizations like the UN to scrutiny.

This is the context of the UN advocacy of human security and related articulations of security. Human security cushions the harshness of the global market—it is the surrogate welfare state, although in a limited way compared to its erstwhile domestic counterpart. In *An Agenda for Peace* 1992, the UN Secretary-General made post-conflict peacebuilding the priority of the UN. Security experts saw underdevelopment as a potential cause for conflict, and the development experts recognized a secure stable state as a prerequisite for development (Williams 2012:

[36] David Harvey proposed the term 'accumulation by dispossession' to describe neoliberal economic policies that rob people of their rights to control and dispose off their own resources, particularly the natural resources (global commons) as in the Global South. 'New mechanisms of accumulation by dispossession' include speculative raiding by hedge funds, intellectual property rights (that enables biopiracy and pillaging of the world's genetic resources by multinational corporations), and commodification of cultural forms' (2004: 75; also see Harvey 2006b).

[37] Pierre Rossanvalon lists a third mechanism—'judgement' where the judicial process is brought to bear on errant political leaders (2008: 227).

16–19). The problem of failed states also served as a major impetus for the convergence of the security and development specialists. In the UNDP's Human Development Report *New Dimensions of Human Security* (1994) the link between security and development was declared immanent. Human security's advocacy of the twin goals of 'freedom from fear' (FFF) and 'freedom from want' (FFW) became a comprehensive 'doctrine' to achieve the goals of security and freedom which underlined the inseparability of the two. Indeed, as far back as 1941 President Franklin D. Roosevelt in his State of the Union Address spoke about the importance of FFF and FFW as two of the 'four freedoms.' These became the foundational principles for the United Nations Declaration of 1 January 1942 and the Universal Declaration of Human Rights (1948).[38] 1994 was not the sudden awakening of the UN to the security and development links, as the move towards this acknowledgement is evident also in the various UN and World Bank sponsored commissions that punctuated the decade of the 1980s (see Bajpai 2000; Thakur et al. 2005).[39]

The more recent measures like High-Level Panel on Threats, Challenges, and Change (2004), *A More Secure World,* ICISS (2001), WSOD (2005), and Peacebuilding Commission (2005) are in this lineage: 'peacebuilding is being rethought so as to reflect the interdependency between security, rights, and development' (Alt 2013: 87). Francis Fukuyama's *End of History* thesis resonates amongst the advocates of R2P as a moral norm (Hehir 2013: 9) and amongst the proponents of liberal peacebuilding who refute the possibility of any other alternative to save people from 'lawlessness, predation, disease and fear' (Paris 2010: 338). Indeed, post-conflict peacebuilding missions 'developed into something of a growth industry in the 1990s' (Paris 2004: 3). Though belonging to different eras, parallels can be drawn between the Marshall Plan (and the Truman Doctrine) of the post-second World War period and the peacebuilding missions inaugurated in the late twentieth century. Both

[38] The other two freedoms were freedom of speech and freedom of worship. See http://www.fdrlibrary.marist.edu/fourfreedoms.

[39] These commissions tasked with re-envisioning security are discussed in Chapter 3. They include the Brandt Commission (1980), Palme Commission 1982, 1987 Brundtland Commission (1987), Report of the South Commission (1990), 1992 Report of the UN Secretary-General (*An Agenda for Peace*) (1992), and the Report of the Commission on Global Governance (1995).

are *post-conflict* responses of the powerful to *socially engineer* afflicted countries to become political democracies and liberalized economies so that peace may prevail (see Paris 2004: 5–6). These moral imperatives in the post-1990s era to secure, save, and protect have also been described as characteristic of the age of 'liberal humanitarianism' (Michael Barnett 2011).[40] Importantly, the ownership claims of the concept of protection have come to be shared amongst a range of national and international actors—'the host state, mandated UN protection agencies, non-governmental organizations and the International Committee of the Red Cross' (Holt et al. 2009: 3). The UNSC itself put an accent on the protection agenda ever since its landmark 'protection of civilian' resolutions 1265 (1999) and 1296 (2000), following which several peacekeeping missions were mandated to protect civilians (Roy and Holmes 2009: iii).

The Critical Security Studies Critique of the UN Security/Development Dispositif as a Liberal Peacebuilding Project

Critical Security Studies literature labels as 'hubris of liberal internationalism', the World Bank-IMF policies that set into motion externally driven 'processes of state-building, dispossession and subjugation' using the carrot and stick policy to create 'liberal market democracies' (Selby 2013: 63–65; also see Chandler 2006; Jahn 2007; Richmond and Franks 2007). Neoliberal economic policies come at the cost of 'democracy and human rights components of the liberal peace' (Cooper et al. 2011: 1995). Those who make a plea for re-embedded liberalism are making an implicit admission that it is not the 'failed state' per se but neoliberal policies that are perilous to the political and economic health of the global order (Abdelal and Ruggie 2009; Levien and Paret 2012). R2P, therefore, serves as a short-term international substitution for a failed state until a local substitute can take over (Warner 2003). I argue that R2P is a *truncated* or *abbreviated* version of the states' and international organizations' embedded liberalism responsibilities in the neoliberal era.

[40] Michael Barnett (2011) periodizes the history of humanitarianism into three ages: (a) 'Imperial humanitarianism' (late eighteenth century to the end of the Second World War; (b) 'neohumanitarianism' (Post-Second World War to the end of the Cold War); (c) 'liberal humanitarianism' (post-Cold War to the present).

The 're-appearance' of the transaction of these responsibilities softens neoliberalism by making it take on a relatively more compassionate avatar of re-embedded liberalism, thus 'regulatory regimes' and 'discourse of governance' are accompanied by 'the moral compass of a basic normative vision' (Beardsworth 2011: 162). The process of re-embedded liberalism, a la embedded liberalism seeks to balance 'economic openness' with 'social protection' (Burgoon 2013: 5).

Within this critical literature there is a growing stream of scholars who employ the Foucauldian lenses of governmentality (and biopolitics) to critique the security/development complex as a liberal peacebuilding project (Alt 2013; Dillon 2010; Duffield 2006, 2007, 2010; Grayson 2010).[41] Though concepts of governmentality and biopolitics are interrelated some scholars employ them as distinct concepts while others use the terms interchangeably. These interrogations do not just see insecurity and violent conflict as a hurdle to development but also a context to talk about change from the 'perspective of end-users' of the security/development package (Luckham and Kirk 2012: 9). HS thus serves as a technology of governance (Duffield and Waddel 2006: 13). Foucauldian insights draw attention to how the biopolitical imperative to 'make live' (in addition to that of 'let die') necessitates the protection mandate of the liberal peacebuilding project (including human security) that also hierarchizes lives. Some lives, for example, those of particular groups—national, religious, or ethnic—are identified as precious while others are deemed expendable on the grounds that their existence threatens the former: 'Liberal peace is a necropolitics of security which makes permanent war against life on behalf of life' (Dillon 2015: 160).[42] The concept of governmentality gives novel insights into liberalism and neoliberalism not just as 'an ideology or philosophy, nor as the most recent political form of the capitalist agenda, but in terms of certain arts, tactics and practices of governing' (Larner and Walters 2004: 4). However, there are also voices of caution advising against the 'scaling up' of Foucauldian concepts to the international realm (Selby 2007).

[41] Also see Brockling et al. (2011); De Larrinaga and Doucet (2008); Dillon (2015); Dillon and Reid (2009); Duffield et al. (2001); Hynek (2010); Lessenich (2011); Mitchell (2010); Rosén (2011).

[42] 'This necropoliticised peace machine—which runs the gamut from peace-keeping and peace-making to "operations other than war" and imperial conquest—is the liberal way of war' (Dillon and Reid 2009 paraphrased in Dillon 2015: 161).

Most of the literature on humanitarian intervention and R2P cites lack of political will of nation-states and political leaders, bureaucratic inertia of international organizations (Barnett 2002), or geoeconomics and geostrategic compulsions as reasons for the non-recourse to military intervention under R2P (see Chandler 2009; Wheeler and Egerton 2009). These arguments are not without merit, but the dominance of these views in the R2P discourse silences other concerns and questions which are the focus of this book. In this regard critical theory's critique of the liberal peacebuilding project is important. R2P discourse echoes the agenda of the liberal peacebuilding project, as like in the latter the burden of responsibility (and guilt) for the crimes is narrowly directed to an individual (e.g., leader/dictator) or a group (e.g., religious, ethnic) and as a consequence the structural linkages/causes that make the crime possible are ignored. For example, one of the components of the liberal peacebuilding project is the growing academic field of conflict resolution/transformation[43] that promotes mechanisms like Truth and Reconciliation Commissions (TRC) to deal with issues of historical wrongs and injustices (including that of genocide). However, as Brownyn Anne Leebaw (2005) observes, the TRC in South Africa omits and thereby absolves the role of Western states and multinational corporations that supported the Apartheid regime. Mahmud Mamdani (2001) similarly points to the erasure of the historical role and legacy of colonial policies/politics in constructing certain tribal identities as antagonistic as was the case of Hutus and Tutsis in Rwanda. Any measure to operationalize R2P pillars cannot be a success if it ignores or perpetuates the dehistoricization and depoliticization of crimes such as genocide. The Foucauldian lens helps us historicize both the crime and the purported response to arrest or prevent the recurrence of the crime.

Conclusion

To summarize, dominant strands of IR scholarship have over a period come to acknowledge the link between security and development, move beyond the military as a singular aspect of security, and recognize the link

[43] The US State Department gives Fulbright Fellowships to students from South Asia and the Middle East for a Master's Programme in Conflict Transformation. Several Universities in the US run dedicated centres on the subject (e.g., George Mason, Eastern Mennonite University). Similar programmes have been introduced in Indian universities.

between the international and the domestic. This is a result of meditations that range from the normative to the critical. Studies on the security/development relationship range from the descriptive to the prescriptive and the critical so the term is accordingly imbued with different meanings. The UN articulation of human security puts the security/development complex in an urgent and favourable light.

Both theorists and practitioners are concerned with the question of whether security and development are equal partners, or has one encroached upon the other perhaps at its own peril or made the entire project futile or inefficient. These discordant reservations are often voiced in discussions on HS and R2P goals of FFF and FFW. For example, soldiers doing development work in conflict zones like Afghanistan and Iran are seen as the military moving away from its core expertise and duty, and therefore, in danger of losing its touch (e.g., with firepower, surveillance, etc.) (Williams 2012: 16). Then there are others who see development being instrumentalized to serve military purposes and thereby, endangering the lives of development workers. Thus, the phenomena of securitization of development and developmentalization of security have both their respective supporters and detractors. International organizations despite the subscription to the nexus belief have separate departments to deal with issues of security and development (Stern and Ojendal 2010: 5–7). This observation was confirmed in my interviews with the personnel and officials of UN agencies and departments who demarcate their respective domain of action as either/or and not as a nexus: each viewed her work as either unadulterated security or unadulterated development work, often there was suspicion or derision for the other's agenda. Agreeing with Bjorne Hettne's view that the security/development relationship is not static, Williams proposes that this be seen as 'selectively co-constitutive' whereby the situation on the ground dictates whether policies be informed by security and/or development (2012: 21–22).

The worlds of academics and policy have seen a parallel growth on the subject of security/development. The policy world (UN, OECD, government departments, and think tanks) since the late 1980s has been the major voice in acknowledging the security/development relationship as benign and has also been a major driver of the burgeoning literature on the subject. In the dialectics between academia and the UN it is difficult to discern whether academic theorizing gives conceptual rigour to the UN ideas/policies, or the latter learns from and is inspired by the academia's criticisms and suggestions.[44]

I have argued that the coinage and wider acknowledgement in the 1990s of the term security-development nexus by the policy/practice and academic worlds does not mean that the nexus did not exist or inform the earlier UN policies and practice. It is the visible though ***unspoken*** link in the *UN Charter's Preamble and Purposes*, development is thus the foundation of the collective security system. That is the collective security system in the Charter is not limited to military security: The founders of the UN affirmed the indivisibility of security, economic development, and human freedom long before the idea of human security gained currency (United Nations 2004: 11). Thus, the contention that there is not a radical shift but only a shift in emphasis in the UN security/development dispositif.

Collective security (as a military and coercive measure) is an indispensable component of human security measures to meet the goal of FFF. Embedded liberalism and neoliberalism are both frameworks of the free market, they disagree only in degree about the distance that the state must maintain vis-à-vis the economy. However, with the crisis in neoliberalism and the chorus for a return to embedded liberalism even that nuanced difference has shrunk. Concepts (and accompanying policies) of human security, corporate social responsibility, peacebuilding, and conflict transformation are necessary to maintain order and stability threatened by the vacuum created by the recession of embedded liberalism, and by the inherent logic of neoliberal policies. Not surprisingly there is a kind of segue of common membership in the various UN-supported commissions including that of the ICISS (Thakur et al. 2005: 11). This epistemic community (Adler and Haas 1992) ensures continuity of ideas, thus the self-answering question: how much out-of-the-box thinking is possible amongst like-minded people in like-minded discourse(s)? But this is not to say that there is no movement in security/development concepts and practices. There is movement, but the movement is within the confines of a liberal framework and it aims to solve the problems generated by the solution to the preceding problem. Governmentality reveals R2P, too as a measure that conforms to this intellection.

To sum up, the liberal/neoliberal security/development dispositif reveals the socio-economic problems endemic to the liberal/neoliberal

[44] See David Chandler's (2015) critique of Roland Paris's writings on R2P, in this context.

political economy, and how this endemicity requires security measures like R2P to maintain order. Unlike the securitization school and the security-development nexus, the security/development dispositif sees the idea of development not discretely but as part of the global political economy. R2P is a part of this dispositif, wherein its advocates oscillate R2P between security (as in pure unadulterated physical security) and security (that is dressed up as benign development to realize security). *The protection act of measures such as R2P is dual one, in its explicit form it saves some populations from atrocity crimes* and *in its implicit guise it saves the neoliberal economy from being devoured by its loss of legitimacy.*

References

Aalberts, Manuel B. 2013. Debate on Neoliberalism in and after the Neoliberal Crisis. *International Journal of Urban and Regional Research* 37 (3): 1053–1057.

Abbott, Phillip, Thomas Barnebeck Anderson, and Finn Tarp. 2010. IMF and Economic Reform in Developing Countries. *The Quarterly Review of Economics and Finance* 50 (1): 17–26.

Abdelal, Rawi, and John G. Ruggie. 2009. The Principles of Embedded Liberalism: Social Legitimacy and Global Capitalism. In *New Perspectives on Regulation*, eds. David Moss and John Cisternino. Cambridge, MA: The Tobin Project, One Mifflin Place.

Abrahamsen, Rita. 2004. The Partnerships in Global Governance. *Third World Quarterly* 25 (8): 1453–1467.

Adler, Emanuel, and Peter M. Haas. 1992. Conclusion: Epistemic Communities, World Order, and the Creation of a Reflective Research Program. *International Organization* 46 (1): 367–390.

African Union. 2004. *Solemn Declaration on a Common African Defence and Security Policy.*

Alt, Suvi. 2013. Beyond Bricks and Mortar: Peace-Building in a Permanent State of Adaptation. In *The Biopolitics of Development: Reading Michel Foucault in the Postcolonial Present*, eds. Sandro Mezzadra, Julian Reid, and Ranabir Samaddar. New Delhi: Springer.

Amin, Samir. 1974. *Accumulation on a World Scale: A Critique of the Theory of Underdevelopment*, trans. Brian Pearce. New York: Monthly Review Press.

Amin, Samir. 1976. *Unequal Development: An Essay on the Formation of Peripheral Capitalism.* New York: Monthly Review Press.

Amin, Samir. 1977. *Imperialism and Unequal Development.* New York: Monthly Review Press.

Ashley, Richard K. 1984. The Poverty of Neorealism. *International Organization* 38 (2): 225–286.

Auerbach, Nancy Neiman. 2007. The Meanings of Neoliberalism. In *Neoliberalism: National and Regional Experiments with Global Ideas*, eds. Ravi K. Roy, Arthur T. Denzau, and Thomas D. Willett. New York: Routledge.

Bajpai, Kanti. 2000. Human Security: Concept and Management. *Kroc Institute Occasional Paper #19:OP:1*. Accessed on 16 September 2015. http://www.hegoa.ehu.es/dossierra/seguridad/Human_security_concept_and_measurement.pdf

Baldwin, David A. 1980. Interdependence and Power: A Conceptual Analysis. *International Organization* 34 (4): 471–506.

Barnett, Michael N. 2002. *Eyewitness to a Genocide: The United Nations and Rwanda*. Ithaca: Cornell University Press.

Barnett, Michael N. 2011. *Empire of Humanity: A History of Humanitarianism*. Ithaca: Cornell University.

Beardsworth, Richard. 2011. *Cosmopolitanism and International Relations Theory*. Cambridge: Polity Press.

Bellamy, Alex J. 2009. Realizing the Responsibility to Protect. *International Studies Perspectives* 10 (2): 111–128.

Booth, Ken, ed. 2005. *Security Studies and World Politics*. London: Lynne Rienner Publishers.

Boutros-Ghali, Boutros. 1995. *An Agenda for Peace: Preventive Diplomacy, Peacemaking and Peace-Keeping*. New York: United Nations.

Brockling, Ulrich, Susanne Krasmann, and Thomas Lemke, eds. 2011. *Governmentality: Current Issues and Future Challenges*. New York: Routledge.

Burgess, J. Peter. 2010a. Editor's Note. *Security Dialogue* 41 (6): 587–588.

Burgess, J. Peter. 2010b. Introduction. In *Routledge Handbook of New Security Studies*, ed. J. Peter Burgess. New York: Routledge.

Burgoon, Brian. 2013. Political Economy of Re-embedding Liberalism. *Inaugural Lecture 482*. Amsterdam: University of Amsterdam. http://www.uva.nl/binaries/content/documents/.../b/u/b...burgoon/.../asset?. Accessed on 16 September 2015.

Burke, Anthony. 2010. Security as Ethics. In *Routledge Handbook of New Security Studies*, ed. J. Peter Burgess. New York: Routledge.

Busumtwi-Sam, James. 2004. Development and Peacebuilding: Conceptual and Operational Deficits in International Assistance. In *Durable Peace: Challenges for Peacebuilding in Africa*, eds. Taisier M. Ali and Robert O. Mathews. Toronto: University of Toronto Press.

Buzan, Barry. 1991a. New Patterns of Global Security in the Twenty-First Century. *International Affairs* 67: 431–451.

Buzan, Barry. 1991b. *People, States, and Fear: An Agenda for International Security Studies in the Post-Cold War Era*. New York: Harvester Wheatsheaf.

Buzan, Barry. 2000. Change and Insecurity' Reconsidered. In *Critical Reflections on Security and Change: Contemporary Security Studies*, eds. Stuart Croft and Terry Terriff. Great Britain: Frank Cass.

Buzan, Barry, Ole Waever, and Jaap de Wilde. 1998. *Security: A New Framework for Analysis*. London: Lynne Rienner Publishers.

Caporaso, James A. 1981. Industrialization in the Periphery: The Evolving Division of Labour. *International Studies Quarterly* 25 (3): 247–284.

Caporaso, James A., and David P. Levine. 1992. *Theories of Political Economy*. Cambridge: Cambridge University Press.

Carment, David, Stewert Prest, and Samy Yiagadeesen. 2010. *Security, Development and the Fragile State: Bridging the Gap between Theory and Policy*. New York: Routledge.

Carr, Edward Hallett. 1962. *Twenty Years' Crisis: An Introduction to the Study of International Relations*. London: Macmillan.

Carroll, William K. 2010. Crisis, Movements, Counter-Hegemony: In Search of the New. *Interface: A Journal for and About Social Movements* 2 (2): 168–198.

Chandler, David C. 2006. *Empire in Denial: The Politics of Statebuilding*. London: Pluto.

Chandler, David. 2008. The Dog that did not Bark. *Security Dialogue* 39 (4): 427–438.

Chandler, David, ed. 2009. *Statebuilding and Intervention: Policies, Practices and Paradigms*. New York: Routledge.

Chandler, David. 2015. The R2P Is Dead, Long Live the R2P: The Successful Separation of Military Intervention from the Responsibility to Protect. *International Peacekeeping* 22 (1): 1–5.

Checkel, Jeffrey T. 1997. *Ideas and International Political Change: Soviet/Russian Behavior and the End of the Cold War*. London: Yale University Press.

Checkel, Jefferey T. 1998. The Constructivist Turn in International Relations Theory Today. *World Politics* 50: 324–348.

Chilcote, Ronald H., ed. 1982. *Dependency and Marxism: Toward a Resolution of the Debate*. Boulder: Westview Press.

Christie, Ryerson. 2010. Critical Voices and Human Security: To Endure, or to Engage or to Critique? *Security Dialogue* 41 (2): 169–190.

Cooper, Neil, Mandy Turner, and Michael Pugh. 2011. The End of History and the Last Liberal Peacebuilder: A Reply to Roland Paris. *Review of International Studies* 37 (4): 1995–2007.

Cox, Robert W. 1987. *Production, Power, and World Order: Social Forces in the Making of History*. New York: Columbia University.

Cox, Robert W. 1996. *Approaches to World Order*. Cambridge: Cambridge University Press.

Cox, Robert W. 2002. *Political Economy of a Plural World: Globalization and Civilization*. London: Routledge.
De Larrinaga, Miguel and Marc G. Doucet. 2008. Sovereign Power and the Biopolitics of Security. *Security Dialogue* 39 (5): 517–537.
Dillon, Michael. 1996. *The Politics of Security: Towards a Political Philosophy of Continental Thought*. New York: Routledge.
Dillon, Michael. 2010. The Biopolitics of Security. In *The Routledge Handbook of New Security Studies*. eds. J. Peter Burgess. New York: Routledge.
Dillon, Michael. 2015. *Biopolitics of Security: A Political Analytic of Finitude*. New York: Routledge.
Dillon, Michael, and Julian Reid. 2009. *The Liberal Way of War: Killing to Make Life Live*. Abingdon: Routledge.
Dreher, Axel. 2006. Does Globalization Affect Growth? Evidence from a New Index of Globalization. *Applied Economics* 38 (10): 1091–1110.
Duffield, Mark. 2001. *Global Governance and the New Wars: The Merging of Security and Development*. London: Zed Books.
Duffield, Mark. 2006. Linking Development and Security in an Age of Terror. In *New Interfaces between Security and Development: Changing Concepts and Approaches*, ed. Stephan Klingebiel. Bonn: German Development Institute.
Duffield, Mark. 2007. *Development, Security and Unending War: Governing the World of Peoples*. Cambridge: Polity Press.
Duffield, Mark. 2010. The Liberal Way of Development and the Development-Security Impasse: Exploring the Global Life-Chance Divide. *Security Dialogue* 41 (1): 53–76.
Duffield, Mark, and Nicholas Waddel. 2006. Securing Humans in a Dangerous World. *International Politics* 43 (1): 1–23.
Duffield, Mark, Joanna Macrae, and Devon Curtis. 2001. Editorial: Politics and Humanitarian Aid. *Disasters, Special Issue: Politics and Humanitarian Aid* 25 (4): 269–274.
Easterly, William. 2005. What did Structural Adjustment Adjust? The Association of Policies and Growth with Repeated IMF and World Bank Adjustment Loans. *Journal of Development Economics* 76 (1): 1–22.
Elshtain, Jean Bethke. 2003. *Just War against Terror: The Burden of American Power in a Violent World*. New York: Basic Books.
Enloe, Cynthia. 1989. *Bananas, Beaches and Bases: Making Feminist Sense of International Politics*. London: Pandora.
European Council. 2008. *Report on the Implementation of the European Security Strategy-Providing Security in a Changing World*. Brussels. S407/08. December 11, 2008.
Evans, Gareth, and Mohamed Sahnoun. 2002. The Responsibility to Protect. *Foreign Affairs* 81 (6): 99–110.

Feltman, Jeffrey. 2013. Politics in Tough Places: UN Diplomacy in Today's Crises. http://un.org.au/2013/07/16/politics-in-tough-places-un-diplomacy-in-todays-crises/. Accessed on 16 September 2015.

Foucault, Michel. 1980. *Power/Knowledge: Selected Interviews and Other Writings 1972–1977*, ed. Colin Gordon. New York: Pantheon Books.

Foucault, Michel. 1990. *The History of Sexuality: An Introduction*, vol. I. New York: Vintage Books.

Foucault, Michel. 1994. Confronting Governments: Human Rights. In *Essential Works of Foucault 1954-1984*, ed. J. D. Faubion, vol. 3. Power. London: Penguin.

Foucault, Michel. 2008. *The Birth of Biopolitics: Lectures at the College de France, 1978–79*. New York: Palgrave Macmillan.

Frank, Andre Gunder. 1966. The Development of Underdevelopment. *Monthly Review* 18 (4): 17–31.

Frank, Andre Gunder. 1967. *Capitalism and Underdevelopment in Latin America: Historical Studies of Chile and Brazil*. New York: Monthly Review Press.

Ghani, Ashraf, and Clare Lockhart. 2008. *Fixing Failed States: A Framework for Building a Fractured World*. New York: Oxford University Press.

Gill, Stephen, ed. 1993. *Gramsci, Historical Materialism and International Relations*. New York: Cambridge University Press.

Gilman, Nils. 2003. Modernization Theory, The Highest Stage of American Intellectual History. In *Modernization, Development, and the Global Cold War*, eds. David C. Engerman, Nils Gilman, Mark H. Haefele, and Michael E. Latham. Massachusetts: University of Massachusetts Press.

Gilpin, Robert. 1987. *The Political Economy of International Relations*. With the Assistance of Jean P. Gilpin. Princeton, NJ: Princeton University Press.

Gilpin, Robert. 2001. *Global Political Economy: Understanding International Economic Order*. With the Assistance of Jean P. Gilpin. Princeton, NJ: Princeton University Press.

Giroux, Henry A. 2004. *The Terror of Neoliberalism: Authoritarianism and the Eclipse of Democracy*. Herndon: Paradigm Publishers.

Glasius, Marlies. 2008. Human Security from Paradigm Shift to Operationalization: Job Description for a Human Security Worker. *Security Dialogue* 39 (1): 31–54.

Gofas, Andreas and Colin Hay. 2010. "Varieties of Ideational Explanations." In *The Role of Ideas in Political Analysis: A Portrait of Contemporary Debates*, eds. Andreas Gofas and Colin Hay. New York: Routledge.

Gourevitch, Peter. 1978. The Second Image Reversed: The International Sources of Domestic Politics. *International Organization* 32 (4): 881–912.

Gourevitch, Peter. 1996. Squaring the Circle: The Domestic Sources of International Cooperation. *International Organization* 50 (2): 349–373.

Grayson, Kyle. 2010. Human Security, Neoliberalism and Corporate Social Responsibility. *International Politics* 47 (5): 497–522.

Harvey, David. 2004. The New Imperialism: Accumulation by Dispossession. *Socialist Register* 40: 63–87.

Harvey, David. 2006a. *Spaces of Global Capitalism: Towards a Theory of Uneven Geographical Development*. New York: Verso.

Harvey, David. 2006b. A Conversation with David Harvey. http://www.logosjournal.com/issue_5.1/harvey.htm. Accessed on 16 September 2015.

Hass, Ernst B. 1958. *The Uniting of Europe: Political, Social, and Economic Forces, 1950–1957*. Stanford: Stanford University Press.

Hass, Ernst B. 1964. *Beyond the Nation-State: Functionalism and International Organization*. Stanford: Stanford University Press.

Hay, Colin. 2007. The Genealogy of Neoliberalism. In *Neoliberalism: National and Regional Experiments with Global Ideas*, eds. Ravi K. Roy, Arthur T. Denzau and Thomas D. Willett. New York: Routledge.

Hehir, Aidan. 2013. *Humanitarian Intervention: An Introduction*. Hampshire: Palgrave Macmillan.

Heilbroner, Robert. 1985. *The Nature and Logic of Capitalism*. New York: Norton.

Helleiner, Eric. 1994. *States and the Re-emergence of Global Finance: From Bretton Woods to the 1980s*. Ithaca: Cornell University Press.

Helman, Gerald B., and Steven R. Ratner. 1993. Saving Failed States. *Foreign Policy* 89: 3–20.

Herbst, Jeffrey. 1990. The Structural Adjustment of Politics in Africa. *World Development* 18 (7): 949–958.

Hodge, Graeme A., and Carsten Greve, eds. 2005. *The Challenge of Public-Private Partnerships: Learning from International Experience*. Cheltenham: Edward Elgar.

Hodge, Graeme A., Carsten Greve, and Anthony E. Boardman, eds. 2010. *International Handbook on Public-Private Partnerships*. Cheltenham: Edward Elgar.

Holt, Victoria and Glyn Taylor with Max Kelly. 2009. *Protecting Civilians in the Context of UN Peacekeeping Operation: Successes, Setbacks and Remaining Challenges*. Independent Study Jointly Commissioned by the Department of Peacekeeping Operations and the Office for the Coordination of Humanitarian Affairs. New York: United Nations.

Howard, Tiffany. 2014. *Failed States and the Origins of Violence: A Comparative Analysis of State Failure as A Root Cause of Terrorism and Political Violence*. Burlington: Ashgate.

Hynek, Nik. 2010. Rethinking Human Security: History, Economy, Governmentality. In *Critical Perspectives on Human Security: Rethinking Emancipation and Power in International Relations*, eds. David Chandler and Nik Hynek. New York: Routledge.

International Commission on Intervention and State Sovereignty. 2001. *The Responsibility to Protect*. Ottawa: International Development Research Centre.

Jahn, Beate. 2007. The Tragedy of Liberal Diplomacy: Democratization, Intervention, Statebuilding (Part I). *Journal of Intervention and Statebuilding* 1 (1): 87–106.

Jooste, Stephan F., and W. Richard Scott. 2012. The Public-Private Partnership Enabling Field: Evidence from Three Cases. *Administration & Society* 44 (2): 149–182.

Kaldor, Mary. 2000. *Global Insecurity: Restructuring the Global Military Sector*. London: Pinter.

Kaldor, Mary. 2007. *Human Security*. Cambridge: Polity.

Kaldor, Mary. 2012. *New and Old Wars: Organized Violence in a Global Era*. Cambridge: Polity Press.

Katzenstein, Peter, ed. 1996. *The Culture of National Security*. New York: Columbia University Press.

Keohane, Robert O. 1984. *After Hegemony: Cooperation and Discord in the World Political Economy*. Princeton: Princeton University Press.

Keohane, Robert O. 2002. *Power and Governance in a Partially Globalized World*. New York: Routledge.

Keohane, Robert O., and Joseph N. Nye. 1976. Introduction: The Complex Politics of Canadian-American Interdependence. In *Canada and the United States: Transnational and Transgovernmental Relations*, eds. Annette Baker Fox, Alfred O. Hero, Jr., and Joseph S. Nye, Jr. New York: Columbia University Press.

Keohane, Robert O., and Joseph N. Nye, Jr. 1977. *Power and Interdependence: World Politics in Transition*. Boston: Little Brown and Company.

Keohane, Robert, O., and Helen Milner, eds. 1996. *Internationalization and Domestic Politics*. Cambridge: Cambridge University Press.

Krasner, Stephen D. 1983. *International Regimes*. Ithaca: Cornell University Press.

Krause, Keith, and Michael C. Williams, eds. 1997. *Critical Security Studies: Concepts and Cases*. Minneapolis, MN: University of Minnesota Press.

Lapid, Yosef, and Friedrich V. Kratochwil, eds. 1996. *The Return of Culture and Identity in IR Theory*. Boulder: Rynne Rienner.

Larner, Wendy and William Walters 2004. Introduction: Global Governmentality. In *Global Governmentality: Governing International Spaces*, eds. Wendy Larner and William Walters. London: Routledge.

Leebaw, Bronwyn. 2005. Transitional Justice, Conflict, and Democratic Change: International Interventions and Domestic Reconciliation. *Draft Report Prepared for the APSA Task Force on Difference and Inequality in the*

Developing World (1–55). http://www.apsanet.org/imgtest/TaskForceDiffIneqLebaw.pdf. Accessed 16 July 2007.

Lessenich, Stephan. 2011. Constructing the Socialized Self: Mobilization and Control in the 'Active Society.'" In *Governmentality: Current Issues and Future Challenges*, eds. Ulrich Brockling, Susanne Krasmann, and Thomas Lemke. New York: Routledge.

Levien, Michael, and Marcel Paret. 2012. A Second Double Movement? Polanyi and Shifting Global Opinions on Neoliberalism. *International Sociology* 27 (6): 724–744.

Linklater, Andrew. 1990. *Beyond Realism and Marxism: Critical Theory and International Relations*. Basingstoke: Macmillan.

Linklater, Andrew. 2007. *Critical Theory and World Politics: Citizenship, Sovereignty and Humanity*. New York: Routledge.

Lipset, Seymour Martin. 1960. *Political Man: The Social Basis of Politics*. Garden City, NY: Doubleday.

Livingstone, Steven G. 1992. The Politics of International Agenda-Setting: Reagan and North-South Relations. *International Studies Quarterly* 36 (3): 313–329.

Lockhart, Clare. 2005. From Aid Effectiveness to Development Effectiveness: Strategy and Policy Coherence in Fragile States. *Overseas Development Institute background paper for the Senior Level Forum on Development Effectiveness in Fragile States*. http://www.oecd.org/dataoecd/33/11/34258843.pdf. Accessed on 21 June 2006.

Loxley, John. 2010. *Public Service, Private Profits*. Fernwood: Black Point.

Loxley, John. 2012. Public-Private Partnerships After the Global Financial Crisis: Ideology Trumping Economic Reality. *Studies in Political Economy* 89: 7–39.

Luckham, Robin and Tom Kirk. 2012. Security in Hybrid Political Contexts: An End-User Approach. *The Justice and Security Research Programme. JSRP Paper 2.*

Luxemburg, Rosa. 2010. *Socialism or Barbarism: Selected Writings*. London: Pluto Press.

Mamdani, Mahmood. 2001. *When Victims Become Killers*. Princeton: Princeton University Press.

Meyer, Bruce D., and James X. Sullivan. 2012. Identifying the Disadvantaged: Official Poverty, Consumption Poverty, and the New Supplemental Poverty Measure. *Journal of Economic Perspectives* 26 (3): 111–136.

Milner, Helen. 1993. The Assumption of Anarchy in International Relations Theory. In *Neorealism and Neoliberalism*, ed. David Baldwin. New York: Columbia University Press.

Mitchell, Audra. 2010. Peace Beyond Process? *Millennium—Journal of International Studies* 38 (3): 641–664.

Mitrany, David. 1975. *The Functional Theory of Politics*. New York: St. Martin's.

Morganthau, Hans Joachim. 1967. *Politics Among Nations: The Struggle for Power and Peace*. New York: Knopf.

Munck, Ronaldo. 2006. Global Civil Society: Royal Road or Slippery Path? *Voluntas: International Journal of Voluntary and Nonprofit Organizations* 17 (4): 325–332.

Murray, Robert W. 2013. Humanitarianism, Responsibility or Rationality? Evaluating Intervention as State Strategy. In *Libya: The Responsibility to Protect and the Future of Humanitarian Intervention*, eds. Aidan Hehir and Robert W. Murray. New York: Palgrave Macmillan.

Mutimer, David. 2010. "Critical Security Studies: A Schismatic History." In *Contemporary Security Studies*, ed. Alan Collins. New York: Oxford University Press.

Oye, Kenneth A. 1986. Explaining Co-operation under Anarchy: Hypotheses and Strategies. In *Co-operation under Anarchy*, ed. Kenneth Oye. Princeton: Princeton University Press.

Ozkan, Gokhan. 2012. Emergence of International Political Economy as a Sub-Discipline of International Relations and Impact of the Global Crisis on International Political Economy. *International Journal of Business and Social Science* 3 (13): 198–204.

Paris, Roland. 2004. *At War's End: Building Peace after Conflict*. Cambridge: Cambridge University Press.

Paris, Roland. 2010. Saving Liberal Peacebuilding. *Review of International Studies* 36 (2): 337–365.

Peterson, V. Spike, and Anne Sisson Runyan. 2010. *Global Gender Issues*. Boulder, CO: Westview.

Phillips, Anne H. 2000. *Power and Influence After the Cold War: Germany in East-Central Europe*. Maryland: Rowman and Littlefield.

Picketty, Thomas. 2014. *Capital in the Twenty-First Century*. Cambridge: Harvard University Press.

Polanyi, Karl. 1957. *The Great Transformation: The Political and Economic Origins of Our Times*. Boston: Beacon Press.

Prashad, Vijay. 2012. *The Poorer Nations. A Possible History of The Global South*. London: Verso.

Pye, Lucian. 1966. *Aspects of Political Development: An Analytic Study*. Boston: Little, Brown and Company.

Richmond, Oliver, and Jason Franks. 2007. Liberal Peace? Virtual Peace in Cambodia. *Security Dialogue* 38 (1): 27–48.

Risse-Kappen, Thomas, ed. 1995. *Bringing the Transnational Back In: Non-State Actors, Domestic Structures and International Institutions*. Cambridge: Cambridge University Press.

Rodrik, Dani. 1999. *The New Global Economy and Developing Countries: Making Openness Work*. Washington DC: Overseas Development Council.

Rodrik, Dani. 2007. *One Economics, Many Recipes: Globalization, Institutions, and Economic Growth*. Princeton: Princeton University Press.

Rosanvallon, Pierre. 2008. *Counter-Democracy: Politics in an Age of Distrust*. Cambridge: Cambridge University Press.

Rosén, Frederik Ferdinand. 2011. No Words will Deliver Anything: Coaching and Mentoring as Neoliberal Governance Strategy in the Afghan State Administration. *Journal of Intervention and Statebuilding* 5 (2): 151–173.

Rostow, Walt Whitman. 1960. *The Stages of Economic Growth: A Non-Communist Manifesto*. Cambridge: Cambridge University Press.

Rostow, Walt Whitman. 1963. *The Economics of Take-Off into Sustained Growth: Proceedings of a Conference Held by the International Economic Association*. London: MacMillan.

Rostow, Walt Whitman. 1971. *Politics and the Stages of Growth*. Cambridge: Cambridge University Press.

Rothschild, Emma. 1995. What Is Security? *Daedalus* 124 (3): 53–98.

Roy, Alain Le, and John Holmes. 2009. Foreword. In *Protecting Civilians in the Context of UN Peacekeeping operation: Successes, Setbacks and Remaining Challenges (Independent Study Jointly Commissioned by the Department of Peacekeeping Operations and the Office for the Coordination of Humanitarian Affairs)*, eds. Victoria Holt and Glyn Taylor with Max Kelly. New York: United Nations.

Ruggie, John, G. 1982. International Regimes, Transactions, and Change: Embedded Liberalism in the Postwar Economic Order. *International Organization* 36 (2): 379–415.

Ruggie, John. G. 2008. Taking Embedded Liberalism Global: The Corporate Connection. In *Embedding Global Markets: An Enduring Challenge*, ed. John Gerard Ruggie. Burlington: Ashgate.

Russett, Bruce, and John R. Neal. 2001. *Triangulating Peace: Democracy, Interdependence, and International Organization*. New York: Norton.

Selby, Jan. 2007. Engaging Foucault: Discourse, Liberal Governance and the Limits of Foucaldian IR. *International Relations* 21 (3): 324–345.

Selby, Jan. 2013. The Myth of Liberal Peace-Building. *Conflict, Security & Development* 13 (1): 57–86.

Serra, Narcis, and Joseph E. Stiglitz, eds. 2008. *The Washington Consensus Reconsidered: Towards a New Global Governance*. New York: Oxford University Press.

Sheehan, Michael. 2005. *International Security: An Analytical Survey*. Boulder: Lynne Rienner.

Slobidian, Quinn. 2018. *Globalists: The End of Empire and the Birth of Neoliberalism*. Harvard University Press.

Smith, Adam. 2010. *The Theory of Moral Sentiments*. New York: Dover Publications.

Spear, Joanna, and Paul D. Williams, eds. 2012. *Security and Development in Global Politics: A Critical Comparison*. Washington DC: Georgetown University Press.

Stein, Howard. 2008. *Beyond the World Bank Agenda: An Institutional Approach to Development*. Chicago: University of Chicago Press.

Stern, Maria, and Joakim Ojendal. 2010. Mapping the Security–Development Nexus: Conflict, Complexity, Cacophony, Convergence? *Security Dialogue* 41 (1): 5–30.

Stiglitz, Joseph. 2002. *Globalization and its Discontents*. New York: W.W. Norton

Strange, Susan. 1984. *Paths to International Political Economy*. London: G. Allen & Unwin.

Strange, Susan. 1986. *Casino Capitalism*. Oxford: Oxford University Press.

Strange, Susan. 1998. *Mad Money*. Manchester: Manchester University Press.

Tadjbakhsh, Shahrbanou, and Anuradha M. Chenoy. 2007. *Human Security: Concepts and Implications*. London: Routledge.

Tarnogorski, Rafal. 2013. Human Security: Reactivation of an Idea? *Strategic File, the Polish Institute of International Affairs* 2 (29): 1–4.

Taylor, Bron, ed. 1995. *Ecological Resistance Movements: The Global Emergence of Radical and Popular Environmentalism*. New York: State University of New York Press.

Thakur, Ramesh, Andrew F. Cooper, and John English, eds. 2005. *International Commissions and the Power of Ideas*. Tokyo: United Nations University.

Tickner, J. Ann. 1992. *Gender in International Relations: Feminist Perspectives on Achieving Global Security*. New York: Columbia University Press.

Tickner, J. Ann. 2001. *Gendering World Politics: Issues and Approaches in the Post-Cold War Era*. New York: Columbia University Press.

Tickner, J. Ann., and Laura Sjoberg. 2011. *Feminism and International Relations: Conversations about the Past, Present and Future*. London: Routledge.

Tschirgi, Necla, Michael S. Lund, and Francesco Mancini. 2010. *Security and Development: Searching for Critical Connections*. Boulder: Lynne Rienner Publishers.

United Kingdom Cabinet Office. 2008. *The National Security Strategy of the United Kingdom: Security in an Interdependent World*. Presented to Parliament by the Prime Minister, by command of her Majesty, March 2008. https://www.gov.uk/government/publications/the-national-security-strategy-of-the-united-kingdom-security-in-an-interdependent-world. Accessed on 16 September 2015.

United Nations. 2004. *A More Secure World: Our Shared Responsibility*. Report of the Secretary-General's High Level Panel on Threats, Challenges and Change, New York: United Nations Publications. UN Doc. A/59/565. 2 December 2004.

United Nations General Assembly. 2005. *World Summit Outcome*. UN Doc. A/RES/60/1. 24 October 2005.

United Nations General Assembly. 1974. *Declaration on the Establishment of a New International Economic Order (NIEO)*. UN Doc. A/RES/S-6/3201. 1 May 1974.

United Nations General Assembly. 2005. *The Peacebuilding Commission*. UN Doc. A/RES/60/2005. 20 December 2005.

United Nations Security Council. 1999. UN Doc. S/RES/1265. 17 September 1999.

United Nations Security Council. 2000. UN Doc. S/RES/1289. 7 February 2000.

United States White House. 2006. *The National Security Strategy of the United States of America*. Washington, D.C. http://www.comw.org/qdr/fulltext/nss2006.pdf. Accessed on 16 September 2015.

United States White House. 2010. *National Security Strategy*. Washington, D.C. https://www.whitehouse.gov/sites/default/files/rss_viewer/national_security_strategy.pdf. Accessed on 16 September 2015.

Uvin, Peter. 2008. Development and Security: Genealogy and Typology of an Evolving International Policy Area. In *Globalization and Environmental Challenges*, ed. Hans Gunter Brauch, et al., vol. 3. Hexagon Series on Human and Environmental Security and Peace. Berlin, Heidelberg: Springer. https://doi.org/10.1007/978-3-540-75977-5_8.

Waever, Ole. 1998. The Sociology of a Not So International Discipline: American and European Developments in International Relations. *International Organization* 52 (4): 687–727.

Walker, R. B. J. 1993. *Inside/Outside: International Relations as Political Theory*. New York: Cambridge University Press.

Walker, R. B. J. 2010a. *After the Globe, Before the World*. New York: Routledge.

Walker, R. B. J. 2010b. *Out of Line: Essays on the Politics of Boundaries and the Limits of Politics*. Abingdon: Routledge.

Wallerstein, Immanuel. 1974. *The Modern World System. Volume 1: Capitalist Agriculture and the Origins of the European World-Economy in the Sixteenth Century*. New York: Academic Press.

Wallerstein, Immanuel. 1979. *The Capitalist World Economy: Essays*. New York: Cambridge University Press.

Wallerstein, Immanuel. 1980. *The Modern World System. Volume 2: Mercantilism and Consolidation of the European World-Economy, 1600–1750*. New York: Academic Press.

Waltz, Kenneth Neal. 1959. *Man, the State, and War: A Theoretical Analysis*. New York: Columbia University Press.

Waltz, Kenneth Neal. 1979. *Theory of International Political*. Reading, MA: Addison-Wesley.

Warner, Daniel. 2003. The Responsibility to Protect and Irresponsible, Cynical Engagement. *Millennium—Journal of International Studies* 32 (1): 109–121.
Warner, Mildres E., and Judith Clifton. 2014. Marketisation, Public Services and the City: The Potential for Polanyian Counter Movements. *Cambridge Journal of Regions, Economy and Society* 7: 45–61.
Weiss, Thomas G. 2001. Researching Humanitarian Intervention: Some Lessons. *Journal of Peace Research* 38 (4): 419–428.
Wendt, Alexander. 1992. Anarchy Is What States Make of It: The Social Construction of Power Politics. *International Organization* 46 (2): 391–425.
Wheeler, Nicholas J., and Frazer Egerton. 2009. The Responsibility to Protect: 'Precious Commitment' or a Promise Unfulfilled? *Global Responsibility to Protect* 1 (1): 114–132.
Williams, Paul D. 2012. Conceptualizing the Security-Development Relationship: An Overview of the Debate. In *Security and Development in Global Politics: A Critical Comparison*, eds. Joanna Spear and Paul D. Williams. Washington, DC: Georgetown University Press.
Williamson, John. 1990. What Washington Means by Policy Reform. In *Latin American Adjustment: How Much Has Happened?* ed. John Williamson. Washington, DC: Institute for International Economics.
World Bank. 2011. *World Development Report: Conflict, Security, and Development*. Washington, DC: World Bank Publications.

CHAPTER 3

Historical Context of R2P

Introduction

The quest for understanding, most often entails, amongst other things, historicization so that the imperatives, forces, purposes, and meanings of the event, phenomenon, or practice are identified. The task of historizing R2P demands moving beyond the immediate, that is, its putative birth certificate of December 2001 and going back to the founding moments of the UN, to recall its liberal philosophy of security/development that informed the UN's Charter and its subsequent journey including that of some its co-travellers. So, this chapter is an exercise in longue duree—an improvised one—wherein we discuss relevant principles of the UN Charter, the UN reports, and the UN-supported or endorsed international commissions on security and development.

The Charter's Preamble lists security and development as discrete goals and emphasizes the urgency of their *simultaneous* pursuit. It reaffirms faith in human rights, 'to promote social progress and better standards of life in larger freedom' which require maintenance of amongst other things 'international peace and security' and 'promotion of the economic and social advancement of all peoples' (read development). Subsequent UN resolutions and reports explicated these further. The exegeses of the last seven decades are a testimony to the UN's continuing fidelity to the goals of peace, security, and development, a confirmation that the UN has

R. Kashyap, *The Political Economy of Security/Development in the Neoliberal Age*, International Political Economy Series, https://doi.org/10.1007/978-3-031-37279-7_3

not departed from the liberal framework. The work of the UN and some international commissions have contributed towards acknowledging what was in the UN Charter only an implied and understated linkage between security and development. The concept of human security, in which R2P is embedded, is the most pronounced articulation and affirmation of the link. Also significant is how peace gradually loses its *speech status* and is subsumed by development: 'The new name for peace (is) development' (Pope Paul VI in Therien 2005: 29).

The UN's acknowledgement of human security serves to reconcile the tensions between key UN principles: (a) sovereignty and human rights; (b) sovereignty and collective security. The administrative decentralization and delegation of duties within various UN bodies forestall frequent confrontations between these principles. Normative status accorded to the concept of human security mellows the antagonism between the principles by forcing a revision of their respective meanings, albeit in all this movement the principle of sovereignty remained relatively moored. Human security and R2P are attempts to unmoor the principle of sovereignty.

Despite the expansion in the UN's membership, structure, and archives—as resolutions and reports have sought to interpret, expand, and extend the principles of its Charter—the liberal/neoliberal underpinnings of its security/development dispositif remain substantially unchanged. Several international commissions—often referred to as the third UN (Jolly et al. 2009)—initiated by the UN system on issues of security and development have been in tandem with the UN principles even when they claim to espouse a paradigm shift. The UNDP *Human Development Report's* (1994) articulation of human security and the ICISS's reiteration of Francis Deng's casting of sovereignty as responsibility are examples of the failure of radical visions to override the principle of sovereignty.

The UN Charter

Written against the backdrop of World War II the Preamble regards security (e.g., 'to save succeeding generations from the scourge of war') and development (e.g., 'to promote social progress and better standards of life in larger freedom') as the primary ends to be pursued by the UN. Security, however, is seen both as an end in itself and as an instrument (e.g., 'to unite our strength to maintain international peace and security') to secure development (e.g., 'to employ international machinery for the promotion of the economic and social advancement of all peoples'). The Preamble underlines the need for the simultaneous pursuit of the *distinct* goals of security and development,[1] but in this simultaneity there is an implied recognition of the linkages between security and development. This framework made possible the subsequent articulation of the doctrine of human security where the boundaries between security and development get blurred, without causing any disruption with the philosophical premises of the UN.

If ink consumed is a criterion, then the goal of security in comparison to development, receives priority in the UN Charter. While development concerns are the specific context of Chapter IX, *International Economic and Social Cooperation;* security is the subject matter of Chapter I, *Purposes and Principles;* Chapter VI, *Pacific Settlement of Disputes;* Chapter VII, *Action with Respect to the Peace, Breaches of the Peace, and Acts of Aggression;* and Chapter VIII, *Regional Arrangements.*

Chapter 1 affirms the UN's commitment to the maintenance of 'international peace and security' (Article 1) and peaceful settlement of disputes (Article 2(3); also Articles 33–38) but makes them contingent on two principles—sovereignty and collective security—that share an uneasy relationship in the world of realpolitiks. Article 2(1) upholds the 'principle of sovereign equality of all its Members,' and Article 2(7) restricts the UN from intervening in domestic jurisdiction, yet adds a qualification or exception—'this principle shall not prejudice the application of enforcement measures under Chapter VII.' Article 1(2)—'the principle of equal rights and self-determination of peoples' along with Article 2(4)—the norm against aggression (Members will not threaten or use force 'against the territorial integrity or political independence of any state')—are central to the UN's vision of security. In order to meet 'any threat to peace, breach of peace, or act of aggression' the Security Council (Article 39) can take the decision for 'partial interruption of economic relations and of rail, sea, air, postal, telegraphic, radio, and other means of communication and the severance of diplomatic relations' (Article 41). If these non-military measures fail, the Security Council can resort to the military option including 'action by air, sea, or land forces as may be seen

[1] This is also reflected in the Charter's Chapter 1 (Article 1).

necessary to maintain or restore peace and security' (Article 42). Articles 43–49 list a range of measures (e.g., establishment of a military staff committee) to be taken once Article 42 is invoked. The chapter concludes by upholding the right of states for 'individual and collective self-defence if an armed attack occurs against a Member' (Article 51 and Chapter 8). The role of the Security Council as the final sanctioning authoritative body on the decision to resort to the military option—outside the use of force for self-defence—is reiterated in Chapter VIII. Regional organizations are encouraged to resolve local disputes but are not allowed to use 'enforcement action' 'without the authorization of the Security Council' (Article 53).[2]

The option of military collective security was used by the UN only once (Korean War) during the Cold War. This gave credence to the view that collective security was designed primarily for action against aggression by relatively minor powers, wherein great powers' consensus is likely. In this virtual 'absence of a universal system for collective security,' UN members often resort to the alternative of collective defence or 'regional arrangements' (Article 51 and Chapter 8). Thus, in the Cold War era collective defence arrangements premised on a 'system of competitive alliances' trumped the UN system of collective security (Busumtwi-Sam and Cohn 2010: 1).

The concern for security provides the rationale for development goals in Chapter IX *International Economic and Social Co-operation.* This suggests that development is valued for its instrumentality in providing security—maintenance of international peace and security. With a view to the creation of conditions of stability and well-being, necessary for peaceful and friendly relations amongst nations based on respect for the principle of equal rights and self-determination of peoples, the UN shall promote:

a. Higher standards of living, full employment, and conditions of economic and social progress and development;
b. Solutions of international economic, social, health, and related problems; and international cultural and educational co-operation; and

[2] The exception to this rule is that the regional organization can take such action against an 'enemy state' (Article 53(1)), i.e. a 'state which during the Second World War has been an enemy of any signatory of the present Charter' (Article 53(2)).

c. Universal respect for, and observance of, human rights and fundamental freedoms for all without distinction as to race, sex, language, or religion (Article 55).

These provisions resonate with the 1994 UNDP Report's two goals of human security—freedom from want and freedom from fear.

The International Commissions

The international commissions—'Brandt, Palme, and Brundtland'[3]—with the mindset of social democrats (Falk 1995; Cooper and English 2005: 13)—belong to the era of neoliberalism (mid-1970s onwards). The commissions' philosophical leaning towards social democracy seeks to extend the 'concept of the welfare state from the domestic to the international arena' (Cooper and English 2005: 15). This paradox of the continuation of welfare state principles in the neoliberal age is discussed in Chapters 5 and 6 of this book. Despite the adoption of different monikers for security and development by these blue-ribbon commissions, they never stray outside of the liberal/neoliberal framework.

There is overlapping membership in these commissions and the Chair of each had been a member of prior commission(s).[4] The sequence of these commissions is the advancement of a set of similar or congenial ideas, thus each commission acknowledged its intellectual debt to the preceding one(s): Olaf Palme acknowledged his commission's affinity with the Brandt Commission's view that both the 'North and the South have a mutual interest in the recovery of the world economy' (1982: xvi),

[3] Willy Brandt was German Chancellor (1969–1974). He belonged to the Social Democratic Party; Olaf Palme was Swedish Prime Minister (1969–1976 and 1982–1986) and belonged to the Swedish Social Democratic party; and Gro Harlem Brundtland is a former Norwegian Prime Minister (1981, 1986–1989, and 1990-1996). She belonged to the Norwegian Labour Party.

[4] Before chairing the *Commission on Environment and Development*, Gro Harlem Brundtland served on the *International Commission on International Development* (Brandt Commission) and *The Independent Commission on Disarmament and Security Issues* (Palme Commission). Olaf Palme was a member in the Brandt Commission. Sridath Ramphal served on Brandt, Palme, and Brundtland Commissions before co-chairing the *Global Governance Commission*. Prior to chairing the *Human Security Commission*, Sadako Ogata was a member of the *Global Governance Commission*. Mohamed Sahnoun, co-chair of the ICISS, was a member of the Brundtland Commission.

Gro Harlem Brundtland spoke of her commission's work as the formulation of a 'third and compelling call for political action: After Brandt's *Programme for Survival* and *Common Crisis*, and after Palme's *Common Security* would come *Common Future*.' (1987: x); Shridath Ramphal justified putting together a common glossary and index for the three commissions—Brandt, Palme, and Brundtland—as they were premised on the idea of 'One World' and had 'substantial common ground' in their work (Ramphal 1990: 7).

The Brandt Commission

The Independent Commission on International Development Issues (ICIDI), or the Brandt Commission as it was popularly known, headed by Wily Brandt, the German Chancellor, set up in 1977 had 18 members including three former heads of government—Eduardo Frei (Chile), Edward heath (UK), and Olaf Palme (Sweden). There were 8 and 10 representatives from the North and South, respectively (Heath 1981: 298). The Commission submitted its report *North–South: A Program for Survival* in 1980.[5] Iterating the link between disarmament and development the report emphasized (a) continuing the process of *détente* via 'confidence-building measures' and a strengthened UN with a revitalized peacekeeping force to protect the integrity of the states (ICIDI 1980:125); (b) a ban on war requires a ban on mass poverty (Brandt 1980: 15–16).

The report argued for a 'new international economic order' following its examination of the 'economic and social disparities of the world,' the 'trends in the world economy' especially in the 'Third World' (ICIDI 1980: 296–297). To improve the 'exchange rate regime, the reserve system, the balance of payment adjustment process,' the world monetary order had to be improved (ICIDI 1980: 289). This 'rearrangement of international relations' requires a 'comprehensive approach to the problem of development' that acknowledges (a) 'the interlocked welfare of nations' (Brandt 1980:18); (b) the inter-linkages between issues of development, environment (sustainable prosperity based on equitably

[5] Lack of political response to the report, compelled some members to write a memorandum *Common Crisis. North–South: Co-operation for World Recovery* (Therian 2005: 29).

shared resources [ICIDI 1980: 124]), population (there must be a 'balance between population and resources,' therefore, the need for family planning programmes) (ICIDI 1980: 283), and disarmament (Brandt 1980: 15). It put forward a 'comprehensive understanding of security' that moved beyond the traditional or military threats to peace (ICIDI 1980: 124–125).

Palme Commission

The Independent Commission on Disarmament and Security Issues (ICDSI) headed by Olaf Palme was set up in 1980 and submitted its report in 1982. The international context of the 'Second Cold War,' renewed the 'hostilities between East and West,' and prompted the need for an international commission on security. However, like the Brandt Commission before it, this commission too viewed the military as only one dimension of security: 'The doctrine of nuclear deterrence offers very fragile protection indeed against the horrors of nuclear weapons.' The 'doctrine of mutual deterrence' needed to be replaced by that of 'common security' (Palme 1982: xiii). Common security was described 'as the organizing principle for efforts to reduce the risk of war, limit arms, and move towards disarmament' (ICDSI 1982: 7–8). The Commission highlighted the economic causes and consequences of conflict that have particularly devastating consequences (including famines) for the security of the third world countries. Therefore, 'poverty and deprivation' and 'economic inequality' are threats to security (Palme 1982: xv) as 'hunger, malnutrition, poverty and ill-health' can lead to violence (ICDSI 1982: 11). Anticipating the decade later 1994 UNDP Report, it underlined that security is contingent on 'economic progress as well as freedom from military fear' (Palme 1982: xvi). It agreed with the Brandt Commission's assertion of the disarmament and development link, and its recommendation of an improved 'peacekeeping machinery' to help the UN in 'anticipating and preventing conflicts' (Palme 1982: xv).

Brundtland Commission

The World Commission on Environment and Development (WCED) or the Brundtland Commission headed by Gro Harlem Brundtland, set up in 1983, submitted its report in 1987. It examined 'the interrelationships between people, resources, environment, and development' (Brundtland

1987: ix). In 1972 the UN Conference on the Human Environment was organized to 'delineate the "rights" of the human family to a healthy and productive environment.' In 1983 the General Assembly called for 'a global agenda for change' so that 'environmental strategies' could be devised to have 'sustainable development by the year 2000 and beyond' (Brundtland 1987: xi).

The events during its tenure made the subject of the commission even more topical—famines in Africa (since the 1970s), Bhopal Gas tragedy (1984), and the Chernobyl nuclear disaster (1986). The commission was also alert to other forms of 'chronic widespread disasters: the debt crisis, stagnating aid to and investment in developing countries, falling commodity prices and falling personal incomes' (Brundtland 1987: xiii).

The Commission's analysis established 'links between poverty, inequality, and environmental degradation' and further contextualized this link with the questions of population and human rights (Brundtland 1987: xiii). 'Poverty' was identified as a 'major cause and effect of global environmental problems' (WCED 1987: 3). Despite this catalogue of ecological, economic, social, and political problems the Commission was optimistic about 'the possibility for a new era of economic growth,' based on policies of sustainable development that would enhance the environmental resource base. 'Such growth' was necessary to alleviate poverty enveloping 'much of the developing world' (WCED 1987: 1).

Referring to the grave danger of nuclear war it pointed out that 'there are no military solutions to "environmental insecurity"' and this fact needed to be factored in 'the concept of sustainable development.' The plea for sustainable development was an argument for expansive notions of security and development and acknowledgement of the link between them (WCED 1987: 19).

Key Security/Development Initiatives in the Decade of the 1990s

An Agenda for Peace: Preventive Diplomacy, Peacemaking, and Peacekeeping 1992

This report by the UN Secretary-General, Boutros Boutros-Ghali, was a response to invite him by the Security Council in 1992 to make recommendations as to how to strengthen preventive diplomacy, peacemaking, and peacekeeping. It was the era where the Cold War had ended and the

First Gulf War (invasion of Kuwait by Iraq and the UN-endorsed, US-led military intervention) had taken place. A key contribution of the report was the emergence of 'peacebuilding as a distinct concept and strategy applied in the context of intra-state war (as distinct from inter-state war)' in the 1990s (Busumtwi-Sam 2004: 315).

The Report identified the UN's 'security arm' as 'a central instrument for the prevention and resolution of conflicts and the preservation for peace' (A/47/277-S/241111/para 15). It pointed out the multi-dimensional nature and causes of conflicts—'poverty, disease, famine, oppression,' problems of refugees and displaced people, and environmental damage (A/47/277-S/241111/para 13). The premise of this broadened understanding of security allowed Boutros Boutros-Ghali to argue that the sequence of preventive diplomacy, peacemaking, and peacekeeping must be followed by 'post-conflict *peace-building*—action to identify and support structures which will strengthen and solidify peace in order to avoid a relapse into conflict' (A/47/277-S/241111/para 20–21).

Preventive diplomacy would include measures to build confidence, fact-finding, and early warning (A/47/277-S/241111/para 24–26). Early warning systems that alert against possible environmental, nuclear, or natural disasters, epidemics, and mass population movement should 'be synthesized with political indicators to assess whether a threat to peace exists' (A/47/277-S/241111/para 26). The Report recommended the formation of UN's own forces under Article 43 of the UN Charter to 'respond to outright aggression, imminent or actual,' that would enhance the 'credibility of the United Nations as a guarantor of international security' (A/47/277-S/241111/para 42–44). As the number of peacekeeping operations had risen and their tasks increased and broadened (A/47/277-S/241111/para 46–49), the report underlined the need to improve the 'logistics, equipment, personnel and finance' of the peacekeepers (A/47/277-S/241111/para 50).

Though the *Human Development Report* 1994 is credited with drawing attention to the concept of human security, the *Agenda for Peace* uses the term as a matter of fact and without fanfare. The 'integrated approach to human security' requires that the 'responsibility for the maintenance of international peace and security be shared by the Security Council with the General Assembly and 'all the functional elements of the world organization' (A/47/277-S/241111/para 16).

The UNDP Human Development Report (1994)

The 1994 UNDP *Human Development Report* (HDR) continues to be one of the most discussed reports and is credited with making a compelling case for the urgent need of the international community to attend to the issue of human security. When human security is threatened 'in any corner of the world' its impact reverberates globally (UNDP 1994: 4). Pointing out the universal nature of human security concerns such as 'unemployment, drugs, crime, pollution, human rights violations,' prudence dictated that in an 'interdependent world these concerns be addressed and prevented in the early stages' (UNDP 1994: 22).

The HDR denounced the separation of security and development as separate arenas. By placing people at the 'centre of development' their capabilities in the 'economic, social, cultural, and political' fields could be enhanced (UNDP 1994: 4). Human security goals require a new development paradigm of 'sustainable human development' marked by 'intragenerational and intergenerational equity' (UNDP 1994: 4). Like the Commission on Global Governance (CGG) subsequently, HDR made a recommendation for a UN Economic Security Council to decide on 'global issues of human security' (UNDP 1994: 6). Clearly the issue of human security was deemed beyond the Security Council's competence since the HDR's emphasis on development put the accent on 'freedom from want' rather than on 'freedom from fear.'

The HDR did not equate human security with human development: 'Human development is a broader concept…a process of widening the range of people's choices. Human security means that people can exercise these choices safely and freely' (UNDP 1994: 23). Though the UN from its inception recognized human security's two components—'freedom from fear' and 'freedom from want,'—the balance gradually came to be eschewed in favour of the former whereby 'national security' was privileged over the 'all-encompassing concept of human security' that includes economic security, food security, health security, environmental security, personal security, community security, and political security (UNDP 1994: 24–25). The report's aim is not to securitize development as much as it is to developmentalize security. Yet critics argue that 'freedom from fear' continues to be the focus of dominant articulations of human security in both policy and practice.

Commission on Global Governance

The Commission on Global Governance (CGG), set up in 1992, was co-chaired by Shridath Ramphal (Secretary-General of the Commonwealth) and Ingvar Carlsson (Prime Minister of Sweden). An initiative of Willy Brandt, it was endorsed by the UN Secretary-General Boutros Boutros-Ghali.[6] The Commission funded by 'UNDP, nine national governments, and private foundations' (Knight 2005: 101–102) was premised on the hope 'that international developments had created a unique opportunity for strengthening global co-operation to meet the challenge of securing peace, achieving sustainable development, and universalizing democracy' (CGG 1995: 359). Its terms of reference were the challenges of globalization where an increasingly interdependent world was faced with contradictory 'forces of both integration and division.' Global governance required the seizing of opportunities that were provided by the decline of East–West tensions (CGG 1995: 366). Echoing the spirit of the earlier commissions, CGG proposed that the concept of global security necessitated broadening 'the traditional focus on the security of states to include the security of people and the security of the planet' (CGG 1995: 338).

Recognizing the growing gap between the rich and poor countries as a problem, it observed that in a globalized economy, national responses were inadequate. Since the 'structures of global governance' were ill equipped to pursue effective 'international public policy' to meet these challenges, it recommended the creation of 'a global forum that can provide leadership in economic, social, and environmental fields. This should be more representative than the Group of Seven or the Bretton Woods institutions, and more effective than the present UN system.' It proposed the establishment of an Economic Security Council (ESC) within the UN, 'structured like the Security Council, though not with identical membership and independent of it' (CGG 1995: 341–342).

The CGG recommended reforms for UN peacekeeping forces and much like the preceding commissions, it foresaw the need for a more

[6] In 1990 on the invitation of West German Chancellor Willy Brandt, members of the Brandt, Palme, Brundtland, and South Commission recommended that 'Ingvar Carlsson (PM Sweden), Shridath Ramphal (Commonwealth Secretary) and Jan Pronk (Minister for Development Co-operation, Netherlands) prepare a report on the opportunities for global co-operation on issues requiring multilateral action.' Subsequent to the report the Commission was set up (CGG 1995: 359).

frequent and robust deployment of peacekeeping forces. While 'the principle of non-intervention in domestic affairs' must be upheld, it should not restrict a UN response on humanitarian grounds' where the 'security of people is endangered.' The UN Charter should be amended to allow such intervention, the final decision for this was to be taken by a 'reformed Security Council' (CGG1995: 339).

International Commission on Intervention and State Sovereignty (2001)

The International Commission on Intervention and State Sovereignty (ICISS), co-chaired by Gareth Evans and Mohamed Sahnoun, set up in 2000, submitted its report *The Responsibility to Protect* in 2001.[7] The commission's composition ensured representation from both the developed and developing countries, its members were Gisele Cote-Harper, Lee Hamilton, Michael Ignatieff, Vladimir Lukin, Klaus Naumann, Cyril Ramaphosa, Fidel Ramos, Cornelio Sommaruga, Eduardo Stein, and Ramesh Thakur (ICISS 1.7). The commission was established by the 'Government of Canada, together with a group of major foundations,' against the backdrop of killings and ethnic cleansing that marked the violent conflicts in Somalia, Bosnia, Rwanda, and the controversial NATO intervention in Kosovo. The commission cautioned against the use of R2P to frame the international response to the 9/11 attacks (Evans and Sahnoun 2001: viii) since recourse for such situations is available under Art 51 of the UN Charter.

The report examining the 'right of humanitarian intervention' (Evans and Sahnoun 2001: vii) put forward two basic principles: first, 'state sovereignty implies responsibility, and the primary responsibility for the protection of its people lies with the state itself.' Second, if a state is unable or unwilling to protect its population from 'suffering serious harm, as a result of internal war, insurgency, or repression or state failure' then

[7] Gareth Evans had been the Australian Foreign Minister (1988–1996) and was an advocate of 'cooperative security' (see Evans 1994). Mohamed Sahnoun, an Algerian diplomat, had served on several prominent assignments including that of Deputy Secretary-General of the Organization of the African Unity (OAU) (1964–1973) and Ambassador to Germany (1975–1979), France (1979–1982), and United States (1984–1989) and United Nations/Organizations of African Unity (OAU) and Special representative for the Great Lakes region of Africa (1997).

'the principle of non-intervention yields to the international responsibility to protect' (Evans and Sahnoun 2001: xi).

The commission rejected the term, humanitarian intervention, as it had acquired negative connotations in the sovereignty–intervention debate. It argued that the term, humanitarian intervention, discounts the needs and concerns of the local people and privileges the claims of the intervening state, and thus at the very outset puts aside the issue of sovereignty (ICISS 2001: 2.27), the term, 'the responsibility to protect,' was deemed more appropriate (ICISS 2001: 2.29). The commission's official rejection of the term, humanitarian intervention, at the same time was accompanied by the acceptance of the latter's philosophy and spirit, albeit with some alterations. Thus, the justification for the concept of R2P is made on a set of arguments that seek to emphasize both historical continuity and contingency. Legitimacy for R2P is sought in the 'old', i.e., UN Charter's human rights provisions and Chapter VII, 'fundamental natural law principles,' 'the Universal Declaration of Human Rights; the Genocide Convention; the Geneva Conventions and Additional Protocols on international humanitarian law; the statute of the International Criminal Court; and a number of other international human rights and human protection agreements and covenants' (ICISS 2001: 2.26). Indeed, a state's subscription to the UN Charter itself is seen as a tacit agreement to the 're-characterization' if not 'dilution' of the concept of sovereignty. As a signatory to the Charter, a state promises to behave as a 'responsible member of the community of nations' which entails a move from '*sovereignty as control* to *sovereignty as responsibility* in both internal functions and external duties' (ICISS 2001: 2.14) (italics in the original). The report contends that 'sovereignty as responsibility' must be a minimum qualification of 'good international citizenship' (ICISS 2001: 1.35).

> It is acknowledged that sovereignty implies a dual responsibility: externally—to respect the sovereignty of other states, and internally, to respect the dignity and basic rights of all people within the state. In international human rights covenants, in UN practice, and in state practice itself, sovereignty is now understood as embracing this dual responsibility. (ICISS 2001: 1.35)

The newness of R2P is found in the international context of the post-Cold War situation whereby new security issues of intrastate violence emerged (ICISS 2001: 1.16). This era saw increasing incidents of 'crimes against humanity' for example, in the Balkans and Rwanda. In some of these cases example, Rwanda (1994), the UN was not more than a talking shop (see Barnett 2002) and in others, for example, the UN guaranteed 'Safe Haven' of Srebrenica (1995), theUN peacekeeping forces were unable to prevent the massacre of Muslims by the Serbs. The ICISS recommendations aimed at addressing certain lacunas in international law and structure so as to ensure that any future international crisis received an adequate and appropriate response. It placed on the international community two additional responsibilities—to prevent and to rebuild, in addition to the responsibility to react, i.e., military intervention (ICISS 2001: 2.29). The report argues that the international responses demonstrate that although not yet a 'new principle of customary international law,' there is 'an emerging guiding principle' which can be named 'the responsibility to protect' (ICISS 2001: 2.24). *The commission is thus claiming not the invention of a new radical idea or norm, but merely a prescient sighting of an already emerging principle, which they are christening and fleshing out.*

The commission trumps the issue of intervention over that of sovereignty by drawing attention to the concept of human security which legitimates 'the security of *people* against threats to life, health, livelihood, personal safety and human dignity' over that of the 'too narrow a concept of "national security."' Human security can be endangered not just by external aggression 'but also by factors within a country, including "security" forces' (ICISS 2001: 2.22). The report outlines its concerns as emerging from the 'compelling human need, about populations at risk of slaughter, ethnic cleansing and starvation' (ICISS 2001: 8.1). This embedding of R2P within human security gave R2P a further conceptual traction whereby violation of human security by the state could become a reason for the international community to intervene. Each of the three responsibilities of R2P specifically services one of the two human security goals 'freedom from want' and 'freedom from fear,' while responsibility to prevent and responsibility to rebuild mainly engage with the former, responsibility to react is primarily concerned with the latter.

Responsibility to React

The report lists six reasons that justify military intervention: 'right authority, just cause, right intention, last resort, proportional means and reasonable prospects' (ICISS 2001: 4.16). Certain precautionary principles must be observed to ensure that the sole purpose of intervention is to protect the people. It recommends that all operations of intervention be multilateral. The military operation must be of a minimum 'scale, duration and intensity' and have 'reasonable prospects' for success so as not to exacerbate the suffering of the people (Evans and Sahnoun 2001: xii). Before taking the military option, 'coercive measures short of military intervention ought first to be examined including in particular various types of political, economic and military sanctions' (ICISS 2001: 4.3).

All authorization for military action must be from the Security Council. A request for such authority should be made to the Security Council or the latter can raise the issue on its own. Also, under Article 99 of the UN Charter, the Secretary-General can draw attention to this issue. The commission suggests that the Security Council responds promptly to the request and verifies facts on the ground. It advises the permanent five to not apply 'their veto power, in matters where their vital state interests are not involved.' In the event of the Security Council rejecting the proposal, the General Assembly in Emergency Session must consider the matter under the 'Uniting for Peace' procedure, or regional organizations can take such action under Chapter VIII of the UN Charter and subsequently seek authorization from the Security Council. The commission also warned the Security Council that its non-action in such situations would lower the 'stature and credibility of the United Nations' (Evans and Sahnoun 2001: xiii).

The just cause according to the Commission would apply in the following circumstances:

> *large scale loss of life, actual or apprehended, with genocidal intent or not, which is the product either of deliberate state action, or state neglect or inability to act, or a failed state situation; or*
>
> *large scale "ethnic cleansing," actual or apprehended, whether carried out by killing, forced expulsion, acts of terror or rape.* If either or both of these conditions are satisfied, it is our view that the "just cause" component of the decision to intervene is amply satisfied. (ICISS 2001: 4.19)

The just cause ambit includes 'crimes against humanity and violations of the laws of war, as defined by the Geneva Conventions and Additional Protocols and elsewhere,' and instances where a collapsed state is unable to protect the population from 'mass starvation and/or civil war' and natural disasters (ICISS 2001: 4.20). R2P was not to be invoked in situations of human rights violations that fall 'short of outright killing' (ICISS 2001: 4.25). To deal with these and similar demands that have been in the past used to justify 'humanitarian intervention,' the international community should take recourse in the appropriate 'international law, and in particular Article 51 of the UN Charter' (ICISS 2001: 4.27).R2P was not intended to replace or substitute existing coercive measures for human protection purposes.

Responsibility to Prevent

Responsibility to prevent like all aspects of R2P is 'first and foremost the responsibility of the sovereign states' which they can transact through institutions of good governance that 'protect human rights, promote social and economic development and ensure a fair distribution of resources' (ICISS 2001: 3.2). Conflict prevention requires the international community's support, which can take the 'form of inducements' or 'punitive measures' (ICISS 2001: 3.3). The UN has recognized its 'vital role' in conflict prevention as is evident from several General Assembly and Security Council resolutions and reports from the Secretary-General's office such as the *Report of the Panel on United Nations Peace Operations* (2000) and *Prevention of Armed Conflict* (2001)(ICISS 2001: 3.5).

A prerequisite for conflict prevention is a good system of early warning and analysis and the UN must make efforts to improve the same (ICISS 2001: 3.15). The UN must take action at the levels of both root cause prevention efforts and direct prevention efforts (ICISS 2001: 3.25). The report legitimates these recommendations by pointing out that the UN Charter mandates itself to do so as is evident from its Article 55, which acknowledges that:

> Solutions to international economic, social, health and related problems; international, cultural and educational cooperation; and universal respect for human rights are all essential for "the creation of conditions of stability and well-being which are necessary for peaceful and friendly relations among nations." (ICISS 2001: 3.18)

The developed countries must assist their developing counterparts in addressing the political, economic, and institutional (including legal and military) dimensions of conflict prevention. The commission recognized that causes of conflict are not just local, since conflicts are also 'fuelled by arms and monetary transfers that originate in the developed world' (ICISS 2001: 1.20), the latter must introspect on the destructive consequences of their policies (ICISS 2001: 3.20–3.24).

The direct prevention efforts include measures like diplomacy including economic sanctions (ICISS 2001: 3.27), '"second track" dialogues' (ICISS 2001: 3.26), 'mediation,' 'arbitration,' and 'adjudication' (ICISS 2001: 3.28), 'specialist tribunals' on war crimes (ICISS 2001: 3.29),International Criminal Court (ICISS 2001: 3.30), and standoff reconnaissance (ICISS 2001: 3.32). The commission urges that the mentality of a 'culture of reaction' be replaced by a 'culture of prevention' (ICISS 2001: 3.42) in which a range of actors—'UN and its specialized agencies, the international financial institutions, regional organizations, NGOs, religious groups, the business community, the media, and scientific, professional and educational communities all have a role to play' (ICISS 2001: 3.36).

Responsibility to Rebuild

The task of rebuilding a country post-military intervention must be undertaken by 'international agents acting in partnership with the local authorities' (ICISS 2001: 5.1). The instruments of responsibility to prevent—institutions of good governance and sustainable economic development—reappear as implements of the third component of R2P, i.e., responsibility to rebuild. In fact, the rationale of responsibility to rebuild is similar if not the same as that of responsibility to prevent, while the former seeks to ensure that a country does not relapse into violent conflict or a civil war, the latter aims to nip in the bud in the possibility of a violent conflict. There is an increasing recognition amongst academics and policymakers that peace agreements rarely sustain peace, therefore, war-torn societies must focus on conflict prevention (responsibility to prevent) and conflict transformation (responsibility to rebuild) to end the vicious conflict cycle (see Busumtwi-Sam 2002, 2004; Lederach 2003, 2005a, 2005b; Lederach and Lederach 2010; Mason & Meernik 2006; Ramsbotham et al. 2011). The Commission quotes extensively from the Secretary-General's 1998 report *The Causes of Conflict and the Promotion of Durable Peace and Sustainable Development in Africa* to underline the imperative of 'post-conflict peacebuilding' so that 'countries emerging from crisis' can move towards 'reconciliation, reconstruction and recovery' (ICISS 2001: 5.5).

Rebuilding must concentrate on 'three crucial areas of security, justice, and economic development' (ICISS 2001: 5.7). The security agenda should ensure amongst other things that the lives and property of the local population are protected (ICISS 2001: 5.8), 'the local security forces' are disarmed, demobilized, and reintegrated (ICISS 2001: 5.9), and the building anew of the 'national armed forces and police' (ICISS 2001: 5.10). Issues of justice are particularly problematic in post-conflict societies as the very institutions of judiciary 'may have deteriorated or disappeared' (ICISS 2001: 5.13), thus, temporary 'justice packages' should be used till the local judicial institutions are established (ICISS 2001: 5.14), '*legal rights of returnees* from ethnic and other minorities' (ICISS 2001: 5.15) and those of refugees and internally displaced people (IDPs) should be protected (ICISS 2001: 5.16). This issue of 'return sustainability' requires that congenial 'social and economic conditions' be created for 'the returnees' (ICISS 2001: 5.18). The commission underlined the crucial role of development in revitalizing a post-conflict society and its return to law and order. The components of development are identified as 'economic growth, the recreation of markets and sustainable development' (ICISS 2001: 5.19). The commission recommends a 'constructive adaptation' of the UN Chapter XII, International Trusteeship System, as a guideline for the intervening authority (ICISS 2001: 5.22), and makes a cautionary note that R2P should not be used for regime change:

> Responsibility to protect is fundamentally a principle designed to respond to threats to human life, and not a tool for achieving political goals such as greater political autonomy, self-determination, or independence for particular groups within the country. (ICISS 2001: 5.23)

Moving on a similar premise, the commission advises that the intervening authorities must never lose focus of the goal that they are there to facilitate local ownership of the post-conflict process of political and economic development. The assumption of sovereignty by the interveners is only temporary and de facto for purposes of logistics of good governance. Therefore, even in the duration of the intervention the local country retains de jure sovereignty, as was the case in Cambodia (1991) (ICISS 2001: 5.26).

The commission concludes that the view of sovereignty and intervention as being 'inherently contradictory and irreconcilable concepts' no longer holds. (ICISS 2001: 8.2). 'Military intervention' under R2P should not be a 'unilateral action' but one that reaffirms 'the collective responsibility of the international community' (ICISS 2001: 8.4). The accent must be on prevention and post-conflict rebuilding (ICISS 2001: 8.5). The mobilization of 'international support' for R2P requires the mobilization of 'domestic support' so that human, military, and financial resources can be allocated to bear the costs of intervention (ICISS 2001: 8.8). The commission suggests that apathy regarding suffering in remote distant lands can be overcome by making a '*moral* appeal' that also underlines the urgency of the situation (ICISS 2001: 8.13). Also, it should be underlined that early action is less costly than later action (ICISS 2001: 8.14). Early action is in a country's national interest as it may stop 'regional security destabilization' and thereby avoid problems such as 'refugee outflows' and disruption of trade and markets (ICISS 2001: 8.15).The UN Secretary-General (ICISS 2001: 8.19), regional organizations, media, and international non-governmental organizations (ICISS 2001: 8.20) must play a role in raising awareness about the issue and mobilizing international support for intervention. The report concludes by saying that it did not aim to weaken sovereignty. On the other hand, it has tried and is optimistic about the possibility of reconciliation between 'two objectives: to strengthen…the sovereignty of states, and to improve the capacity of the international community to react decisively when states are either unable or unwilling to protect their own people' (ICISS 2001: 8.31).

Key Security/Development Initiatives Between 2001 and 2005

Commission on Human Security

The Commission on Human Security, co-chaired by Sodako Ogata and Amartya Sen,[8] was set up in 2001 'through the initiative of the Government of Japan and in response to the UN Secretary-General's call at the 2000 Millennium Summit for a world "free of want" and "free of fear."'[9] The report *Human Security Now,* presented to the UN Secretary-General in 2003, observes that in the era of globalization 'security of all people' is interlinked. This era has spawned both 'new opportunities for people' and 'new fault lines.' The ensuing conflicts from 'political and economic instabilities' have created conditions of increasing insecurity for people in both the developing and developed states. These new security challenges require a paradigm shift from state security to human security (CHS 2003: 1). Having said this, the report then adds that the two are not antagonistic as 'human security complements "state security"' (CHS 2003: 4). Humansecurity is also complementary to both human development and human rights (CHS 2003: 10). Thus, the scope of human security is wide and envelops the social, economic, and political domains:

> Human security means protecting vital freedoms. It means protecting people from critical and pervasive threats and situations, building on their strengths and aspirations. It also means creating systems that give people the building blocks of survival, dignity and livelihood. Human security connects different types of freedoms—freedom from want, freedom from fear and freedom to take action on one's own behalf. To do this, it offers two general strategies: *protection* and *empowerment*. Protection shields people from dangers. It requires concerted effort to develop norms, processes and institutions that systematically address insecurities. Empowerment enables people to develop their potential and become full participants in decision making. Protection and empowerment are mutually reinforcing, and both are required in most situations. (Outline of the Report of the Commission on Human Security 2003: 1)

[8] The work of the Commission received financial support from the Ministry of Foreign Affairs of Japan, the Government of Sweden, the World Bank, the Rockefeller Foundation, and the Japan Center for International Exchange. The United Nations Office for Project Services lent its administrative support (Ogata and Sen 2003: v).

[9] See http://www.unocha.org/humansecurity/chs/.

Human security concerns raise a range of issues that were addressed by previous international commissions and UN reports on the issues of security and development, for example protection of civilians in violent conflict (Chapter 2), protection of migrants (Chapter 3), the need for effective governance, development, and reconciliation as a means to provide protection of people in post-conflict societies (Chapter 4), economic security (Chapter 5), health services (Chapter 6), and education (Chapter 7). Human security requires an integrated approach in which 'public, private and civil actors' must work together (CHS 2003: 142). These 'disparate human security actors' must built 'a strong global alliance around the United Nations and the Bretton Woods organizations' (CHS 2003: 143).

Report of the Secretary-General's High-Level Panel on Threats, Challenges and Change (2004)

The Secretary-General set up the High-Level Panel on Threats, Challenges and Change to 'assess current threats to international peace and security,' to examine how effectively those threats had been addressed by the UN and to suggest how the UN could best 'provide collective security' (Annan 2004: vii). The panel was chaired by, Anand Panyarachun, the former Prime Minister of Thailand.

The Panel's report *A More Secure World: Our Shared Responsibility* argued for 'a *broader, more comprehensive concept* of collective security: one that tackles new and old threats and addresses the security concerns of all States—rich and poor, weak and strong.' The link between security and development was emphasized—problems of poverty, terrorism, or civil war could not be dealt with in isolation (A/59/565/para 5). Development was viewed as 'the *indispensable foundation* of a new collective security' therefore, the urgency to focus on meeting the Millennium Development Goals (A/59/565/para 7). Drawing attention to the late and weak response to the HIV/AIDS pandemic, the report highlighted the challenges to the global health system's 'vulnerability to new infectious diseases and the promise and peril of advances in biotechnology.' Kofi Annan welcomed the focus on issues of *biological security* (A/59/565/para 8). This broad aspect of security was the subject of the report's Chapter III, while other aspects of security—interstate and intrastate conflicts, nuclear, radiological, chemical and biological weapons, terrorism, transnational organized crime, and the role of sanctions were the focus of Chapters IV to VIII. Suggestions for measures to fortify the nuclear non-proliferation regime included 'voluntary time-bound moratorium on the construction of uranium enrichment and processing facilities' and negotiation of a fissile material cut-off treaty (A/59/565/ para 12). While urging governments to strengthen the tools of sanctions and mediation to meet these challenges, the panel also underscored the need for governments to arrive at criteria regarding the use of force (A/59/565/para 9 and 10). It also proposed that states work towards enhancing the UN's peace enforcement and peacekeeping capability (see the report's Chapter X).

The report returns to the development aspect of security in Chapter XI on post-conflict peacebuilding. Peace enforcement and peacekeeping forces play an important role 'in terminating conflicts but are not sufficient for long-term recovery,' therefore the need for peacebuilding activities to reconstruct and rebuild post-conflict societies so that they do not 'relapse into conflict' (A/59/565/para 224). The report identifies 'a key institutional gap' in the UN system that ill-equips it to help countries transit 'from war to peace.' It recommends the establishment of a Peacebuilding Commission that could partner with the national government and 'martial and sustain the efforts of the international community in post-conflict peacebuilding over whatever period may be necessary' (A/ 59/565/para 264 and 265).[10]

Recognizing protection of human rights as an important component of security, the report pushed for changes in the Human Rights Commission so that the human rights mechanisms could be made more effective and credible (A/59/565/para 15). It proposed that the Human Rights Commission be upgraded 'a Human Rights Council that is no longer subsidiary to the Economic and Social Council but a Charter body standing alongside it and the Security Council' (A/59/565/para 291).[11]

Section 3 of Chapter IX, *Using Force: Rules and Guidelines*, frames the issue of internal threats in the UN Charter's Chapter VII, in the context of R2P. Citing the humanitarian disasters in Somalia, Bosnia, Rwanda, and Darfur it drew attention to the increasing 'recognition that the issue

[10] The Peacebuilding Commission was established on 20 December 2005 by the UN General Assembly.

[11] The Human Rights Council was established on 15 March 2006 by the UN General Assembly. It is not at par with the UNSC or ECOSOC.

is not the "right to intervene" of any State but the "responsibility to protect" of *every* State when it comes to people suffering from avoidable catastrophe—mass murder and rape, ethnic cleansing by forcible expulsion and terror, and deliberate starvation and exposure to disease' (A/59/565/para 201). It went further than the preceding ICISS Report 2001 and the subsequent World Summit Outcome Document 2005 in delineating the criteria for international response, by adding development or the freedom from want as a criterion. It also identified and endorsed 'the emerging norm' of 'collective international responsibility to protect, exercisable by the Security Council authorizing military intervention' (A/59/565/para 203).

Secretary-General's Report, in Larger Freedom: Towards Development, Security and Human Rights for All (2005)

UN Secretary-General, Kofi Annan, prepared the report, *In Larger Freedom: Towards Development, Security and Human Rights for All,* on the request of the General Assembly to draft a comprehensive account on the 'implementation of the Millennium Declaration' (A/59/2005/para 3). The report identified the challenges that face the international community—extreme poverty, migration, climate change, and HIV/AIDS (A/59/2005/9). Evoking the UN Charter's 'notion of larger freedom,' it emphasized that 'development, security and human rights go hand in hand.' (A/59/2005/14). Though poverty and human rights denial may not '"cause" civil war, terrorism or organized crime, they all greatly increase the risk of instability and violence' (A/59/2005/16). The interconnectedness of the threats and challenges requires collective action of nation-states (A/59/2005/19), regional and global intergovernmental institutions (A/59/2005/21), civil society, and private sector (A/59/2005/20).

Freedom from want is imperative as poverty today is 'intellectually and morally indefensible' (A/59/2005/27). In addition, other aspects of development like gender equality, health, education, and environment must also be worked on (A/59/2005/28). The Secretary-General's articulation of the concept of freedom from fear embraced a 'broad vision,' a 'comprehensive concept of collective security' that was cognizant of both old threats—war and conflict and new challenges in the form of 'civil violence, organized crime, terrorism and weapons of mass destruction.' Significantly, he also included in this list the threats to freedom from want—'poverty, disease, and environmental degradation since these have equally catastrophic consequences' and can lead to death (A/59/2005/78). The report recalled that the Millennium Declaration's list of promises includes the guarantee of the right to live in dignity, freedom from want, and freedom from fear. Rule of law, human rights, and democracy are important instruments in realizing these promises, and, therefore, must be promoted.

World Summit Outcome Document (2005)

At the World Summit 2005 the UN General Assembly adopted the principle of R2P via resolution A/RES/60/1. The Heads of States and Governments resolved 'to provide multilateral solutions to problems in the four following areas: Development; Peace and collective security; Human rights and the rule of law; Strengthening of the United Nations' (A/RES/60/1/para 16). R2P is included in the section, *Human rights and the rule of law* as 'Responsibility to protect populations from genocide, war crimes, ethnic cleansing and crimes against humanity' (Paragraphs 138–140).

The World Summit Outcome Document (WSOD) states that it is the responsibility of the state to protect its people from four crimes: 'genocide, war crimes, ethnic cleansing and crimes against humanity' (A/RES/60/1/para 138). In the event of the 'national authorities' failing to do so the 'international community, through the United Nations' must assume the responsibility and use 'appropriate diplomatic, humanitarian and other peaceful means, in accordance with Chapters VI and VII of the Charter.' This includes the option of collective action, under Chapter VII; the Security Council should work in close 'co-operation with relevant regional organizations.' The WSOD underlines the commitment of the international community to help build and strengthen individual state capacity to deal with such crimes (A/RES/60/1/para 139). Support was extended for 'the mission of the Special Adviser of the Secretary-General on the Prevention of Genocide' (A/RES/60/1/para 140).[12]

Even though the promise to help build state capacity to protect its populations is reminiscent of responsibility to prevent, it is evident that the WSOD trimmed R2P essentially meant responsibility to react. The

[12] In 2004 the UN Secretary-General, Kofi Annan, appointed Juan Mendez as Special Adviser to look into the problem of genocide violence.

pithy articulation of a truncated R2P in WSOD focuses on the horror of crimes such as genocide and the need for a proactive national and international response to stop the same. Though responsibilities to prevent and rebuild find no mention in these paragraphs, they are present as pseudonyms in other sections of the WSOD. For example, the section 'Human rights and the rule of law' in addition to R2P talks about human rights (A/RES/60/1/para 121–131), internally displaced people (A/RES/60/1/para 132), refugee protection and assistance (A/RES/60/1/para 133), and human security (A/RES/60/1/para 143) while the section 'Peace and collective security' discusses peacekeeping (A/RES/60/1para 92–96) and peacebuilding (A/RES/60/1para 97–105), also issues like 'debt problem of developing countries' (A/RES/60/1para 26), 'employment' (A/RES/60/1para 47), and 'sustainable development' (A/RES/60/1para 48–56) are the subject matter of the section 'Development.'

Collective Security to Human Security: A Security Continuum?

The post-World War Two era to the present has seen various articulations of security—collective, common, cooperative, comprehensive, and human. As argued earlier in this chapter each of these expressions is accompanied by a certain notion of development. All these concepts reside on a security continuum, which includes the apparent 'outlier'—collective security. Collective security's pariah status is evident from the argument that the search for alternative concepts of security was an admission of the failure of collective security (see Busumtwi-Sam and Cohn 2010: 3).

Common Security

The concept of common security put forward by the Palme Commission emerged in Europe as a reaction to the arms race and deteriorating East–West relations (Dewitt 1994: 4). While affirming the right of all nations to security irrespective of 'ideological or political convictions,' it underlines that 'security cannot be attained through military superiority.' However, it upholds the right of 'collective defence of victims of aggression' as guaranteed by the UN Charter. It recommends restraint in national policy expressions and reduction of armaments and declares that the use of military to resolve disputes is not legitimate (ICDSI 1982: 8–10). Common security advocates underline the indivisibility of security in the age of interdependence that requires states to work with rather than against each other. Though the concept acknowledges development concerns and therefore, the 'multi-dimensional nature of security, most discussions of common security in the European Cold War context focused on military changes, and the promotion of non-provocative defense and military confidence building measures' (Busumtwi-Sam and Cohn 2010: 4). In its espousal of military issues, common security echoes the principles of collective security (Dewitt 1994: 5).[13]

Cooperative Security

Cooperative security—a term not used by any of the above commissions—although not 'Euro-centred,' like common security seeks to move beyond deterrence to promotion of interdependence and confidence-building measures amongst adversaries. However, whereas 'common' security assumes a degree of similarity amongst participating states and their security policies, 'cooperative' security is open to the idea that cooperation can exist amongst a wider group of states with divergent policies, and is therefore, more inclusive. 'Cooperative security advocates include possibilities for collective security as a residual guarantee to member states in response to aggression, but they assume that collective security sanctions would be unnecessary because major aggression would become a remote possibility' (Busumtwi-Sam and Cohn 2010: 4–5). Cooperative security does not privilege the hegemon's right to set the agenda or treat the 'military as a repository' of all security wisdom and recognizes non-military challenges to security. It regards both the state and non-state entities as critical security actors, therefore, not surprisingly 'track two' diplomacy is one of its key operative features in the security domain. It is a more imaginative concept of security as the accent is not on 'common' but 'cooperative' that allows for a more comprehensive way of thinking

[13] The success of the Conference on Security and Cooperation in Europe (CSCE), formed in 1973, in narrowing the gap between East–West relations gave fillip to the common security concept: 'The CSCE represented the operationalization of the core principles of common security' (Dewitt 1994: 5).

about 'state and trans-boundary interests' which include issues of environmental degradation, demography, human, and other threats (Dewitt 1994: 8–9). Cooperative security is thus relatively bolder than common security in breaching the military security bastion.

Comprehensive Security

The Japanese coined the term, comprehensive security, employed by the Brandt Commission and the Brundtland Commission, in the 1970s to propose an alternative to the national security concept. The term was also an instrument that helped Japan charter a more active role in international politics (later Japan moved beyond comprehensive security to become along with Canada a foremost promoter of human security). The comprehensive security concept takes cognizance of 'different functional areas of security— economic and political as well as military; and different levels of security— ranging from national to bilateral, regional, and global' (Busumtwi-Sam and Cohn 2010: 5). The Association of Southeast Asian Nations (ASEAN) version of comprehensive security is 'generally more inward looking than the Japanese notion,' as is evident from their inclusion of domestic stability and regime survival as security concerns (Dewitt 1994: 3). Environmental and health concerns are also a part of comprehensive security doctrines.

The Brandt, Palme, and Brundtland Commissions contributed to fleshing out the comprehensive security concept by expanding the notions of both security and development. All three were critical of the negative economic consequences of the 'arms race' as it 'pre-empts resources that might be used more productively to diminish the security threats created by environmental conflict and the resentments that are fuelled by widespread poverty' (WCED 1987: 7).

Human Security

Amongst all the non-traditional or alternative or non-military[14] articulations of security, it is human security that is credited with having created a paradigm shift in the security discourse by shifting the focus from the state to the needs of the people. Human security is viewed as creating a

[14] The alternative approaches do include the military component in the conceptualization of security but do not privilege it.

possibility for setting up of a new political agenda (Glasius 2008; Maclean et al. 2006; Tadjbakhsh and Chenoy 2007). In the post-Cold War security terrain where wars are 'increasingly within states rather than between states' (Boutros-Ghali in Duffield 2005), humansecurity has moved from the shadows of domestic affairs onto the international political agenda. Though human security became 'an umbrella norm for various treaties and conventions that aim to protect vulnerable people from persecuting actors' (Kerr 2007: 93), there is a tension between human security as a critical tool and as policy paradigm (Owens 2008: 450). Scholarship on human security is identified under two schools of thought: the narrow school which promotes 'freedom from fear' and the broad school(s) that advocates 'freedom from want' (Kerr 2007: 95). However, UNDP's (1994: 23) formulation of human security combines notions of 'freedom from want' and 'freedom from fear.' Dominant articulations of human security at national and international forums evoke notions of protection of individuals/communities.

Not all scholars accord the paradigmatic status to human security. Human security is also contextualized in the 1990s 'liberal internationalism,' which jettisoned the idea of 'national self determination' (Stanley Hoffmann in Rothschild 1995: 56). In this reading the ideas of liberal internationalism and human security are further dated back to the 'preoccupations of late Enlightenment liberalism' whereby the human became the centre of political concerns. Therefore, 'the new political rhetoric of human security in the 1990s is also the old rhetoric of natural or international rights' (Rothschild 1995: 67). However, notwithstanding the lineage of human security, it cannot be denied that human security is the most inclusive of all *latest* security concepts.

Collective Security

The concept of collective security contends that in the context of international anarchy, stability is better ensured not by the self-help imperative but a 'regulated, institutionalized balancing' (Kupchan and Kupchan 1995: 52). Chapter VII of the Charter aims at such institutionalization of collective security in the UN's Security Council so that international peace and security are maintained. The collective security premise rests on (a) disavowal of use of force to change the status quo by all states; (b) states band together irrespective of national interest against the state violating the norm; (c) trust among states that other states will come to their aid, in case they are victim of military aggression' (Mearsheimer 1995: 14).

The new articulations of security have not led to the erasure of collective security and the UN has not denounced the idea and as the international commissions' recommendations reveal the push is for reforming the concept and its office (Security Council) and not its abandonment. This is because the concept of collective security in the UN Charter's Chapter VII appears as a mechanism, an instrument aimed at confronting military aggression that threatens international peace and security. That is, it is concerned with only one form of security—military security. The Charter's framers did not make it available for their own proposed expansive notions of security, i.e., 'larger freedom.' The expansive or broad articulations of security since the decade of the 1980s are a push for an interventionary UN role in the case of non-military threats. To overcome the limitation of politics of great powers in the Security Council that make action difficult, the aforementioned Commissions have proposed UN reforms including that of Security Council, creation of an Economic and Social Security Council at par with the Security Council. The advocates of expansive notions of security seek to bring about changes in the structures or instruments of security so as to make its decision-making more democratic and reflective of the reality of a post-decolonized international order.[15] Therefore, there is no principled opposition or fundamental incompatibility between collective security and human security at the UN.

Conclusion

The above discussion shows that the core ideas of R2P are in consonance with the security/development mandate of the UN Charter. The blue-ribbon international commissions are also similarly placed vis-à-vis the Charter. There are some themes that are common to the commissions and UN reports post-1980s: (a) the issue of questioning the notion of absolute sovereignty; (b) the relative devaluing of the state and the promotion of civil society actors as more reliable agents of good governance in the domains of politics, security, and development. I discuss the implication of these themes for R2P in subsequent chapters.

[15] For a discussion on Security Council reforms (see Alvarez 1996; Kuziemko and Werker 2006; Luck 2006; Weiss 2003; UN 2004).

References

Alvarez, Jose E. 1996. Judging the Security Council. *The American Journal of International Law* 90 (1): 1–39.

Annan, Kofi. 2004. "Foreword." In *A More Secure World: Our Shared Responsibility. Report of the Secretary-General's High Level Panel on Threats, Challenges and Change.* New York: United Nations Publications. UN Doc. A/59/565, 2 December 2004.

Barnett, Michael N. 2002. *Eyewitness to a Genocide: The United Nations and Rwanda.* Ithaca: Cornell University Press.

Brandt, Willy. 1980. A Plea for Change: Peace, Justice, Jobs: An Introduction. In *North-South, a Programme for Survival Co-operation for World Recovery.* Independent Commission on International Development Issues (chaired by Willy Brandt) (1980). Cambridge, Mass.: MIT Press.

Brundtland, Gro Harlem. 1987. Chairman's Foreword. In *Our Common Future.* World Commission on Environment and Development. Oxford: Oxford University Press.

Busumtwi-Sam, James. 2002. "Development and Human Security: Whose Security and From What?" International Journal Spring: 239-258.

Busumtwi-Sam, James. 2004. Development and Peacebuilding: Conceptual and Operational Deficits in International Assistance. In *Durable Peace: Challenges for Peacebuilding in Africa*, eds. Taisier M. Ali, and Robert O. Mathews. Toronto: University of Toronto Press.

Busumtwi-Sam, James, and Ted Cohn. 2010. *International Organization and Global Governance: Theory and Practice.* Unpublished Book Draft.

Commission on Global Governance. 1995. *Our Global Neighbourhood.* Oxford: Oxford University Press.

Commission on Human Security. 2003. *Human Security Now.* New York: Commission on Human Security.

Cooper, Andrew F., and John English. 2005. International Commissions and the Mind of Global Governance. In *International Commissions and the Power of Ideas*, eds. Ramesh Thakur, Andrew F. Cooper, and John English. Tokyo: United Nations University.

Dewitt, David. 1994. Cooperative Security: A Canadian Approach to the Promotion of Peace and Security in the Post-Cold War Era. *Canadian Defence Quarterly* 23 (3): 11–18.

Duffield, Mark. 2005. Getting Savages to Fight Barbarians: Development, Security and the Colonial Present. *Conflict, Security & Development* 5(2): 141–159.

Evans, Gareth. 1994. Cooperative Security and Intrastate Conflict. *Foreign Policy* 96: 3–20.

Evans, Gareth, and Mohamed Sahnoun. 2001. Foreword. In *The Responsibility to Protect*. International Commission on Intervention and State Sovereignty. Ottawa: International Development Research Centre.

Falk, Richard A. 1995. Liberalism at the Global Level: The Last of the Independent Commissions? *Millennium—Journal of International Studies* 24 (3): 563–576.

Glasius, Marlies. 2008. Human Security from Paradigm Shift to Operationalization: Job Description for a Human Security Worker. *Security Dialogue* 39 (1): 31–54.

Heath, Edward. 1981. North–South: A Programme for Survival. *The Geographical Journal* 147 (3): 298–306.

Independent Commission on International Development Issues (chaired by Willy Brandt). 1980. *North South, A Programme for Survival Co-operation for World Recovery*. Cambridge, Mass.: MIT Press.

International Commission on Intervention and State Sovereignty. 2001. *The Responsibility to Protect*. Ottawa: International Development Research Centre.

Jolly, Richard, Louis Emmerij, and Thomas G. Weiss. 2009. *UN Ideas that Changed the World*. Bloomington: Indiana University Press.

Kerr, Pauline. 2007. Human Security. In *Contemporary Security Studies*, ed. Alan Collins. Oxford: Oxford University Press.

Knight, W. Andy. 2005. Equivocating on the Future of World Order: The Commission on Global Governance. In *International Commissions and the Power of Ideas*, eds. Ramesh Thakur, Andrew F. Cooper, and John English. Tokyo: United Nations University.

Kupchan, Charles, and Clifford A. Kupchan. 1995. The Promise of Collective Security. *International Security* 20 (1): 52–61.

Kuziemko, Ilyana, and Eric Werker. 2006. How Much is a Seat on the Security Council Worth? Foreign Aid and Bribery at the United Nations. *Journal of Political Economy* 114 (5): 905–930.

Lederach, John Paul. 2003. *The Little Book of Conflict Transformation*. Intercourse, PA: Good Books.

Lederach, John Paul. 2005a. *The Moral Imagination. The Art and Soul of Peacebuilding*. New York: Oxford University Press.

Lederach, John Paul. 2005b. *Building Peace: Sustainable Reconciliation in Divided Societies*. Washington, DC. United Services Institute of Peace Press.

Lederach, John Paul, and Angela Jill Lederach. 2010. *When Blood and Bones Cry Out: Journeys through the Soundscape of Healing and Reconciliation*. New York: Oxford University Press.

Luck, Edward C. 2006. *UN Security Council: Practice and Promise*. New York: Routledge.

Maclean, Sandra J., David R. Black, and Timothy M. Shaw, eds. 2006. *A Decade of Human Security: Global Governance and New Multilateralisms*. Ashgate: Aldershot & Burlington VT.

Mason, T. David., and James D. Meernik, eds. 2006. *Conflict Prevention and Peacebuilding in Post-War Societies: Sustaining the Peace*. New York: Routledge.

Mearsheimer, John. 1995. The False Promise of International Institutions. *International Security* 19 (3): 5–49.

Ogata, Sadako, and Amartya Sen. 2003. Foreword. In *Human Security Now*. New York: Commission on Human Security.

Owens, Taylor. 2008. The Critique that doesn't Bite: A Response to David Chandler's 'Human Security: The Dog that didn't Bite.' *Security Dialogue* 39: 445–453.

Palme, Olaf. 1982. Introduction. In *Common Security: A Blueprint for Survival*. The Independent Commission on Disarmament and Security Issues. New York: Simon and Schuster.

Ramsbotham, Oliver, Tom Woodhouse, and Hugh Miall. 2011. *Contemporary Conflict Resolution: The Prevention, Management and Transformation of Deadly Conflicts*. Cambridge, UK: Polity.

Ramphal, Sridath S. 1990. Introduction. In *Common Index and Glossary to the Brandt, Palme and Brundtland Reports of the Independent Commissions on International Development, Disarmament and Security, and Environment and Development*. London: Commonwealth Secretariat.

Rothschild, Emma. 1995. What is Security? *Daedalus* 124 (3): 53–98.

Tadjbakhsh, Shahrbanou, and Anuradha M. Chenoy. 2007. *Human Security: Concepts and Implications*. London: Routledge.

The Independent Commission on Disarmament and Security Issues. 1982. *Common Security: A Blueprint for Survival*. New York: Simon and Schuster.

Therien, Jean-Phillipe. 2005. Brandt Commission: The End of an Era in North-South Politics. In *International Commissions and the Power of Ideas*, eds. Ramesh Thakur, Andrew F. Cooper, and John English. Tokyo: United Nations University.

United Nations. 1945. *Charter of the United Nations*. https://www.un.org/en/about-us/un-charter.

United Nations. 2004. *A More Secure World: Our Shared Responsibility*. Report of the Secretary-General's High Level Panel on Threats, Challenges and Change, New York: United Nations Publications. UN Doc. A/59/565, 2 December 2004.

United Nations. 2005. Addendum 2, Peacebuilding Commission: Explanatory note by the Secretary-General, Background. In *Larger Freedom: Towards*

Development, Security and Human Rights for All, Report of the Secretary-General. New York: United Nations. Available at http://www.un.org/largerfreedom/add2.htm. Accessed on 23 May 2006.

United Nations Development Program. 1994. *Human Development Report—1994.* New York: Oxford University Press.

United Nations General Assembly. 2021. *The Responsibility to Protect and the Prevention of Genocide, War Crimes, Ethnic Cleansing and Crimes Against Humanity.* UN Doc. A/RES/75/277. 18 May 2021.

United Nations Secretary-General. 2005. *In Larger Freedom: Towards Development, Security and Human Rights for All.* Report, of the Secretary-General. UN Doc. A/59/2005. 26 May 2005.

Weiss, Thomas G. 2003. The Illusion of UN Security Council Reform. *Washington Quarterly* 26 (4): 147–161.

World Commission on Environment and Development. 1987. *Our Common Future.* Oxford: Oxford University Press.

CHAPTER 4

The Material and the Ideational Dimensions of R2P: R2P in the UN's Security/Development Dispositif

Introduction

This chapter maps the nature and dimensions of R2P's ideational and material presence in the UN to demonstrate its incorporation in the latter's security/development dispositif. The indicators of the materiality of R2P are the UN (and non-UN) bodies[1] that are mandated with the implementation of R2P, and these are identified by no less than the Secretary-General himself, via his annual reports on R2P. So in addition to the Special Adviser on R2P, the R2P *job* belongs to various UN bodies including the General Assembly, Secretariat, Security Council, Human Rights Council, Peacebuilding Commission, particular UN programmes, funds, specialized agencies, country teams, World Bank, certain enti ties outside the UN too have a similar responsibility: the International Criminal Court, states especially the 'neighbouring states,' regional, sub-regional organizations, and civil society (A/68/947 S/2014/449/paras 21–24). The identification of the ideational dimension of R2P requires bringing forth how the above entities (a) fleshed out the conceptual details of the skeletal R2P of the WSOD (2005) (b) incorporated the principles of R2P as a basis of their respective practices.

[1] This is not to suggest that this study covers all institutions and organizations outside the UN, which deal with R2P.

R. Kashyap, *The Political Economy of Security/Development in the Neoliberal Age*, International Political Economy Series,
https://doi.org/10.1007/978-3-031-37279-7_4

The Official Conceptual 'State of Being' of R2P at the UN

R2P owes its conceptual development—the SOD's three pithy paragraphs (138–140)—to the Secretary-General and the Office of the Special Adviser on Prevention of Genocide (OSAPG). The Secretary-General's annual reports[2] on R2P along with the 'Framework of Analysis' (FOA)[3]—a toolkit to identify countries most at risk of atrocity crimes—developed in 2014 by the United Nations Office on Genocide Prevention

[2] The first report (2009) developed the three pillars of R2P and mentioned the significance of early warning and assessment (A/63/677/2009). The second report (2010) 'focused on early warning, assessment and the responsibility to protect' (A/64/864/2010). The third report (2011) discussed the role of regional and sub-regional arrangements in implementing the responsibility to protect (A/65/877-S/2011/393). The fourth report (2012) focused on timely and decisive response (A/66/874-S/2012/578), and 'took stock of the Charter-based tools available to respond to situations of concern and the partnerships that could be utilized, as well as ways of protecting responsibly' (A/67/929-S/2013/399/para 3). The fifth report (2013) was on the responsibility of the state to protect and prevent. It focused on the causal dimensions of atrocity crimes and suggested preventive measures that a state can take in this regard (A/67/929-S/2013/399). The sixth report (2014) was on the second pillar and identified the 'actors, approaches and principles to guide efforts to assist States through encouragement, capacity building and protection assistance' (http://www.un.org/en/preventgenocide/adviser/responsibility.shtml) (A/68/947-S/2014/449). The seventh report, *A Vital and Enduring Commitment: Implementing the Responsibility to Protect*, assesses the work done in the last ten years to implement R2P (A/69/981-S/2015/500). The eighth report (2016) was on how to craft an agenda to mobilize collective action for the implementation of R2P in the coming decade (A/70/999-S/2016/620). The ninth report discussed how despite the theoretical commitment to R2P by actors, the atrocity crimes against populations have continued. It suggested the fixing of accountability (at the levels of government, intergovernmental organization, and the United Nations) for the non-implementation of R2P (2017) (A/71/1016-S/2017/556). The tenth report (2018) underlined the need for improved and efficient early warning systems that would make early action on prevention of atrocity crimes possible (A/72/884-S/2018/525). The eleventh report (2019) was about lessons learned so far and the recommended actions for prevention of atrocity crimes. The twelfth report (2020) focused on the protection of women and drew attention to how the pandemic had deepened structural inequalities including that of gender (A/74/964-S/2020/501). The thirteenth report (2021) was an overview of how the OSAPG had led the task of operationalization of R2P throughout the UN (A/75/863-S/2021/424). The fourteenth report (2022) argued for the need to prioritize the protection of children and young people as they are targeted distinctly during commission of atrocity crimes (A/76/844-S/2022/428).

[3] United Nations Office on Genocide Prevention and the Responsibility to Protect. 2014. *Framework of Analysis for Atrocity Crimes: A Tool for Prevention*. New York: United Nations.

and the Responsibility to Protect (UNOGPR2P) can be regarded as the UN's authoritative expansive explanation of R2P. These annual reports—began in 2009, during the tenure of the then Secretary-General, Ban Ki-moon, a keen advocate of R2P—are committed to 'move the principle from the realm of rhetoric into concrete action' (A/68/947-S/2014/449/para5). The reports self admittedly draw from the ideas put forward and work done by former Secretary-Generals, particularly Boutros Boutros-Ghali and Kofi Annan, and other UN organs/agencies/departments on R2P-related issues.

R2P is founded on the 'well-established legal obligations' that emerge from the Convention on the Prevention and Punishment of the Crime of Genocide, Geneva Conventions, and 'legal obligations and interpretations' of the International Court of Justice 2007, February 27 judgement in the *Case Concerning Application of the Convention on the Prevention and Punishment of the Crime of Genocide* (Bosnia and Herzegovina v. Serbia and Montenegro) (UNOGPR2P 2014: 2–3).

R2P aims to protect populations from four atrocity crimes—genocide, crimes against humanity, war crimes, and ethnic cleansing. The Secretary-General has argued against R2P's application to other calamities like 'HIV/AIDS, climate change' as it would undermine the 2005 consensus and stretch the concept beyond recognition or operational utility (A/63/677).

a. The norm against genocide draws from the Convention on the Prevention and Punishment of the Crime of Genocide (Article 2), Rome Statute of the International Criminal Court (Article 6), Statute of the International Criminal Tribunal for the former Yugoslavia (Article 4(2)), and Statute of the International Criminal Tribunal for Rwanda (Article 2(2)) (UNOGPR2P 2014: 26).
b. Crimes against humanity have come to be defined 'under customary law through the jurisdiction of international courts,' the Rome Statute of the International Criminal Court (Article 7(1)), Statute of the International Criminal Tribunal for the former Yugoslavia (Article 5), and Statute of the International Criminal Tribunal for Rwanda (Article 3). We may note that the statutes do not exactly replicate each other's definition of crimes against humanity (UNOGPR2P 2014: 27).
c. War Crimes are those 'violations of international humanitarian law that place individual criminal responsibility' on perpetrators

under international humanitarian law and international criminal law treaties, as well as international customary law (Geneva Conventions (1949) and Additional Protocol (1977)), Rome Statute of the International Criminal Court (Article 8), Statute of the International Criminal Tribunal for the former Yugoslavia (Article 2 & 3), and the Statute of the International Criminal Tribunal for Rwanda (Article 4). Again, we may note that these conventions and statutes differ in their respective cataloguing of war crimes (UNOGPR2P 2014: 28).

d. Ethnic cleansing, although not deemed 'an independent crime under international law' came to be defined by the United Nations Commission of Experts that was established in the 'context of the war in former Yugoslavia' (UNOGPR2P 2014: 32).[4] 'It includes acts that are serious violations of international human rights and humanitarian law that may themselves amount to one of the recognized atrocity crimes, in particular crimes against humanity' (UNOGPR2P 2014: 1).

Prevention of atrocity crimes is necessary to 'preserve human life,' and maintain 'national,' 'regional and international peace and stability.' Prevention is cheaper than the costs of post-conflict intervention and also reinforces a state's sovereignty by averting 'more intrusive forms of response from other States or international actors' (UNOGPR2P 2014: 2).

The UN's elaborate setup for early warning assessment is an optimistic 'pre-emptive strike' against potential situations of atrocity crimes. The United Nations Interagency Framework for Coordination on Preventive Action ('Framework team') is an informal forum where '21 United Nations agencies, departments, funds and programmes share information and analysis on selected situations that display early signs of growing

[4] See Interim Report of the Commission of Experts Established Pursuant to Security Council Resolution 780 (1992), *U.N. SCOR*, *U.N. Doc. S/25274 (26 January 1993)*. Ethnic cleansing includes making a region 'ethnically homogeneous' through coercive acts like murder, rape, ghettoization of civilian population, torture, and extrajudicial executions. Importantly, the Commission also observed that these acts '... constitute crimes against humanity and can be assimilated to specific war crimes. Furthermore, such acts could also fall within the meaning of the Genocide Convention' (UNOGPR2P 2014: 32).

tension' (A/64/864/para 9).[5] Better assessment tools and capacity, efficient sharing and processing of information through an R2P lens, would ensure 'system-wide coherence' for a better implementation of R2P (A/64/864/para 10).[6]

The FOA identifies fourteen risk factors that 'include behaviors, circumstances or elements that create an environment conducive to the commission of atrocity crimes, or indicate the potential, probability or risk of their occurrence.' Risk factors include both structural and 'dynamic circumstances or events' that serve as triggers to convert a 'general risk into an increased likelihood' of the commission of crimes. In addition, the indicators (i.e., manifestations) of each risk factor are also identified. While eight[7] of these fourteen risk factors are 'common to all crimes,' there are

[5] The Framework team is housed 'in the Bureau of Crisis Prevention and Recovery of the United Nations Development Programme, whose Conflict Prevention Unit works with the Department of Political Affairs (DPA) to formulate conflict prevention strategies and implement programmes with United Nations country teams in the field. Both the Department of Peacekeeping Operations (DPKO) and the United Nations International Children's Emergency Fund (UNICEF) maintain round-the-clock situation centres in New York to receive information from their extensive field operations. The Office of the United Nations High Commissioner for Human Rights (OHCHR) and the Office of the United Nations High Commissioner for Refugees (UNHCR) continuously monitor and assess developments related to their mandates, both of which have important implications for implementing the responsibility to protect. The work of the special rapporteurs established by the United Nations Human Rights Council (UNHCR) and of the human rights treaty bodies can also be of assistance in particular cases' (A/64/864/para 9).

[6] Poor information management and analysis is identified as one of the factors that led to the failure of prevention of 'Rwandan genocide' and the 'fall of Srebrenica' (A/64/864/para 7).

[7] The eight risk factors (along with an example of its indicator) are: Situations of armed conflict or other forms of instability (indicator—'Security crisis' resulting from violations of 'peace agreements, armed conflict in neighboring countries, threats of external interventions or acts of terrorism') (UNOGPR2P 2014: 10); Record of serious violations of international human rights and humanitarian law (indicator—'past acts of genocide, crimes against humanity, war crimes or their incitement') (UNOGPR2P 2014: 11); Weakness of State structures (Indicator—'National institutions, particularly judicial, law enforcement and human rights institutions that lack sufficient resources, adequate representation or training') (UNOGPR2P 2014: 12); Motives or incentives (Indicator—'Economic interests, including those based on the safeguard and well-being of elites or identity groups, or control over the distribution of resources') (UNOGPR2P 2014: 13); Capacity to commit atrocity crimes(Indicator—Strong culture of obedience to authority and group conformity') (UNOGPR2P 2014: 14); Absence of mitigating factors (Indicator—'Lack of a strong, organized and representative national civil society and of a free, diverse and independent national media.') (UNOGPR2P 2014: 15); Enabling circumstances or

two specific risks for each of the 'three international crimes- namely genocide,[8] crimes against humanity[9] and war crimes'[10] (UNOGPR2P 2014: 5–6).

The Three Pillars

The SG in his 2009 annual report on R2P proposed a 'three-pillar strategy' for implementing R2P in accordance with the mandate of paragraphs 138 and 139 of the 2005 SOD. These pillars were detailed at length in subsequent reports. *Pillar one* describes the protection responsibilities of the State, *pillar two* refers to the international assistance and capacity building responsibility of international community while *pillar three* is the timely and decisive response of the UN Member States. The report values strategies of prevention but acknowledges that when prevention fails 'early and flexible response' must be made to address the situation.

preparatory action (Indicator—'Acquisition of large quantities of arms and ammunition or of other objects that could be used to inflict harm.') (UNOGPR2P 2014: 16); Triggering factors (Indicator—'Sudden changes that affect the economy or the workforce, including as a result of financial crises, natural disasters or epidemics.') (UNOGPR2P 2014: 17).

[8] The two specific risk factors (along with an example of its indicator) for genocide are: Intergroup tensions or patterns of discrimination against protected groups (Indicator—'Past or present serious discriminatory, segregational, restrictive or exclusionary practices, policies or legislation against protected groups.') (UNOGPR2P 2014: 18); Signs of an intent to destroy in whole or in part a protected group (Indicator—'Official documents, political manifests, media records, or any other documentation through which a direct intent, or incitement, to target a protected group is revealed, or can be inferred.') (UNOGPR2P 2014: 19).

[9] The two specific risk factors (along with an example of its indicator) for crimes against humanity are: Signs of a widespread or systematic attack against any civilian population (Indicator—'Signs of development or increased use of means or methods of violence that are incapable of distinguishing between civilian and military targets or that are capable of mass destruction, persecution or weakening of communities') (UNOGPR2P 2014: 20); Signs of a plan or policy to attack any civilian population (Indicator—'Adoption of discriminatory security procedures against different groups of the civilian population.') (UNOGPR2P 2014: 21).

[10] The two specific risk factors (along with an example of its indicator) for war crimes are: Serious threats to those protected under international humanitarian law (Indicator—'Promotion of ethnicity or religion as a determinant of national allegiance or allegiance to a party of the conflict.') (UNOGPR2P 2014: 22); Serious threats to humanitarian or peacekeeping operations (Indicator—'Interference, limitation or prohibition of access or movement of humanitarian or peacekeeping operations or their personnel.') (UNOGPR2P 2014: 23).

All three pillars are projected as being equally important in upholding the 'edifice' of R2P. The report underlines their simultaneity and treats them as non-sequential. This is deemed as necessary for two reasons, *first*, it allows for a tailored or a more appropriate response to a situation that may demand the deployment of tools from more than one of the three pillars. *Second*, this also helps the SG stress the point that R2P's prevention strategy requires a continuous, permanent, always active responsibility of the State, regional organizations, and the international community (A/63/677/2009).

For example, in order to ensure that a State fulfils its responsibility under pillar one, it may need to be educated, trained, or persuaded (publicly or confidentially) by other States or international[11] and regional organizations. This latter action requires activation of pillar two (A/63/677/para 30). Pillar two is also needed when a State is too weak to stop the commission of atrocities by an armed opposition. In addition to the persuasive measures and positive incentives, pillar two could also encompass military assistance to the 'beleaguered State.' In such an instance pillar two's measures 'supplement the policy tools under pillar one and complement those under pillar three because none of the pillars is designed to work in isolation from the others' (A/63/677/para 30).

However, if a State is determined to commit the crime, then the international community must organize its 'capacity and will for a "timely and decisive" response' under pillar three (A/63/677/para 29). The tools to implement R2P under pillar three include the range of non-coercive measures available under Chapter VI of the UN Charter—'negotiation, enquiry, mediation, conciliation, arbitration, judicial settlement, resort to regional agencies' (A/66/874-S/2012/578/para 22). And if these non-coercive measures fail, then the Security Council must authorize action under the UN Charter's Chapter VII (A/66/874-S/2012/578/para 21). Actions under pillar three must enable the 'future achievement of pillar one goals' (A/66/874-S/2012/578/para 15). For this reason, it

[11] This would include the services of the 'United Nations High Commissioner for Human Rights, the United Nations High Commissioner for Refugees, the Emergency Relief Coordinator, the Special Adviser on the Prevention of Genocide, other special advisers, special representatives and envoys of the Secretary-General, and ranking officials of the United Nations, its development agencies and the Bretton Woods institutions' (A/63/677/para 30, also see para 33).

is essential to observe 'responsibility while protecting'[12] so that R2P is operationalized 'in a manner that is responsible, sustainable and effective' (A/66/874-S/2012/578/para 49).

In contrast to the ICISS Report, which segregated and sequenced the responsibilities of prevention, reaction, and rebuilding, the mandate of the three pillars is not so neatly categorized. Prevention of atrocity crimes is clearly a responsibility of all three pillars. For example, both the state (pillar one) and the international community (pillar two) are expected to promote economic development and prosperity of the population so as to address the root causes of atrocity crimes. Pillar three though associated primarily with responsibility to react, also has the prevention component in the range of its initiatives. Diplomatic negotiations and economic sanctions are pillar three's tools that aim to stop atrocity crimes so that recourse to military intervention can be avoided. Pillar two's option of military assistance by the regional organization/international community to a 'beleaguered state' is comparable to pillar three's responsibility to react, though unlike the latter it is taken with the consent of the state. The responsibility to rebuild belongs to both the state (pillar one) and the international community (pillar two).[13]

The Special Adviser on the Responsibility to Protect at the Office of the Special Adviser on the Prevention of Genocide

The Special Adviser on the Responsibility to Protect (SAR2P) works 'under the overall guidance' of the Office of the Special Adviser on the Prevention of Genocide (OSAPG). The Special Adviser on Prevention of Genocide's (SAPG) task is to 'raise awareness of the causes and dynamics of genocide, to alert relevant actors where there is a risk of genocide, and to advocate and mobilize appropriate action.'[14] The task of SAR2P is to develop the 'conceptual, political, and operational aspects' of R2P. The SAPG and SAR2P have distinct but complementary mandates and are

[12] The Brazilian President introduced the 'initiative on responsibility while protecting' in the UN General Assembly debate in 2011 (A/66/874-S/2012/578/para 50).

[13] For further analysis of the responsibilities under the three pillars see the book's Chapter 6.

[14] http://www.un.org/en/preventgenocide/adviser/index.shtml.

therefore supported by a joint office to ensure efficient synergy between their respective tasks. In this chapter the word, *Office*, refers to OSAPG.

In 2004 the post of Special Advisor to the Secretary-General on the Prevention of Genocide (SAPG) was created by a Security Council Resolution (S/RES/1366) to fill critical gaps in the international system that allowed the genocides in Rwanda and the Balkans go unchecked; Juan Mendez was appointed as the Special Adviser. In 2007, Secretary-General Ban Ki-moon appointed Francis M. Deng on a full-time basis at the level of Under-Secretary-General. In 2008 Edward Luck was appointed as the SAR2P.[15] While the SAR2P holds the rank of an Assistant Secretary-General, this is not a 'regular budget post' which some argue slows down the R2P work (Luck 2011: 391).

Under the UN's regular budget, there is one full-time Under-Secretary-General USG (Special Advisor on Prevention of Genocide), one part-time Assistant Secretary-General (Special Advisor on Responsibility to Protect), six professional positions (P5 Senior Political Affairs Officer, Head of Office), three P4s (two Political Affairs Officers, one Human Rights Officer), two P3s (Political Affairs Officers), and two support staff. One of the P4s supervises one of the P3s.[16] Other temporary staff (varying in number) are supported by voluntary contributions and work under the supervision of the regular staff.[17]

The core functions of the Office are listed as the following: (a) Monitoring and risk assessment of situations in countries that are at risk of the four atrocity crimes. This involves information collection/assessment from the UN and other sources and the maintenance of 'internal database' on the subject. The Office uses its *Framework of Analysis* to assess such situations and identify factors that could lead to atrocity crimes; (b) Advising the Secretary-General and through him, the Security Council, about situations at risk of atrocity crime and consequently 'mobilizing' the UN system, individual states, regional and sub-regional organizations for the same. In pursuit of this goal the

[15] Subsequent SAPGs are Adama Dieng (2012–2020) and Alice Wairumu Nderitu (2020–). Subsequent SAR2Ps Jennifer Welsh (2013–2015), Ivan Simonovic (2016–2018), Karen Smith (2019–2021), and George Okoth-Obbo's (2021–).

[16] In the UN staff category parlance P5 denotes a professional with minimum 10 years of work experience, P4 indicates a professional with minimum 7 years of work experience, and P3 indicates a professional with minimum 5 years of work experience.

[17] This information was given to me by an OSAPG Official via email.

Office 'issues(s) public statements and engages(s) in quiet diplomacy' and may on the instructions of the Secretary-General 'convene key Under-Secretaries-General in crisis situations' in order 'to discuss policy and strategy options'; (c) Enhancing capacity of the UN, individual states, civil society, regional and sub-regional organizations through its various training programmes; (d) Advancing R2P through its 'conceptual, political and institutional/operational development' and working towards its implementation by the UN, individual states, civil society, regional and sub-regional organizations. The 'associated activities' in this regard include (i) Engagement and consultations with the above actors to develop a 'political and institutional consensus on the implementation of the responsibility to protect'; (ii) Assisting the SG in the drafting of reports and statements on R2P; (iii). Persuading other intergovernmental organizations to incorporate R2P in their programmes and policies; (iv) Assisting other UN bodies including the General Assembly and the Security Council to deliberate on R2P and organizing 'high-level events' on the same; (v) Exploring means to assimilate R2P into the 'work of the UN system'; and (e) Raising awareness about the 'causes and dynamics' of atrocity crimes and the 'responsibility of the States and the international community' in this context (OSAPG *Brief Overview*). In pursuit of these functions the Office[18] undertakes key missions[19] and outreach.[20] The Office organizes workshops/seminars for 'UN staff, government officials and civil society' to train them to dissect and analyse information on atrocity crimes 'within the United Nations system' and identify 'effective and practical means' of atrocity prevention. Workshops in various countries are organized in collaboration with other training institutes such as Auschwitz Institute for Peace and Reconciliation (United States), Clingendael Institute (The Netherlands), Nonviolent Peaceforce, (Belgium), International Institute for Humanitarian Law (Italy), and

[18] See http://www.un.org/en/preventgenocide/adviser/responsibility.shtml.

[19] Edward Luck as SAR2P undertook such missions: Berlin, Germany 2011, Hanoi Vietnam 2011, UK 2011, Washington, US 2011, 2012 (SAPG also attended the same). The SAPG compared to the SAR2P has headed most of the missions probably because unlike the latter the post of SAPG is full time.

[20] http://www.un.org/en/preventgenocide/adviser/key_missions.shtml.

OXFAM (Australia).[21] The Office undertakes extensive outreach activities such as conferences, lectures, brown bag lunches, and meetings with both UN and non-UN bodies. The non-UN partners include:

a. regional/sub-regional organizations—the Organization of American States (OAS), the European Union (EU), the African Union (AU), the Intergovernmental Authority on Development (IGAD), the Economic Community of West African States (ECOWAS), International Committee on the Great Lakes Region (ICGLR), and the Association of South-East Asian Nations (ASEAN).
b. society organizations—Amnesty International, Asia Pacific Centre for the Responsibility to Protect, Auschwitz Institute for Peace and Reconciliation, Genocide Watch, Global Action to Prevent War, Global Center for the R2P, Human Rights Watch, ICC Coalition, International Association of Genocide Scholars (IAGS), International Center for Transitional Justice, International Coalition on RtoP, International Crisis Group, Minority Rights Group International, Stanley Foundation, and WFM-IGP (The World Federalist Movement).

The Office and Its Interface with the Rest of the UN

The work of the Office involves close interaction with other UN departments, programmes, agencies, and independent experts.[22] Its task of coordination aims at avoiding 'duplication' and ensuring that the actions of individual UN units are in tandem so as to best address a given situation. In addition to ad hoc relationships, the Office engages on a regular basis with some UN entities which come under the four principal UN organs—the General Assembly, the Security Council, Economic and Social Council, the Secretariat including the Human Rights Council (a

[21] For more details see http://www.un.org/en/preventgenocide/adviser/training.shtml.

[22] http://www.un.org/en/preventgenocide/adviser/engagement_partners.shtml.

subsidiary body of the General Assembly).[23] Evidently the OSAPG seeks to move the principle of R2P beyond the confines of its office into other departments and agencies of the UN organs.

General Assembly

R2P officially entered the UN via the General Assembly (GA) adoption of the World Summit Outcome Document (2005). Subsequently, the GA resolution (A/RES/63/308) underlined the need to continue consideration of the R2P. There have been five formal debates (2009, 2018, 2019, 2021, and 2022) and informal interactive dialogues (2010–2017) on R2P following the presentation of the SG's annual reports on R2P. These GA dialogues, albeit informal, are significant since unlike in the Security Council, all Member States 'are represented with equal votes' at the GA. The deliberations of the GA legitimize 'norms, rules, and actions,' making it an influential advocacy forum for policy issues (Peterson 2007: 97; also see Claude 1967; Barnett and Finnemore 2007: 41). The debates 'forge a shared understanding and consolidate global consensus on R2P' (Thakur 2012: xiii). In addition, the GA provides 'broad supervision' over other UN organs including the Economic and Social Council and the Secretariat (Peterson 2007: 98–99). The GA serves as a forum to 'elaborate international norms and principles that facilitate the protection of populations, and galvanize resources to support States to fulfill their commitment' (A/68/947-S/2014/449/para 21).

The informal interactive dialogues on R2P are thus an important resource to delineate the ideational/normative dimensions of R2P.[24] Post-2009 each of these dialogues built upon the previous discussion(s), while further debating an aspect of R2P. Despite their differences the participating Member States have reached a consensus on the prevention mandate of R2P (i.e., pillars one and two).[25] Another consequence of these regular annual dialogues is the emergence of a broad consensus that acknowledges the respective responsibilities of the State(s) and the international community in atrocity prevention. The debate is about

[23] The Human Rights Council has replaced the former United Nations Commission on Human Rights.

[24] See Chapter 5.

[25] Pillars one and two are analysed in Chapter 5.

which instruments can best operationalize R2P. Along with the Secretary-General's reports, these discussions essay the UN's understanding of the ideational and normative aspects of R2P. Vide its 2021 resolution the GA formalized inclusion of the debate on R2P in its annual agenda (A/RES/75/277/2021).

Security Council

The 'rites of passage' of R2P's incorporation in the UN's dispositif includes its endorsement at the Security Council (SC)—the 'UN's most powerful (and mediagenic) forum' whose decisions are 'binding on all member states' (Malone 2007: 117). Whenever the international community requires taking coercive action to fulfil its responsibility to protect, it must do so with the approval of the Security Council—the primary UN organ tasked by the Charter to maintain international peace and security:

> When a State does not respond to diplomatic and other peaceful means, paragraph 139 of the Summit Outcome calls for "timely and decisive" collective action, in accordance with the Charter. Such collective measures may be authorized by the Security Council, under Articles 41 and 42 of the Charter...
>
> Only the Security Council can authorize the use of force, under Chapter VII, Article 42, of the Charter. Coercive military force can be utilized in various forms, through the deployment of United Nations-sanctioned multinational forces for establishing security zones, the imposition of no-fly zones, the establishment of a military presence on land and at sea for protection or deterrence purposes, or any other means, as determined by the Security Council. (A/66/874-S/2012/578/paras 31 & 32)

The ICISS report had pointed out the flaws in the SC's structure and its working that immobilize its response to the commission of atrocity crimes. Yet it underlined the SC as being crucial in the move from 'analysis to action' and did not propose any alternative 'source of authority' (2001: 8.4). In view of this important role of the SC in sanctioning the various forms of coercive measures to operationalize R2P, the SC resolutions are another source to map out the ideational/normative dimensions of R2P at the UN. There have been 90 occasions (between 27 January 2006 and

26 May 2023) when the SC resolutions and Presidential statements have referenced R2P. The SC reaffirmed R2P in its 'resolutions 1674 (2006), 1894 (2009), 2117 (2013 and 2150 (2014)' (A/68/947-S/2014/449/ para3).

Two aspects of these resolutions deserve attention. *First*, while the specific term R2P in these resolutions is mainly used to denote and remind the particular state of its responsibility to protect, R2P is implicitly present in other terms (and forms of practice) such as conflict prevention and peacebuilding measures. These tasks are in conformity with the agenda of R2P's pillars one and two. The resolutions are punctuated with terms from the field of security/development: for example, the role of regional and sub-regional organizations,[26] International Criminal Court,[27] civil society and NGO's,[28] Peacebuilding Commission, peacebuilding,[29] peacekeeping,[30] justice and reconciliation measures,

[26] See (S/RES/2150), (S/RES/1973/2011/para 9), S/RES/1653/2006/para17), (S/RES/1674/2006/para 24), (S/RES/1975/2011/para 1 & 2), (S/RES/1996/2011), (S/RES/2014/2011), (S/RES/2085/2012), (S/RES/2095/2013/para 14(b)), (S/RES/2100/2013), (S/RES/2109/2013), (S/RES/2117/2013), S/RES/2127/2013), ([2]/2014), (S/RES/2171/2014/para 25).

[27] See S/RES/2211) (S/RES/1894/2009), (S/RES/2011/para 4 & 5), (S/RES/1973/2011), (S/RES/1975/2011), (S/RES/2040/2012), (S/RES/2085/2012/para 19), (S/RES/2095/2013), (S/RES/2100/2013), (S/RES/2100/2013/ para 16(g)), (S/RES/2127/2013), (S/RES/2134/2014), (S/RES/2150/2014), (S/RES/2171/2014).

[28] See (S/RES/1653/2006/para 12).

[29] See (S/RES/1653/2006/para 18), (S/RES/1996/2011), (S/RES/1996/2011/para18 & 20), (S/RES/2171/2014/para 7 & 23), (S/RES/2185/2014).

[30] See (S/RES/1894/2009), (S/RES/2185/2014), (S/RES/2187/2014).

illicit arms/arms embargo,[31] disarmament/demobilization,[32] internally displaced people/refugees,[33] education,[34] and media incitement.[35]

The *second* aspect of these SC resolutions is the twinning of R2P and protection of civilians (POC) concerns. This parallel emergence of POC and the R2P principle (Francis and Sampford 2012: 3) is not a coincidence and echoes the protection component that since the 1990s informs the humanitarian agenda (Barnett 2010). Long before the R2P principle was formally articulated, the SC in the late 1990s had made 'explicit reference to the protection of civilians' (Ferris 2011: xiv). UNSC S/RES/1265/1999 is credited with first specifically formally noting the concern for the protection of civilians who bear various forms of violence and hardships during armed conflict. The resolution affirms 'the primary responsibility of states' to ensure the protection of refugees and internally displaced persons 'in particular by maintaining' their 'security and civilian character.' It also emphasizes 'the responsibility of States to end impunity and to prosecute those responsible for genocide, crimes against humanity and serious violations of international law' (S/RES/1265/1999/6). POC became an integral part of the UN's agenda through S/Res/1296/2000) (Ferris 2011: xiv). Both address matters of physical violence with an emphasis on mass atrocities, despite sharing a 'common terminology' there are key differences between the two. *First*, POC has a firm basis in international law because it is grounded in existing international humanitarian law (IHL) (based on the 1949 Geneva Conventions of the Laws of War and the 1977 Additional Protocols) and international refugee law (IRL). R2P, by contrast, has no legal basis in international law. The endorsement of a version of R2P by the UNGA

[31] See (S/RES/1674/2006), ((S/RES/1894/2009/para 29), (S/RES/2011/para 9 & 10), (S/RES/1973/2011), (S/RES/2040/2012 para 8), (S/RES/2095/2013), (S/RES/2095/2013/para 9–12), (S/RES/2127/2013/para54-55), (S/RES/2134/2014), (S/RES/2149/2014), (S/RES/2187/2014).

[32] See (S/RES/1996/2011/para 15), (S/RES/2085/2012), (S/RES/2100/2013/para 11 and 16(v)), (S/RES/2109/2013/para24), (S/RES/2121/2013para 8, 17, 18), (S/RES/2127/2013/para11-13) (S/RES/2134/2014/para2(d)), (S/RES/2149/2014/para 30(g)), (S/RES/2171/2014), (S/RES/2185/2014).

[33] See (S/RES/1674/2006/para 14), (S/RES/1894/2009), (S/RES/1975/2011, para 10), (S/RES/2016/2011), (S/RES/2014/2011), (S/RES/2085/2012/para 9 (e)), (S/RES/2155/2014), (S/RES/2165/2014), (S/RES/2187/2014/para 4(vi)).

[34] See (S/RES/1674/2006).

[35] See (S/RES/1975/2011/para 9), (S/RES/2155/2014/para 12, 16, 17).

via the WSOD in 2005 gave R2P some legitimacy. The key here is the difference between legality and legitimacy.[36] *Second*, POC as part of the UN peacekeeping agenda requires the consent of the host state, 'R2P maybe invoked without the consent of the host state, specifically when the host state is failing to protect its population. R2P…goes beyond the principles of peacekeeping' (United Nations Department of Peace Operations 2019: 21). *Third*, while POC is concerned with crimes against civilians—non-combatants in active hostilities—R2P is applied to crimes against populations that could include those involved in hostilities, for e.g., in 'genocidal regimes…egregious violations of duties towards enemy combatants' may involve an 'R2P atrocity crime.' Relatedly, while POC concern for civilians can be prompted by 'small-scale attacks against individuals,' R2P's theatre of action requires an assault on populations on a 'larger-scale' (Breakey 2012: xi). The explicit and specific reference to one or more of the atrocity crimes distinguishes an R2P resolution from a 'mere' PoC resolution. This is because R2P's scope narrows the focus and raises the threshold of the potential/actual harm to a population from a 'mere' violation of broader IHL, IHRL, or IRL to the level of atrocity crimes (which have the status of *jus cogens* peremptory norms). Thus, while all R2P-specific resolutions also invoke PoC, PoC resolutions do not automatically imply R2P. Post WSOD (2005) most of these resolutions that reference R2P also draw attention to the issue of protection of civilians (POC).[37] This adjacent placing of R2P and POC concerns has

[36] See Chapter 5.

[37] The POC references include phrases protection of civilians or condemnation of attacks against civilians: (a) Security Council resolutions that mention both R2P and POC are S/ Res/1674/2006;S/RES/1894/2009 on POC; S/RES/1970/2011 (Libya); S/RES/1973/2011 (Libya); S/RES/1975/2011 (Cote d'Ivoire); S/RES/1996/2011 (South Sudan); S/RES/2014/2011(Yemen); S/RES/2040/2012(Libya); S/RES/2085/2012 (Mali); S/RES/2085/2012 (Mali); S/RES/2093/2013 (Somalia); S/RES/2095/2013 (Libya); S/RES/2100/2013 (Mali); S/RES/2109/2013 (South Sudan); S/RES/2117/2013 (Small Arms and Light Weapons); S/RES/2121/2013 (Central African Republic); S/RES/2127/2013 (Central African Republic); S/RES/2134/2014 (Central African Republic); S/RES/2139/2014 (Syria); S/RES/2149/2014 (Central African Republic); S/RES/2155/2014 (South Sudan); S/RES/2165/2014 (Syria); S/RES/2170/2014 (Threats to International Peace and Security Caused by Terrorist Acts); S/RES/2171/2014 (Maintenance of International Peace and Security—Conflict Prevention); S/RES/2185/2014 (Maintenance of International Peace and Security—Policing in UN); S/RES/2187/2014 (South Sudan); S/RES/2196/2015 (Central African Republic); S/RES/2206/2015 (South Sudan); S/RES/2211/2015 (Democratic Republic of Congo), (b) Security Council resolutions on POC that do not mention R2P are: SC/RES/1738

possible implications for the practice of R2P, particularly in the light of several recent peacekeeping operations with POC missions.[38]

The operationalization of pillar three's responsibilities is contingent on the Security Council's power to sanction coercive measures. Therefore, advocates of R2P have urged the Council to exercise voluntary restraint on the use of veto so that a decisive action can be taken in situations of atrocity crimes. At the 68th Session of the UNGA (2013d), the President of France, Francois Hollande exhorted the P5 to 'collectively renounce their veto powers' in such contexts.

Economic and Social Council

The Economic and Social Council (ECOSOC) as one of the principal organs of the UN is responsible for the 'coordination, policy review, policy dialogue and recommendations on economic, social and environmental issues.' Its mandate includes the coordination of the activities

2006 condemning attacks against journalists and media in conflict situations, (c) Security Council resolutions that mention R2P but not POC are: S/RES/1653/2006 (conflict prevention and peaceful resolution of disputes in the Great lakes region 27 Jan 2006); S/RES/2150/2014 (Threats to International Peace and Security—Prevention of Genocide).

[38] The POC missions are: UNOMSIL (United Nations Observer Mission in Sierra Leone 1999); it was given a revised mandate that included protection of civilians via S/RES/1289/2000; UNTAET (East Timor, 1999); it was succeeded by the United Nations Mission of Support in East Timor (UNMISET) in 2002; MONUSCA (United Nations Organization Stabilization Mission in the Democratic Republic of the Congo 2010); MONUSCA took over from the earlier peacekeeping mission—MONUC (United Nations Organization Mission in the Democratic Republic of the Congo 1999) via C/RES/1925/2010; it was given the mandate to protect civilians; UNIFIL (United Nations Interim Force in Lebanon 1978); it was given an additional mandate that included protection of civilians via S/RES/1701/2006; UNMIL (United Nations Mission in Liberia 2003); UNOCI (United Nations Operation in Cote D'Ivoire 2004); MINUSTAH (United Nations Stabilization Mission in Haiti (2004); ONUB (United Nations Operation in Burundi, 2004); UNMIS (United Nations Mission in the Sudan (2005)); UNAMID (African Union-United Nations Hybrid Operation in Darfur 2007); MINURCAT (United Nations Mission in the Central African Republic and Chad, 2007), UNISFA (United Nations Organization Interim Security Force for Abyei 2011), UNMISS (United Nations Mission in the Republic of South Sudan (2011)); UNSMIS (United Nations Supervision Mission in Syria 2012); MINUSMA (United Nations Multidimensional Integrated Stabilization Mission in Mali, 2013); MINUSCA (United Nations Multidimensional Integrated Stabilization Mission in the Central African Republic, 2014); and UNMIT (United Nations Integrated Mission in Timor-Leste, 2006) (See S/RES/1912/2010; S/RES/1969/2011).

of the 'subsidiary and expert bodies' in the above fields.[39] In addition to economic and social issues ECOSOC works towards the promotion 'respect for, and observance of human rights and fundamental freedoms for all' (UN Charter Article 62(2)). ECOSOC is also the 'main "portal of entry" to the United Nations' for non-governmental organizations (Rosenthal 2007: 136). This UN organ is important in the context of the work of R2P's pillars one and two. More specifically, the Office works closely with the following programmes and specialized agencies of the Economic and Social Council: United Nations International Children's Emergency Fund (UNICEF), United Nations Development Programme (UNDP), United Nations Entity for Gender Equality and Women's Empowerment (UN Women), and the World Food Programme (WFP).

Secretariat

The UN Secretary-Generals (SG) have played a major role in the promotion of R2P. The ICISS Report (2001) received the previous SG Kofi Annan's strong support. The SG's annual reports on R2P contribute significantly to the explication of the concept. Moreover, the Secretariat's reports and recommendations to the Security Council do contribute to shaping the latter's deliberations including those on the range of options (2001: 8.19).

Cold War politics, particularly post the tenure of Dag Hammarskjold (1953–1961), witnessed the marginalization of the SG. However, the post-Cold War period rescued the office from 'irrelevance' and the SG has come to 'represent an organ of authority and facilitation in the roles of creative mediation and conflict resolution' (Newman 2007: 182). It is through the Secretariat that the UN has come to exercise 'international executive action.' Hammarskjold argued that such a mandate exists in the UN Charter's Article 99—'The Secretary-General may bring to the attention of the Security Council any matter which in his opinion may threaten the maintenance of international peace and security.' Boutros Boutros-Ghali too has argued that through Article 99 'preventive diplomacy is a particular responsibility of the Secretary-General. Early Warning, fact finding, confidence-building measures, personal contacts, and good

[39] http://www.un.org/en/ecosoc/about/index.shtml.

offices, all are instruments of this' (Newman 2007: 178). Developing her argument on similar lines Anne Orford views R2P as providing a 'normative' basis to such 'practices of international executive action' (2011: 10). In this light the advocacy of R2P by Ban Ki-moon is a significant input into transforming R2P from 'principle to practice' (Hoffmann and Nollkaemper 2012).

OSAPG works closely with the following departments, programmes, and offices of the Secretariat: Department of Political Affairs (DPA), Office of the High Commissioner for Human Rights (OHCHR), Department of Peacekeeping Operations (DPKO), Office for the Coordination of Humanitarian Affairs (OCHA), Office of Legal Affairs (OLA), United Nations High Commissioner for Refugees (UNHCR), and the United Nations Network on Racial Discrimination and Protection of Minorities.[40]

In addition, the Office works on a regular basis with the Secretariat's inter-departmental bodies: The Secretary-General's Policy Committee[41]; The Executive Committee on Peace and Security[42]; The Meeting of the Secretary-General Senior Management Team and senior advisers; The Inter-Agency Framework for Coordination on Preventive Action (Framework Team), including: (a) Inter-Departmental working groups on countries under Framework Team review and (b) The Expert Reference Group, to enhance Framework Team follow-up; Country-specific working inter-agency groups and task forces and crisis teams.

Human Rights Council

The Human Rights Council (HRC), a subsidiary body under the UNGA, was established in 2006 to replace the Commission on Human Rights.

[40] http://www.ohchr.org/EN/Issues/Minorities/Pages/UNNetworkRacialDiscriminationProtectionMinorities.aspx.

[41] Policy Committee of the Secretary-General Manual (2008) ST/SGB/2005/16/page 3.

[42] ECPS, also set up in 1997, is a high-level body for inter-agency and inter-departmental coordination, chaired by the Under-Secretary-General for Political Affairs, where complex crises require contributions from a range of UN entities. ECPS briefs about, or formulates advice for the Secretary-General on, overall political frameworks within which political, developmental, and humanitarian dimensions must be reflected. (Inter-Agency Standing Committee IASC Working Group Retreat (17–19 September 2007) *ECHA and other Executive Committees*: 1–3. WO/0709/2371/7).

Some speculate that the HRC may become a principal organ of the UN (Ramcharan 2007: 450; also see Ramcharan 2011). This intergovernmental body comprises 47 states and is 'responsible for the promotion and protection of all human rights around the globe.'[43] HRC by virtue of this role itself becomes a significant platform for the prevention of the four atrocity crimes identified under R2P; that is, there is a clear overlap between the R2P and HRC concerns. Also, as Kofi Annan reiterated at the 2005 World Summit, 'human rights constitute one of the three pillars— along with peace and security and economic and social development— that form the base of all the UN's work' (Terlingen 2007: 167). Ban Ki-moon observed that the Human Rights Council along with 'human rights treaty bodies and special procedures mandate-holders encourage and make recommendations to States to meet their pillar 1 responsibility to protect, and help to identify potential risks of atrocity crimes through their ongoing monitoring role' (A/68/947-S/2014/449/para 21).

Since 2011 R2P has been a point of discussion every year at the HRC. In 2011, in a joint statement the Australian Permanent Mission to the United Nations and 55 Member States emphasized the HRC's role in ensuring that states fulfil their responsibility to protect. In 2012, once again the Australian Permanent Mission took the initiative (on behalf of Australia, Hungary, Nigeria, Thailand, and Uruguay) and urged the HRC to take measures to operationalize R2P.[44]

Endorsement for R2P has also come from Ms. Navanetham 'Navi' Pillay, UN High Commissioner for Human Rights, who underscored the link between R2P and contemporary crises as in Syria (2013).[45] The Report of the HRC on its 23rd session called upon the 'Syrian authorities to meet their responsibility to protect the Syrian population' (A/HRC/23/2/para 3; also see A/HRC/52/30). In 2013 the HRC commemorated the 65th anniversary of the adoption of the Convention on the Prevention and Punishment of the Crime of Genocide (A/HRC/22). At the 25th regular session of the Human Rights Council in 2014, Special

[43] Http://www.ohchr.org/en/hrbodies/hrc/pages/hrcindex.aspx.

[44] The statement was made at the General Debate in the Council on Technical Assistance and Capacity Building.

[45] Opening Statement by the UN High Commissioner for Human Rights Navi Pillay at the 23rd Session of the Human Rights Council, Geneva, 27 May 2013. http://www.ohchr.org/EN/NewsEvents/Pages/DisplayNews.aspx?NewsID=13358&LangID=E.

Adviser on the Prevention of Genocide, Adama Dieng, stressed the need to detect 'early warning signs…so as to prevent the escalation of conflict into serious widespread human rights abuses like those outlined within the scope of RtoP' (ICR2P 2014: 4–7).

R2P 'Outside' the UN

The civil society partners of OSAPG play a collaborative role—particularly that of advocacy—with the UN in the sedimentation of the idea of R2P. The Global Centre for the Responsibility to Protect (GCR2P), the International Coalition for the Responsibility (ICR2P), and the Asia Pacific Centre for Responsibility to Protect (APR2P)—are examples of such partnership. The first two organizations, in particular, have a symbiotic relationship with OSAPG. They also serve to establish that an understanding of the dispositif of R2P at the UN must include an appreciation of its extension outside the UN.

The UN does not exist in a hermetically sealed environment of its own, therefore, the word 'outside' in these paragraphs is used *only* to connote the non-official UN status of the civil society and international non-governmental organizations (INGOs) which work closely with the UN.[46] The role of civil society organizations or INGO[47] outside of the UN is significant in R2P's swift movement from just an idea of yet another international commission in 2001 to a principle that was endorsed in 2005 by the GA and invoked in subsequent Security Council resolutions. That civil society organizations can be crucial in the advocacy and promotion of R2P is the reason why the ICISS, 'built a large civil society component within the ongoing structure of its activities' (Cooper and English 2005: 19).

GCR2P, ICR2P, and APR2P are illustrations of INGO advocacy of R2P, they serve as an important 'R2P lobby' (Pingeot and Obenland

[46] The UN has a tradition of hearing representations from NGOs on various issues.

[47] The terms civil society and international non-governmental organizations (INGOs) are used interchangeably in the UN documents. Academic literature that treats the two as different though related entities. Civil society is seen to include all non-market and non-state organizations while INGOs are regarded as a subset of civil society that deals with development related issues. see 2007–2008 Advisory Group on CSOs and Aid Effectiveness in http://www.cn.undp.org/content/dam/china/docs/Publications/UNDP-CH03%20Annexes.pdf.

2014: 27). The examples also demonstrate that these proliferating 'presences' of R2P outside the UN are intimately connected with the UN and with each other. While the OSAPG lists several INGOs as its outreach partners, the examples of GCR2P, ICR2P, and APR2P are significant as unlike other INGOs whose agenda includes issues other than R2P, the raison d'être of these three organizations is solely R2P.[48] GCR2P and ICR2P, in particular, aided in no small measure by their geographical and physical proximity to the UN Headquarters in New York[49] have a relatively more robust operationalization of their advocacy mandate.

These three organizations are linked together not just by the theme of R2P but also by some common membership[50] that partly overlaps with the ICISS Commission: Mohamed Sahnoun and Gareth Evans, the co-chairs of the ICISS are the co-chairs of GCR2P's International Advisory Board; Gareth Evans along with Ramesh Thakur, an ICISS member is a Patron at APR2P; Simon Adams, former Executive Director, GCR2P is on the International Advisory Board of APR2P; Lloyd Axworthy, President of WFM-IGP is a patron of both GCR2P and APR2P. The ICR2P's Steering Committee members include the APR2P as an organization.[51] Some of the individuals of these three organizations are also members of OSAPG's other INGO partners. Examples: Former Special Advisers at the OSAPG, Francis Deng, Edward Luck, and Juan Mendez are on the Board

[48] These three organizations along with the World Federalist Movement are the only four civil society organizations that participated in the 2014 Informal Interactive Dialogue of the UN General Assembly on the Responsibility to Protect. GCRtoP and ICR2P have participated in all General Assembly's interactive dialogues on R2P between 2010 and 2014. In 2010 and 2012 GCR2P and ICR2P were the only two civil society organizations to participate while in 2011 they were amongst the only four civil society organizations to participate.

[49] GCR2P is located at the Ralph Bunche Institute for International Studies, The Graduate Center, City University of New York, 365 Fifth Avenue, Suite 5203, New York. ICR2P is hosted by GCR2P.

[50] This chapter highlighted the fact of overlap in membership of the international commissions.

[51] Other members are: Coordinadora Regional de Investigaciones Economicas y Sociales (CRIES, Argentina), East Africa Law Society (Tanzania), Human Rights Watch, Initiatives for International Dialogue (The Philippines), International Refugee Rights Initiative (USA & Uganda), Pan African Lawyers Union (Tanzania), The Stanley Foundation (USA), The West Africa Civil Society Institute (Ghana), and World Federalist Movement-Institute for Global Policy (USA, The Netherlands). See http://www.wfm-igp.org/content/icrtop-steering-committee.

of Directors, Auschwitz Institute for Peace and Reconciliation; the Board of Advisors Genocide Watch include SAPG, Adama Dieng; Advisory Board of the ICC Coalition includes Juan Mendez, Lloyd Axworthy, and Kofi Annan; and President Emeritus, International Center for Transitional Justice, is Juan E. Mendez. This overlapping membership is indicative of a growing R2P epistemic community whereby stakes in arguing for the relevance of R2P no longer come *only* for the purpose of atrocity crime prevention; at times, the career of an idea parallels the careerism of its advocates, the liberal peacebuilding project has spawned a few cottage industries based on its ideas such as human security and peace itself.

'Lobbying' for R2P by some INGOs preceded R2P's 2005 entry into the UN. Following the ICISS Report (2001), the World Federalist Movement-Institute for Global Policy (WFM-IGP)[52] created 'the first civil society project on RtoP called R2P-Engaging Civil Society (R2PCS).'[53] This loose network of NGOs strongly advocated R2P as 'an emerging norm' in its engagement with civil society and governments. This network claims to have played a crucial role in the 'inclusion of R2P in the 2005 World Summit Outcome Document.'[54] This led to the creation of two parallel initiatives: (1) the Global Center for the Responsibility to Protect was launched in February 2008 and (2) in 2009 the International Coalition of Responsibility to Protect (ICR2P) was launched, as an international NGO coalition for the Responsibility to Protect, similar to earlier successful NGO human security campaigns. The purpose was to not lose the momentum for R2P that had been created by the 2005 SOD, and to ensure the prevention of 'backsliding among governments at the international level.' The aim was also to advance the

[52] The WFM-IGP itself is listed as an Outreach Partner of the OSAPG. WFM-IGP, the World Federalist Movement-Institute for Global Policy, a non-governmental organization, founded in 1947, works in partnership with the UN, national governments, international organizations, and individuals for 'peace, prosperity, and security.' It regards the role of democratic institutions and international law crucial in this regard. Its programmes include the goal to protect civilians from the threat of genocide, war crimes, and crimes against humanity. See http://wfm-igp.org/about/overview.

[53] The R2PCS project received support of the governments of Sweden and the United Kingdom, the John D. and Catherine T. MacArthur Foundation, the Oak Foundation, the Arsenault Family Foundation and individual donations. See http://www.responsibilitytoprotect.org/index.php/former-r2pcs-project.

[54] See http://www.wfm-igp.org/content/international-coalition-responsibility-protect.

cause of R2P by increasing 'basic knowledge of RtoP' amongst not just governments but also international and regional organizations.[55]

The ICR2P founded in 2009 was hosted by WFM-IGP which integrated its Responsibility to Protect-Engaging Civil Society (R2PCS) project into the Coalition initiative.[56] From May 2021 the GCR2P is hosting the ICR2P Secretariat.[57] It mobilizes and connects NGOs across the world to build up the normative consensus for RtoP and increase 'the understanding of the norm' and strengthen their capacity for atrocity crimes prevention.[58] ICR2P's educational tool's understanding of R2P is in consonance with that of OSAPG. For example, a 2015 educational tool[59] suggestion of 'advocacy points' for NGOs to advance R2P at the national,[60] regional,[61] and international[62] levels, is in accordance with the FOA. ICR2P advocacy efforts include mapping global action on R2P and compiling information on crisis situations where R2P could be applicable.

Established in 2008, the GCR2P[63] aims for an effective operationalization of R2P by transforming the R2P principle 'into a practical guide for

[55] See http://responsibilitytoprotect.org/index.php/former-r2pcs-project/2008-roundtables.

[56] See www.responsibilitytoprotect.org.

[57] Prior to being hosted by GCR2P, the International Coalition for the Responsibility to Protect used the acronym ICRtoP.

[58] See http://www.responsibilitytoprotect.org/index.php/about-coalition.

[59] See ICR2P (2014). *RtoP at the United Nations: An Educational Tool by the International Coalition for the Responsibility to Protect*. Accessed on September 25, 2015. Available at http://responsibilitytoprotect.org/Sept%202014%20UN%20and%20RtoP.pdf.

[60] For example NGOs must urge governments for the incorporation of FOA into the national early warning mechanisms, ratification of 'international instruments pertinent to RtoP, including international human rights and humanitarian law treaties/instruments and the Rome Statute of the International Criminal court'.

[61] For example NGOs must call upon regional organizations to strengthen the early warning mechanisms in accordance with the FOA.

[62] For example NGOs must 'encourage the next Secretary-General to enhance implementation of RtoP and support the mainstreaming of the norms into all UN departments.' They must also urge for the incorporation of the FOA 'into the monitoring and early warning actions conducted by the UN departments' like UNDP and DPKO (Department of Peacekeeping Operations).

[63] Countries which support it—Australia, Belgium, Canada, Denmark, France, Germany, Luxembourg, Mexico, The Netherlands, Norway, Rwanda, Slovenia, Sweden, Switzerland, and United Kingdom. It is supported by the following foundations: Arsenault Family Foundation, Carnegie Corporation of New York, Humanity United, Open Society

action in the face of mass atrocities' for governments and international/regional organizations. An impressive array of influential international figures that includes political leaders, diplomats, activists, and academics are associated with the Centre in various capacities. GCR2P's range of advocacy measures to promote R2P include holding annual[64] meetings of the R2P Focal Points initiative, a global network of the national R2P Focal Points (represented by senior level officials of the respective countries) launched in 2010.[65] The network is a support system for states committed to R2P objectives.[66] It supports the work of the OSAPG by engaging with the UN Member States at various fora. It engages with the UN through State Missions in New York, Geneva, and national capitals and also with the rest of the UN system: holds 'bilateral meetings, workshops and events for member state representatives'; publishes 'policy briefs on relevant thematic issues'; facilitates 'the participation of a diverse group of supportive member states in the UNGA's annual R2P dialogue'; and 'encourages them to' affirm their support for R2P during the opening session of the General Assembly, in the Security Council and in the Human Rights Council.'[67] The Centre conducts the Annual Ministerial Meeting on R2P during the opening of the General Assembly session that creates a dialogue on R2P amongst 'cross-regional group of states.'[68] These meetings are co-hosted by the Centre along

Foundations, The David and Anita Keller Foundation, The John D. and Catherine T. MacArthur Foundation, The Stanley Foundation.

[64] The first meeting (May 2011) was attended by thirty one countries; the second meeting (September 2012) saw the participation of thirty-six countries; in attendance at the third meeting (June 2013) were thirty-five countries and three regional organizations; thirty-one countries and the UN Special Adviser on the responsibility to protect attended the fourth meeting (June 2014). See http://www.globalr2p.org/our_work/r2p_focal_points.

[65] At present forty-three countries are members of the Global Network of R2P Focal Points: Albania, Argentina, Australia, Austria, Belgium, Bosnia–Herzegovina, Botswana, Bulgaria, Chile, Costa Rica, Cote d'Ivoire, Croatia, Czech Republic, Democratic Republic of the Congo, Denmark, Finland, France, Georgia, Germany, Ghana, Greece, Guatemala, Hungary, Ireland, Italy, Liberia, Liechtenstein, Lithuania, Luxembourg, Montenegro, Mozambique, Netherlands, New Zealand, Paraguay, Poland, Republic of Korea, Slovenia, Spain, Sweden, Switzerland, Uruguay, United Kingdom, and United States.

[66] See http://www.globalr2p.org/our_work/r2p_focal_points.

[67] http://www.globalr2p.org/our_work/united_nations_engagement.

[68] http://www.globalr2p.org/our_work/annual_r2p_ministerial_meeting.

with a different Member State each year.[69] A key part of the Centre's strategy is to advance and institutionalize R2P in its effort to seek a more proactive involvement of the 'emerging powers and regional bodies' on this issue. With this in mind it organizes regional policy forums.[70] Its range of publications—R2P Monitor, media releases, open letters, statements, background briefings, policy briefs, occasional paper series, and reports—describe and analyse situations from an R2P lens and also monitor international response to such crisis.[71]

The APR2P at the University of Queensland, Australia was established in February 2008 by former Foreign Minister of Canada, Lloyd Axworthy and former SAR2P, Edward Luck. The Centre's Director, Alex Bellamy is a prominent academic voice on R2P. Other such influential R2P voices include former Executive Director of GCR2P, Simon Adams as a member International Advisory Board.[72] Its patrons include Lloyd Axworthy, Gareth Evans, Ramesh Thakur, and former SAR2P, Jennifer Welsh. An associate of GCR2P and a member of ICR2P, the Centre's primary goal is to advance the R2P principle 'through research and public dialogue.' For example, (a) In 2009 it funded fourteen two-year projects to advance the understanding of R2P; and (b) It publishes a journal *GCR2P Global Responsibility to Protect* (four issues annually). Promotion of R2P in Southeast Asia is a key focus of the Centre and through its country-specific programmes it seeks to create a 'domestic constituency around this norm.' The Centre's strategies include:

[69] Past co-hosts have been 'foreign ministers of Australia, Botswana, Brazil, Denmark, Ghana, Gautemala, the Netherlands, Nigeria, Rwanda and Timor-Leste'.

[70] Three regional policy forums have been organized so far: Conversation on the 'Responsibility While Protecting' in Brazil (2012), ECOWAS Regional Policy Forum on R2P (2012) in Abuja, Nigeria, Regional Forum for Latin America and the Caribbean on Responsibility to Protect in Mexico city in 2009. http://www.globalr2p.org/our_work/policy_forums.

[71] http://www.globalr2p.org/publications/.

[72] Other members are: Alister Gee, Executive Director of Act for Peace NCCA, a humanitarian protection agency; Amina Rasul-Bernardo, President, Phillipine Centre for Islam and Democracy; Amitav Acharya, Professor of International relations, University of Bristol, United Kingdom; Jacqui True, Professor of Politics and International Relations, Monash University, Australia; Liu Tiewa, Research Fellow at the Centre; Mely Caballero-Anthony Associate Professor, S. Rajaratnam School of International Studies (RSIS); Pranee Thiparat, Assistant professor, International Relations, Chulalongkorn University, Thailand; Rizal Sukma, Deputy Executive, Centre for Strategic Studies, Jakarta, Indonesia.

> Translation of RtoP documents...into major Southeast Asian languages; inclusion of RtoP in university curricula; and workshop and training seminars for teachers and educators, civil society groups, local government officials, law enforcement personnel and government/state bureaucrats. (Morada 2012: 242)

Conclusion

The OSAPG reaches out to various UN bodies in ways and processes that aim to introduce and embed R2P in the latter's work. The process is undertaken in four ways by: (a) embedding R2P within the existing premise, philosophy of the department; (b). emphasizing R2P's compatibility with and potential to enrich the existing premise, philosophy of the department; (c) ensuring that the existing tasks of the department are informed by the R2P ethos/agenda; and (d) adding R2P tasks to the existing tasks of the department.

Advocates of R2P present the term as both new and old. The newness is evident from the fact that it has to be nurtured by the Special Advisor whose mandate is to ensure the 'conceptual, political and institutional development and further refinement of the responsibility to protect concept as well as consensus-building to assist the General Assembly to continue consideration of this issue.' On the other hand, R2P is also presented as an idea that is in consonance with the existing UN Charter (see Welsh 2013). In this trope the newness is restricted to emphasizing R2P as only a new instrument to ensure the fulfilment of an old promise, that is, the Charter's promise. R2P thus becomes an instrument that seeks to access other (mostly existing) UN instruments (sanctions, development assistance, military intervention, etc.) to ensure their robust use in the appropriate situations.

References

Barnett, Michael N. 2010. *The International Humanitarian Order*. New York: Routledge.

Barnett, Michael N., and Martha Finnemore. 2007. "Political Approaches." In *The Oxford Handbook of the United Nations*, ed. Thomas G. Weiss and Sam Daws. New York: Oxford University Press.

Breakey, Hugh. 2012. "The Responsibility to Protect: Game Change and Regime Change." In *Norms of Protection: Responsibility to Protect, Protection of Civilians and their Interaction*, ed. Charles Sampford, Angus Francis and Vesselin Popovski. Geneva: United Nations University.

Claude, Inis L. Jr. 1967. *The Changing United Nations* New York: Random House.

Cooper, Andrew F., and John English. 2005. "International Commissions and the Mind of Global Governance." In *International Commissions and the Power of Ideas,* ed. Ramesh Thakur, Andrew F. Cooper, and John English. Tokyo: United Nations University.

Ferris, Elizabeth G. 2011. *The Politics of Protection: The Limits of Humanitarian Action.* Washington DC: Brookings Institution Press.

Francis, Angus and Charles Sampford. 2012. "Introduction." In *Norms of Protection: Responsibility to Protect, Protection of Civilians and Their Interaction,* ed. Angus Francis, Vesselin Popovski, and Charles Sampfor. Tokyo: United Nations University Press.

Hoffmann, Julia and Andre Nollkaemper. 2012. "Introduction." In *Responsibility to Protect: From Principle to Practice*, ed. Julia Hoffmann and Andre Nollkaemper. Amsterdam: Pallas Publication.

ICR2P. 2014. *RtoP at the United Nations: An Educational Tool by the International Coalition for the Responsibility to Protect.* Accessed on September 25, 2015. Available at http://responsibilitytoprotect.org/Sept%202014%20UN%20and%20RtoP.pdf.

International Commission on Intervention and State Sovereignty. 2001. *The Responsibility to Protect.* Ottawa: International Development Research Centre.

Luck, Edward. 2011. The Responsibility to Protect: The First Decade. *Global Responsibility to Protect* 3 (4): 387–399.

Malone, David, M. 2007. "Security Council." In *The Oxford Handbook of the United Nations,* ed. Thomas G. Weiss and Sam Daws. New York: Oxford University Press.

Morada, Noel M. 2012. "ASEAN Responses to Responsibility to Protect: Challenges, Opportunities, and Constraints." In *Responsibility to Protect: From Principle to Practice*, ed. Julia Hoffmann and Andre Nollkaemper. Amsterdam: Pallas Publication.

Newman, Edward. 2007. "Secretary-General." In *The Oxford Handbook of the United Nations*, ed. Thomas G. Weiss and Sam Daws. New York: Oxford University Press.

Opening Statement by the UN High Commissioner for Human Rights Navi Pillay at the 23rd Session of the Human Rights Council, Geneva. 27 May 2013. http://www.ohchr.org/EN/NewsEvents/Pages/DisplayNews.aspx?NewsID=13358&LangID=E.

Orford, Anne. 2011. *International Authority and the Responsibility to Protect*. Cambridge: Cambridge University Press.

Peterson, M.J. 2007. "General Assembly." In *The Oxford Handbook of the United Nations*, ed. Thomas G. Weiss and Sam Daws. New York: Oxford University Press.

Pingeot, Lou and Wolfgang Obenland. 2014. *In Whose Name?: A Critical View of the Responsibility to Protect*. Bonn: Global Policy Forum.

Ramcharan, Bertrand G. 2007. "Norms and Machinery." In *The Oxford Handbook of the United Nations*, ed. Thomas G. Weiss and Sam Daws. New York: Oxford University Press.

Ramcharan, Bertrand G. 2011. *The UN Human Rights Council*. New York: Routledge.

Rosenthal, Gert. 2007. "Economic and Social Council." In *The Oxford Handbook of the United Nations*, ed. Thomas G. Weiss and Sam Daws. New York: Oxford University Press.

Terlingen, Yvonne. 2007. The Human Rights Council: A New Era in UN Human Rights Work? *Ethics & International Affairs* 21 (2): 167–178.

Thakur, Ramesh. 2012. "Emerging Powers and the Responsibility to Protect after Libya." *Policy Brief 15*. Oslo: Norwegian Institute of International Affairs.

United Nations Department of Peace Operations. 2019. *The Protection of Civilians in United Nations Peacekeeping*. (DPO Unclassified Policy) Ref. 2019.17.

United Nations General Assembly. 2005. *World Summit Outcome*. UN Doc. A/RES/60/1, 24 October 2005.

United Nations General Assembly. 2013a. Human Rights Council. Good Practices in National Criminalization, Investigation, Prosecution and Sentencing for Offences of Torture. UN Doc. A/HRC/52/30. 13 March 2023.

United Nations General Assembly. 2013b. Human Rights Council. Report of the Special Rapporteur on Torture and Other Cruel, Inhuman or Degrading Treatment or Punishment, Juan E. Méndez. UN Doc. A/HRC/22/53. 1 February 2013.

United Nations General Assembly. 2013c. Human Rights Council. Report of the Human Rights Council on its Twenty Third Session. UN Doc. A/HRC/23/2. 27 August 2013.

United Nations General Assembly. 2013d. 68th Session, 5th Plenary Meeting. UN Doc. A/68/PV.5/2013.

United Nations General Assembly. 2021. The Responsibility to Protect and the Prevention of Genocide, War Crimes, Ethnic Cleansing and Crimes Against Humanity. UN Doc. A/RES/75/277. 18 May 2021.

United Nations General Assembly. 2023. Human Rights Council. Good Practices in National Criminalization, United Nations General Assembly. *Human Rights Council*. Good Practices in National Criminalization,

United Nations Office on Genocide Prevention and the Responsibility to Protect. 2014. *Framework of Analysis for Atrocity Crimes: A Tool for Prevention*. New York.

United Nations Secretary-General. 2011. *The Role of Regional and Sub-Regional Arrangements in Implementing the Responsibility to Protect*. Report of the Secretary-General. UN Doc. A/65/877-S/2011/393. 28 June 2011.

United Nations Secretary-General. 2014. *Fulfilling our Collective Responsibility: International Assistance and the Responsibility to Protect*. Report of the Secretary-General. UN Doc. A/68/947-S/2014/449. 11 July 2014.

United Nations Secretary-General. 2016. *Mobilizing Collective Action: The Next Decade of the Responsibility to Protect*. Report of the Secretary-General. UN Doc. A/70/999-S/2016/620. 22 July 2016.

United Nations Secretary-General. 2017. *Implementing the Responsibility to Protect: Accountability for Protection*. Report of the Secretary-General. UN Doc. A/71/1016-S/2017/556. 10 August 2017.

United Nations Secretary-General. 2018. *Responsibility to Protect: From Early Warning to Early Action*. Report of the Secretary-General. UN Doc. A/72/884-S/2018/525. 10 June 2018.

United Nations Secretary-General. 2020. *Prioritizing Prevention and Strengthening Response: Women and the Responsibility to Protect*. Report of the Secretary-General. UN Doc. A/74/964-S/2020/501. 23 July 2020.

United Nations Secretary-General. 2021. *Advancing Atrocity Prevention Work and and the Responsibility to Protect*. Report of the Secretary-General. UN Doc. A/75/863-S/2021/424. 3 May 2021.

United Nations Secretary-General. 2022. *Responsibility to Protect: Prioritizing Children and Young People*. Report of the Secretary-General. UN Doc. A/76/844-S/2022/428. 26 May 2022.

United Nations Security Council. 2000. UN Doc. S/RES/1296. 19 April 2000.

United Nations Security Council. 2006. Responsibility to Protect. UN Doc. S/RES/1674. 28 April 2006.

United Nations Security Council. 2006. UN Doc. S/RES/1701. 11 August 2006.

United Nations Security Council. 2006. UN. Doc. S/RES/1653. 27 January 2006.

United Nations Security Council. 2009. UN Doc. S/RES/1894. 11 November 2009.

United Nations Security Council. 2010. UN Doc. S/RES/1912. 26 February 2010.

United Nations Security Council. 2011. UN Doc. S/RES/1969. 24 February 2011

United Nations Security Council. 2011. UN Doc. S/RES/1970. 25 February 2011.

United Nations Security Council. 2011. UN Doc. S/RES/1973. 17 March 2011.
United Nations Security Council. 2011. UN Doc. S/RES/1975. 30 March 2011.
United Nations Security Council. 2011. UN Doc. S/RES/1996. 8 July 2011.
United Nations Security Council. 2011. UN Doc. S/RES/2011. 12 October 2011.
United Nations Security Council. 2011. UN Doc. S/RES/2014. 21 October 2011.
United Nations Security Council. 2011. UN Doc. S/RES/2016. 27 October 2011.
United Nations Security Council. 2012. UN Doc. S/RES/2040. 12 March 2012.
United Nations Security Council. 2012. UN Doc. S/RES/2085. 20 December 2012.
United Nations Security Council. 2013. UN Doc. S/RES/2109. 11 July 2013.
United Nations Security Council. 2013. UN Doc. S/RES/2117. 26 September 2013.
United Nations Security Council. 2013. UN Doc. S/RES/2127. 5 December 2013.
United Nations Security Council. 2013. UN Doc. S/RES/2093. 6 March 2013.
United Nations Security Council. 2013. UN Doc. S/RES/2095. 14 March 2013.
United Nations Security Council. 2013. UN Doc. S/RES/2100. 25 April 2013.
United Nations Security Council. 2013. UN Doc. S/RES/2121. 10 October 2013.
United Nations Security Council. 2014. UN Doc. S/RES/2134. 28 January 2014.
United Nations Security Council. 2014. UN Doc. S/RES/2139. 22 February 2014.
United Nations Security Council. 2014. UN Doc. S/RES/2149. 10 April 2014.
United Nations Security Council. 2014. UN Doc. S/RES/2150. 16 April 2014.
United Nations Security Council. 2014. UN Doc. S/RES/2155. 27 May 2014.
United Nations Security Council. 2014. UN Doc. S/RES/2165. 14 July 2014.
United Nations Security Council. 2014. UN Doc. S/RES/2170. 15 August 2014.
United Nations Security Council. 2014. UN Doc. S/RES/2171. 21 August 2014.
United Nations Security Council. 2014. UN Doc. S/RES/2185. 20 November 2014.
United Nations Security Council. 2014. UN Doc. S/RES/2187. 25 November 2014.

United Nations Security Council. 2015. UN Doc. S/RES/2206. 3 March 2015.

United Nations Security Council. 2015. UN Doc. S/RES/2196. 22 January 2015.

United Nations Security Council. 2015. UN Doc. S/RES/2211. 26 March 2015.

Welsh, Jennifer. 2013. Norm Contestation and the Responsibility to Protect. *Global Responsibility to Protect* 5 (4): 365–396.

CHAPTER 5

Understanding the Map: Locating R2P in the UN Security/Development Dispositif

Introduction

New normative-ideational constructs are characterized by inherent ambiguity and contestability, which make them susceptible to different interpretations. The diversity of interpretations notwithstanding, the meaning of R2P is constantly being revised so that it is in greater congruence with the UN Charter. This thread of sameness that runs through these differences is analysed by moving R2P beyond the realm of a mere idea via Foucauldian concepts of governmentality, biopolitics, and dispositif in order to bring forth the materiality of ideas.

Indicators of Incorporation

To answer questions about ways in which R2P was incorporated into the UN and its impact, if at all, and its normative and political implications in the way the UN approached the relationship between security and development, two broad 'indicators' are used to gauge the degree or form of R2P's incorporation. The *first* is institutional/operational, that is, the material dimensions of R2P, and entails identifying via an examination of reports, resolutions, declarations, etc., the UN entities (General Assembly, Security Council, Secretary-General, and the different departments and agencies under them including that of Office of the Special Adviser on

R. Kashyap, *The Political Economy of Security/Development in the Neoliberal Age*, International Political Economy Series,
https://doi.org/10.1007/978-3-031-37279-7_5

Responsibility to Protect (OSAR2P)) that have adopted (in whole or in part) the normative/ideational components of R2P articulated in the 2001 ICISS report. The *second* 'indicator' is ideational/normative, which entails discovering the ideational and normative aspects/dimensions of R2P contained in the resolutions, declarations, reports, and practices of these UN bodies, as well as in the views of key UN officials, and academics and NGOs associated with R2P. R2P's 'conceptual development' by its advocates (including the SG and the OSAPG) involves tweaking R2P in response to questions and concerns raised by its critics (which include the General Assembly). The modification includes frequent assertions such as—(a) R2P does not undermine but strengthens sovereignty; (b) Pillar three (timely and decisive action) is only a last resort; (c) The last resort contains the military option along with a range of non-military measures.

The identification of the indicators of incorporation recognizes that there are varying degrees/forms of incorporation that range from a cold or distant acknowledgement of R2P presence in a UN space(s) to a welcome embrace by a UN 'unit'(s). The reports and resolutions of the three key UN organs—GA, SC, and the Secretariat accent their respective endorsements differently. The smaller UN departments and offices too relate to R2P in dissimilar ways, for example, while the Department of Political Affairs (DPA) has come around to welcoming it, the Office for the Coordination of Humanitarian Affairs (OCHA) seeks to maintain a distance from R2P lest it be 'polluted' by the latter. The noteworthy aspect of the OCHA reaction to R2P is that it indicates not just a presence but a significant enough presence, albeit a notorious one from the OCHA perspective (Anonymous OCHA official 1 Interview August 2013) compelling this office to denounce any association with R2P. And then there are some who dismiss R2P simply as a passing fad with a catchy acronym (Anonymous UNDPKO official Interview August 2013) or as a small office with no significance (Anonymous UNOCC official interview August 2013). A similar range of stances is visible in the UN's official documents—there is unequivocal incorporation, cautious and qualified incorporation, and incorporation that underlines R2P's distinctiveness from other principles (e.g., sovereignty).

The presence of R2P cannot be gauged only through one clear manifest indicator—OSAR2P and documents (resolutions, reports) emerging from the OSAGP—its institutional manifestations must also be sought in how the three key organs of the UN (General Assembly, Security Council, and the Secretariat) view it and react to it. Interviews conducted with UN officials and R2P-related experts in INGOs and academia not only shed light on the empirical mapping of R2P in Chapter 4 but also help understand *how* R2P came to be incorporated at the UN, that is, the *nature* of R2P's incorporation.

R2P is *unevenly* incorporated at the UN.[1] Importantly, the individual ranges of the supports and criticisms of R2P vary from full to partial, i.e., R2P as a broad spectrum of three pillars of responsibility or R2P as narrowly confined to one or two pillars of responsibilities which essentially echo the human security agenda. This unevenness is taken into account while outlining the normative and ideational aspects of R2P.

The chapter is divided into five sections. It begins with a brief analysis of the key features of R2P that emerge from the empirical mapping in Chapter 4. Section 'Key Features of R2P' is a discussion of the institutional manifestations of R2P in three key UN organs—the Secretariat (where OSAPG is located), General Assembly, and the Security Council. The discussion is punctuated with interviews of officials from different UN agencies, offices, departments, and academics (that includes supporters and detractors of R2P) to bring forth the nature of R2P's uneven incorporation into this organization. The additional purpose is to also demonstrate that different UN bodies highlight and promote different aspects (or even truncated versions) of R2P. Section 'The Institutional Manifestations' delineates the normative/ideational dimensions of R2P by identifying the key themes—legality, morality, sovereignty, responsibility, and protection—that emerge from the mapping, which also provides the context where the contestation over R2P is played out. That is the themes serve as the terrain on which grounds of R2P's incorporation are played out. These themes are inter-related and exist with each other in dynamic dialectics. For example, the idea of sovereignty as complete independence of a state in its domestic jurisdiction (also upheld by the UN Charter Article 2(7)) has to be *tweaked* in response to issues of morality, responsibility, and protection that are raised by R2P. Similarly, sovereignty too impacts the meanings of the other themes. The significance of responsibility and protection is evident from the moniker of R2P itself. Though responsibility and protection are two distinct concepts, in different R2P advocacies the two take cues from one another and

[1] Chapter 6 analyses whether this unevenness is of any significance and whether it diminishes or dilutes the incorporation of R2P at the UN. That is what are the implications of this unevenness.

are thus framed in synchronicity. The discussion of these dimensions is carried forward via an interrogation of the conceptual challenges to R2P. Section 'The Normative and Ideational Dimensions of R2P' works as a preface to Chapter 6 as it examines whether R2P is a radical departure from or is embedded in the UN Charter and existing international law. It also briefly re-introduces two claims about the consequences of and the peculiar nature of this 'unevenness' (explored further in Chapter 6): (a) This 'unevenness' makes possible the wholeness of R2P; (b) This 'unevenness' demonstrates the flexibility, malleability, and resilience of the R2P concept and also reveals insights into the nature of the UN's liberal/neoliberal security/development dispositif.

Key Features of R2P

The Purpose of R2P

The purpose of R2P is to protect people from the four atrocity crimes—'genocide, war crimes, ethnic cleansing and crimes against humanity' (*A/RES/60/1/*para138). While the ICISS Report spoke about the protection of population in the context of 'serious harm' suffered 'as a result of internal war, insurgency, or repression or state failure' (Evans and Sahnoun 2001: xi), the purpose of R2P was made more specific by the 2005 World Summit Outcome Document (see *A/RES/60/1/* para138–140). Theoretically, the targets of protection are clearly identified as potential and current victims of the atrocity crimes, but the complex reality on the ground during times of conflict makes such clarity elusive.

The Agents of Protection

The agents of protection are the state, regional organizations, and international community (UN and the individual states). The first and primary responsibility is of the state and the responsibility of the international community is to be activated only if the state fails. However, in view of the already existing 'weak, failed, failing, fragile states' the international community is expected to assume the responsibility to help in capacity building, e.g., preventive measures. Within the UN, the General Assembly has been the forum of most R2P discussions. There are two views in this regard—one says that the Security Council should be brought back into the conversation, the other view is that the General Assembly should wrest control of decision-making on such issues, which so far often are hostage to the politics of the Permanent Five (P5). The Security Council has invoked R2P via pillar one to remind the *errant* state—for example, Democratic Republic of Congo (S/RES/1674/2006, S/RES/2211/2015, S/RES/2277/2016, S/RES/2360/2017, 2018 S/RES/2409/2018, S/RES/2439/2018), South Sudan (S/RES/2155/2014, S/RES/2187/2014, S/RES/2206/2015, S/RES/22522015, S/RES/2363/2017, 2018 S/RES/2428/2018) and Central African Republic (S/RES/2196/2015, S/RES/2217/2015, S/RES/2339/2017)—of its responsibility to protect its population. The Security Council's role in R2P is nowhere more significant than in the sanctioning of coercive action including that of military intervention (pillar three). The OSAPG works closely with other UN departments and offices in operationalizing preventive and rebuilding measures of R2P.

The inclusion of regional organizations as R2P's agents of protection is no surprise since these organizations in recent times have been in prominence as conflict resolution mechanisms (Chigas et al. 1996; Pinder 1996; Peck 2001). The ICISS Report and the subsequent annual Secretary-General Reports on R2P recognize their significance in lending legitimacy to R2P actions. For example, the Arab League's request for a 'no-fly zone to protect civilians in Libya' made possible the Security Council Resolution 1973 (Welsh 2012: 189). In addition, the SG has emphasized the role of civil society organizations and individuals as R2P agents even though no specific formal role has been given to them. The OSAPG regularly partners with civil society organizations in R2P advocacy. Individual citizens are encouraged to play a proactive role by not being mute spectators to atrocity crimes: 'The premise of responsibility is that personal or individual responsibility segues into state responsibility' (Anonymous OSAPG official 1 Interview, June 2012).

The Mandates and Instruments of the Agents

The mandates and instruments of the agents are delineated under the three pillars, which are not sequential despite the numbering. As pointed out in Chapter 4 that unlike the ICISS Report that segregated and sequenced the responsibilities of prevention, reaction, and rebuilding, the mandates of the three pillars overlap. Prevention of atrocity crimes is clearly a responsibility of all three pillars and therefore of the state (under pillar one 'the protection responsibilities of the state') and the international community (under pillar two 'international assistance and capacity building' and pillar three 'timely and decisive response'). Prevention involves political (rule of law, independent judiciary, free press, minority rights, 'gender-responsive justice and security sector reforms' (A/63/677/2009/paras14–27)) and economic measures (that ensure employment 'equity in the distribution of resources, assets, income and opportunities' to all groups in a country (A/67/929-S/2013/399/para45) that a state must undertake. Similarly, in the fulfilment of its responsibility to prevent the international community is expected to promote economic development and prosperity of the population so that root causes of atrocity crimes are addressed (A/63/677/2009/para43). Pillar three's 'timely and decisive action' mandate is popularly understood as UN Security Council-sanctioned military intervention. However, this responsibility to react also has preventive components in the range of its initiatives, e.g., diplomatic negotiations and economic sanctions: The three pillars of sovereignty as responsibility have been 'expanded.' People assume R2P is 'largely about the third pillar' 'the third pillar, although it has variations, has military intervention as a component of last resort' (Deng 2010: 85).

Also, note that military assistance by the regional organization/international community offered to a 'beleaguered state' under pillar two is comparable to pillar three's military intervention, though the latter option is exercised without the consent of the state. The responsibility to rebuild a country post military intervention belongs to both the state (pillar one) and the international community (pillar two) and this involves political and economic initiatives similar to preventive measures.

Thus, the instruments and techniques of the agents encompass the entire paraphernalia of conflict prevention and peacebuilding measures[2] and early warning assessment and mechanisms which must be undertaken by all agents in different degrees and at different times. Therefore, these measures belong to all three pillars. It is misleading to view the three pillars as exact individual replicas of the ICISS's report's 'three-part structure' of responsibilities—of prevention, reaction, and rebuilding. The 2005 WSOD and the 2009 Secretary-General's Report on R2P cast

[2] Anne Orford sees R2P as 'consolidating and streamlining the existing practices of protection that have developed and been institutionalized since the late 1950s, such as administration, surveillance, fact-finding, quiet diplomacy, management, capacity-building and policing' (2011: 103).

the ICISS's sequential and 'temporal model' as a 'continuum of tasks' whereby all responsibilities particularly of prevention and rebuilding were to be undertaken simultaneously by the concerned actors (Luck 2012: 41).

The Institutional Manifestations

Incorporation of R2P entails embedding it in various UN departments like UNDP, OCHA, UNHCR, and the UN Peacebuilding Commission as there are limitations even in terms of logistics and infrastructure of the Office of the Special Adviser on the Responsibility to Protect.

The institutional manifestations of R2P are evident in the creation of the post of the Secretary-General's Special Adviser on Responsibility to Protect (SAR2P), reports and resolutions of the three key organs of the UN even though they emphasize different aspects of R2P and do not endorse it in its entirety of the three pillars. The creation of the post of the Secretary-General's Special Adviser on Responsibility to Protect (SAR2P) at the UN, in 2008, is in a sense the *formalization* of R2P's official *presence* at the UN. However, the idea or the *phrase* R2P had been raised and discussed in various UN documents prior to 2008, for example, the 2005 WSOD. Indeed, the creation of the post of SAR2P within three years of the 2005 WSOD, and within eight years of its articulation by the 2001 ICISS, is suggestive of R2P's fast-track course at the UN. Promoters of R2P see this telescoped span of time as recognition of an idea whose time has come and has come with urgency. Others see the SAR2P along with the SAPG as being of no significance or consequence at the UN. These positions are viewed as mere honorifics created to 'accommodate people' (Anonymous Academic 1 Interview in July 2013). A UNDPKO official described specialized offices such as the OSAPG as 'little boutiques with no leverage.' In his view, a specialized office is a problem because it has unintended side effects:

> When the OSAPG was created, I was opposed to it. My view on genocide prevention and to some extent R2P is that making it the job of one person has the side effect that no one else feels responsibility for it and especially when it comes to genocide prevention, if this is not the job of every senior UN official then what is? (Anonymous UNDPKO official Interview August 2013)

However, using the same premise Simon Adams, former Executive Director, GCR2P makes a case for the post of special advisers as a way to avert the apathy of 'everybody's job becoming nobody's job.' But he adds that this should not mean the confinement of R2P to the OSAPG, on the other hand, R2P must be mainstreamed in other departments (Interview August 2013). The defence for a specialized office is also made on the ground that the UN itself is a work in progress:

> The UN is an idea always in the making, whereby new offices are possible. The UN did not start with a UN Commission on Human Rights but as human rights became important, you have human rights commission. Just like you need a doctor who is generic and specialist, you need a generic UN in the sense of political processes that will lead to resolution of conflicts, genocide prevention, good governance. At the same time, you need a specialist UN with special knowledge to understand and engage with certain kind of threats. (Andrea Bartoli interview August 2013)[3]

A frequent refrain amongst those who support the post of the SAR2P is that its relevance gets undermined because it is not a full-time 'regular budget post' (Luck 2011: 391; also, Thomas Weiss interview August 2013). The former SAR2P, Jennifer Welsh, operating from Florence, Italy, and not from the UN Headquarters in New York is viewed as a handicap, for example, it does not allow for a regular and continuing engagement with state diplomats at the UN: The post of the SAR2P should be 'a full-time, regular budget post with the incumbent in residence in New York. You have to be around when things happen, it cannot be a part-time engagement by a consultant who schedules "quality-time" with delegates' (Thomas Weiss interview August 2013). Therefore, though the post of the SAR2P is a significant step forward for the institutionalization of R2P at the UN, its *delivery potential* and influence are almost entirely contingent on the personality of the special adviser. Most interviewees from academia, INGOs, and the UN observed that Edward Luck's personal commitment and astute understanding of UN politics were valuable contributions to the Secretary-General's efforts to put R2P on the agenda of the Security Council and the General Assembly.

[3] Andrea Bartoli, representing a civil society perspective, participated in the 2011 and 2010 Informal Interactive Dialogue of the UN General Assembly on the Responsibility to Protect. An international conflict resolution expert, he is currently Dean of the School of Diplomacy and International Relations, Seton Hall University, New Jersey, USA.

Advocacy for R2P, especially in the initial years, was not without challenges. One complex task was reaching out and addressing the concerns of three different constituencies: (a) Member states who needed to be assured that R2P is not an intrusive but collaborative mandate to help them transact their responsibilities; (b) UN colleagues who see the very title, 'genocide prevention,' as making their work with governments difficult. These UN officials were the 'first line of resistance'; (c) The NGO community that wants a more 'assertive role' to 'name and shame' (Deng 2010: 85). The package of three pillars (of R2P) definitely helps advocates in presenting R2P as a benign measure.

The Secretary-General's seven consecutive annual reports on R2P (2009–2023) enjoy an encyclopaedic stature of sorts where through conceptual expansion of the three SOD paragraphs, the *official* meaning of R2P has been established. The Secretary-General and the Secretariat are credited with bringing the UN's (particularly, the Security Council's) focus onto R2P (Bellamy and Williams 2011b: 826). The reports emphasize the non-military prevention (and peacebuilding) aspects of R2P and underline that the military intervention option is the last resort to stop atrocity crimes. The accent on pillar one ('the protection responsibilities of the state') and pillar two ('international assistance and capacity building') seeks to de-stigmatize R2P from the charge of being a tool of modern-day imperialism in the hands of the powerful states. The reports' template's contextualization of R2P in the UN Charter is an adroit manoeuvre to claim (and bestow) legitimacy for R2P while retaining the military intervention option. Critics of R2P while acknowledging the Secretary-General's interest and entrepreneurial zeal in R2P promotion downplay the significance of these reports:

> A better indicator for the institutionalization of R2P at the UN would be if, in addition to these reports, the Secretary-General's reports on Mali, Congo, DRC where atrocity crimes have been committed make a reference to R2P. But the fact is that the vast majority of these reports do not make a reference to R2P. (Anonymous UNDPKO official interview 2013)

A similar observation can be made regarding the General Assembly (GA) resolutions, exceptions to which are the 2005 SOD (paras138–140) and the 2009 resolution (A/RES/63/308), whereby the Assembly decided to continue consideration of R2P through informal debates. Although GA resolutions do not enjoy the status of binding international law, they often presage future progress in that realm 'and they are in themselves evidence of the potential emergence of *opino juris* on a matter' (Breakey et al. 2012: 39). While R2P detractors caution against overestimating the significance of these debates/dialogues on account of their informal status, R2P proponents view the interactive dialogues as 'productive' (Luck 2012: 41) in the creation of a 'shared understanding' on R2P as different from humanitarian-intervention (Thakur 2012: 3). These deliberations have seen espousal of strong criticism of R2P including the famous 2009 Noam Chomsky speech in which he referred to R2P as a cousin of humanitarian-intervention. Ngugi wa Thiong'o[4] and Jean Bricmont[5] were the other two prominent R2P critics at the event and they echoed concerns about the misuse of R2P by the powerful states.[6] The President of the General Assembly while summing up the debate iterated that the Member States favoured a crisis prevention approach that included both crisis management and dealing with root causes: 'We should thereby avoid any impression of a continuum from diplomatic means, through coercion, to the ultimate use of force' (A/63/PV.101/2009/page 20). Significantly such criticisms (which were made even in subsequent debates) raise questions about the intentions of powerful countries in the North, without denying that prevention of atrocity crimes is imperative. The GA's concern is to preserve the principle of sovereignty and therefore, its annual informal dialogues repeatedly iterate the significance of the first two pillars as 'prevention is at the heart of R2P.' Issues like early warning, early engagement, good governance, and the rule of law are emphasized in these dialogues because these are seen as preventative actions (see ICR2P 2010, 2011). The GA, clearly, has been influential in making the Secretary General focus on the prevention aspects of R2P. The GA's acceptance of pillar three as a last resort comes with caveats that lay stress on (a) the range of pillar three measures that include pacific and coercive means (Chapters VI and VII of the UN Charter,

[4] Ngugi wa Thiong'o is a Kenyan novelist and post-colonial theorist.

[5] Jean Bricmont is a Belgian physicist and activist.

[6] The UN webcast of this event (23 July 2009) is available at the following link: http://www.un.org/webcast/2009.html. The text of these speeches is available at the following link: http://www.responsibilitytoprotect.org/index.php/component/content/article/35-r2pcs-topics/2493-general-assembly-debate-on-the-responsibility-to-protect-and-informal-interactive-dialogue.

respectively); (b) that intervention must be accompanied by a responsibility while protecting (RWP) so that the international response can be monitored and be made accountable.[7] This de-emphasizing of military intervention is the GA's domestication of R2P as decisions under Chapter VII are in the Security Council's domain. GA's de-emphasising of R2P's military intervention—a task that under Chapter VII is clearly in the purview of the SC—should not be seen as the defanging of R2P but a way to claim/assert greater control over R2P. Not surprisingly, the thrust of these dialogues has also been on the need for reform of the Security Council's veto powers so that there is a consistency in the application of R2P and concerns about double standards can be dispelled (see ICR2P 2011).[8]

The Security Council has invoked R2P in its resolutions not just to condemn atrocity crimes but also to sanction operational mandates under Chapter VII of the UN Charter. On two occasions the Security Council authorized the use of force i.e., in Libya (S/RES/1973/2011)[9] and in

[7] See http://www.responsibilitytoprotect.org/index.php/component/content/article/35-r2pcs-topics/5004-united-nations-general-assembly-holds-fifth-informal-interactive-dialogue-on-the-responsibility-to-protect.

[8] The above reference to the views of the General Assembly does not suggest homogeneity of opinion amongst the Member States. There are different reservations about R2P expressed by different members, for example, Cuba and Venezuela do not support it, countries like India support it with reservation, Brazil has raised the issue of the need to observe responsibility while protecting. Also not all Member States participate in these informal dialogues.

[9] The resolution reiterates 'the responsibility of the Libyan authorities to protect the Libyan population and reaffirming that parties to armed conflicts bear the primary responsibility to take all feasible steps to ensure the protection of civilians.' The Security Council's acting under Chapter VII of the UN Charter authorized Member States to act 'nationally or through regional organizations or arrangements' to take measures to protect civilians and civilian populated areas under threat of attack in the Libyan Arab Jamahiriya' (para4), declared a no fly zone (S/RES/1973/2011para6–12), enforced an arms embargo (para13–16), banned flights (S/RES/1973/2011/para17 18) and froze assets of the Libyan authorities (S/RES/1973/2011/para19–21).There are some who argue that Resolution 1970 is the first example of the Security Council's authorization for a coercive intervention (Zifcak 2012: 61). However, it must be clarified that Resolution 1970 did not authorize military intervention. Acting under Chapter VII (S/RES/1970/2011/Article 41) of the UN Charter the Security Council referred the Libyan situation to the ICC (S/RES/1970/2011/para4–8), imposed an arms embargo on Libyan Arab Jamahiriya (9–14), a travel ban on certain listed individuals (S/RES/1970/2011/para15–16), froze assets of certain listed individuals and entities (S/RES/1970/2011/paras17–21).

Cote d'Ivoire (S/RES/1975/2011).[10] UNSG Ban Ki-moon termed this 'NATO-led, UN mandated intervention in Libya' as the '"coming of age" of the "R2P" concept' (Morris 2013: 1265). However, the ensuing regime change in Libya as a result of the intervention reignited suspicions that R2P was a ruse to pursue the foreign policy goals of the powerful countries. This Libyan experience became the primary reason for the Security Council's non-use of Chapter VII in the case of Syria. UN officials in UNDP and in DPKO whom I interviewed in 2013 cited this as a proof of the faded currency of R2P that would soon go out of circulation even in terms of discourse. Such criticisms miss three points, *first* the Security Council has not ceased to reference R2P in its subsequent resolutions. *Second* R2P's pillar three is not only about military intervention but it includes a range of non-coercive measures. *Third*, R2P is also constituted by pillars one and two. Indeed, all three pillars contain the entire spectrum of measures of conflict prevention/ resolution/transformation and peacebuilding, which are stressed upon in these resolutions. Some of these measures are authorized under the UN Charter's Chapter VII[11]; clearly, besides Resolutions 1973 and 1975, there are other Security Council resolutions that are R2P operational

[10] Resolution 1975 points out that the attacks in Cote d'Ivoire 'could amount to crimes against humanity.' It must be noted that prior to Resolution 1975 the Security Council, acting under Chapter VII of the UN Charter, in its Resolution 1528 had authorized UNOCI to protect Civilians and had also authorized the French forces to use 'all necessary means' to support UNOCI (S/RES/1528/2004). Resolution 1975 recalls this prior authorization to the (a) UNOCI to use all necessary means to protect civilians' (SRES/ 1975/2011/para6); (b) French forces to support UNOCI fulfill its mandate (SRES/ 1975/2011/para7). Therefore, the United Kingdom argued that Resolution 1975 was merely reaffirming the earlier resolution.

[11] Some examples of the Security Council resolutions paragraphs that invoke the UN Charter's Chapter VII include: establishment of UNMISS (S/RES/1996/2011/para1); restraining Libyan authorities to refrain from reprisals (S/RES/2016/2011/para4); calling upon Libyan authorities to promote human rights (S/RES/2040/2012/para3); encouraging Libya and its neighbours to work towards regional cooperation and ensure stability in Libya (S/RES/2040/2012/para5); extension of the UNSMIL mandate (S/RES/ 2040/2012/para6); imposition of arms embargo (S/RES/2040/2012/para8); imposition of asset freeze (S/RES/2040/2012/para9); demanding that rebel groups in Mali cut off all ties to terrorist organizations (S/RES/2085/para2); urging member states, regional and international organizations to provide coordinated assistance, expertise and training to the Malian Defence and security forces (S/RES/2085/para9); authorizing member states of the African Union to maintain the deployment of AMISOM (S/RES/ 2093/para1); requesting the African Union to keep the Security Council informed on the implementation of AMISOM's mandate through written reports to the SG (S/RES/

mandates, albeit non-coercive ones. It is, therefore, not useful to derive the Security Council's stance on R2P only in the context of its power to authorize military action. The Security Council's engagement with R2P is not limited to pillar three, Security Council's *non-military* resolutions on R2P are an endorsement of pillars one and two. Thus, the three main UN organs end up supporting similar R2P *practices*. This is not surprising as all three are part of the UN's liberal/neoliberal security/development dispositif, which ensures an alignment of views in the *long run*. As noted earlier the twinning of R2P and POC in these resolutions is not welcomed by the UN Humanitarian Agencies: 'We at OCHA with our POC mandate cannot be part of a discussion on military intervention' (Anonymous OCHA official 1 Interview in August 2013).

The empirical mapping shows the institutional manifestations of R2P in the agencies, offices, and departments under the key UN organs. The OSAPG through its engagement with them, particularly on the issues under pillars one and two, aims to mainstream R2P in the UN. For example, the officials from these agencies participate in the workshops conducted by OSAPG to raise awareness about R2P and train participants on how to use the R2P lens in atrocity crime prevention as laid down in the 2014 *Framework of Analysis*. The Human Rights Council has been relatively proactive in referencing R2P: 'The High Commissioner for Human Rights has referred to RtoP on a number of occasions, while the Human Rights Council employed it in the Libyan and Syrian situations, preempting the Security Council both times' (Luck 2011: 392).

The mapping also reveals an interesting fact about civil society organizations' engagement with the UN on the R2P issue, their role goes beyond that of interest group lobbying for a particular policy. In fact, the common membership (including that of former UN officials, ICISS commissioners, and State Heads) and work profile make these organizations an *extension* of the UN. ICR2P and GCR2P are not, what

2093/para8); asking the Libyan government to cooperate with the International Criminal Court (S/RES/2095/para4) ICC; requesting the Secretary-General, African Union, and the ECOWAS to support the transitional road map in Mali including the work of the Dialogue and Reconciliation Commission (S/RES/2100/para2); urging the Transitional Authority in the Central African Republic to develop and implement disarmament, demobilization and reintegration (SC/RES/2127/2013/para11); urging security sector reforms (SC/RES/2127/2013/para12); authorizing the deployment of MISCA (SC/RES/2127/2013/para28–33); mandating the European Union operation in the Central African Republic (S/RES/2134/para43–50).

Slaughter, Tullumello, & Wood described in another context, mere 'international analogues of U.S. public interest groups' (1998: 371). Indeed, these two organizations are crucial in UN's interface with civil society on R2P as is evident from their respective mission statements. A pressure or interest group approach (Keck & Sikkink 1998; Risse-Kappen 1995, 2002) is inadequate in understanding the relationship between these specific INGO's and the UN. That is, it is analytically limiting to view these individual groups as discrete entities aiming to merely claim a share in the pie. The concept of dispositif moves beyond the intentions of the actors and shows how they are located in the same discursive space and driven towards discursive congeniality.

The Normative and Ideational Dimensions of R2P

R2P advocates emphasize that the ideational origins of R2P lie in a non-western context. This is a useful argument to counter the accusations of R2P being a Trojan horse for western imperialism. The 2009 Report of the Secretary-General on implementing R2P traces the intellectual heritage of the WSOD's conceptualization of R2P to (a). Francis Deng's notion of 'sovereignty as responsibility' that emerged from his work on internally displaced persons; (b). African Union's 'thought and practice' of 'non-indifference' instead of non-intervention in case of the commission of atrocity crimes in any member-state; (c). the 2001 ICISS Report (since the ICISS also had commissioners from the Global South); (d). the 2004 Secretary-General's *High-Level Panel on Threats, Challenges and Change* that included several of the ICISS report's recommendations; (e). Secretary-General's Report *In Larger Freedom: Towards Development, Security and Human Rights for All* (A/63/677/2009/para7–9). The R2P intellectual lineage is further enriched by including in it Kofi Annan's 'two concepts of sovereignty' speech in 1999 (see Weiss 2007: 89; Bellamy 2008: 617). Edward Luck sees R2P as emerging from a the history that includes the movement towards human security—the privileging of people's security over that of the state with a focus on the protection of civilians and the prevention of gender-related violence, and mass rape. R2P was made possible by so many different things coming together.[12] Embedding R2P in this history provides it with a normative basis and builds an argument for its legal status thereby giving it an additional context of legitimacy, that is, the *legal as an instrument of legitimization*. While legality and legitimacy are conceptually distinct, in politics they may not only coexist but get conflated. This was Max Weber's question: 'how political legitimacy can result from legality' (Benhabib 1997: 725). R2P advocates seek legitimation for R2P not only by constructing it as a moral imperative but also by imputing *some form* of legality to R2P. This is done by emphasizing R2P's *likeness* to the existing international laws (including the UN Charter).

Legal Dimension of R2P

R2P is neither a part of an international treaty nor does it have a 'status of customary international law. The World Summit Outcome Document provisions on R2P were only included in the UNGA resolution and therefore, are not a formal source of law' (Garwood-Gowers 2015: 6). Through the resolutions/reports of the GA, SC, and the SG, the advocates of R2P seek to embed it in the UN Charter provisions and the existing international laws (for example, the Genocide Convention). By virtue of this embeddedness, a *vicarious sort of legality* is constructed for R2P. Also, the ostracism of atrocity crimes and the advocacy of R2P are made on both legal and moral grounds. The WSOD by equating the R2P scope with atrocity crimes made possible a 'distinct legalization of the principle' (Hoffmann and Nollkaemper 2012b: 359) since genocide, crimes against humanity, and war crimes are designated as crimes under international law. Although the fourth atrocity crime, ethnic cleansing, is not an 'independent crime under international law,' the OSAPG imputes it with that status by referencing the condemnation of ethnic cleansing by the United Nations Commissions of Experts (1992) appointed in the context of the war in Yugoslavia (UNOGPR2P 2014: 32).[13] Not all see

[12] See http://www.un.org/en/preventgenocide/adviser/videos/video_5.shtml. Accessed in November 2013.

[13] The terms genocide and ethnic cleansing emerge from the twentieth century European experience: Raphel Lemkin introduced the term 'genocide' to refer to Nazi policies, while the expression 'ethnic cleansing' gained wide currency after the Yugoslav wars of the 1990s (Ferrara 2015: 1). Also see Pegorier (2013) for a detailed exploration of the international legal dimensions of the crime of ethnic cleansing.

this legalization as fast tracking of R2P's legitimacy and point out that creating 'endless chains of legal obligations' would be inimical to the interests of 'endangered populations.' Instead, the R2P goal of protection is more likely to be realized if—as suggested by the 2006 proposal of S5 (Costa Rica, Jordan, Liechtenstein, Singapore, and Switzerland)—there is an imposition of '*procedural* obligations' on 'Security Council members to justify their vote' (or veto) (Peters 2012: 207–208).[14]

The concern of most countries of the Global South, as underlined in the GA informal dialogues on R2P, is that these attempts to give R2P a legal status are aimed at the dilution of the legal principle of non-intervention in the 'domestic jurisdiction of any state' (UN Charter Article 2(7)). This fear gets credence in the thesis that 'hegemonic law-making' ensures that the 'power of norms and the norms of the powerful are two sides of the same coin' (Reinold 2013: 4). The impact of the R2P discourse is 'more political than legal; from a legal perspective, an attempt to induce a state to stop killing its population has never been qualified as intervention, as long as it was not pursued by coercion' (Hoffmann & Nollkaemper 2012b: 363).

Sovereignty and R2P

This relative privileging of the political over the legal not only reinforces the role of power (and possibly its arbitrariness) but also magnifies the element of contingency in international politics or what Kenneth Waltz (1959) described as 'international anarchy.' Concurring with this view an OCHA official 1 criticized R2P's dilution of sovereignty because it erases the *certainty* built by international law over a long period of time:

> The concept of R2P undermines the basic foundations of international law— the concept of sovereignty. The whole system of the UN is built on that. It is good to have predictability and certainty in international relations. If you put together a concept that undermines this principle of sovereignty, you need to make sure that it brings in as much certainty and predictability than you remove. And this is not the case with R2P. It is seen as a tool used by the more powerful countries to undermine the sovereignty of the less powerful ones. Whether it is the right or wrong perception can be discussed. But this is the way that it is perceived. So, I

[14] Also see Peters (2012: 210 fn 44).

> think that OSAPG needs to work on this aspect i.e., how to bring certainty and predictability. At the moment the concept of R2P is vague in its application i.e., why should we apply it only in certain contexts. I don't think there are concepts of justice, fairness and predictability in R2P. Those are missing. (Anonymous OCHA official 1 Interview 2013)

Having clearly anticipated this criticism (i.e., violation of the principle of non-intervention and therefore a violation of the international architecture's key premise of sovereignty), R2P advocates have strongly endorsed Francis Deng's casting of 'sovereignty as responsibility' and made it the very premise of R2P. In such conceptualization, R2P strictly speaking is not a violation of the UN Charter as Article 2(7) itself contains the qualification that the principle of non-intervention 'shall not prejudice the application of the enforcement measures under Chapter VII.' It is in a similar light that the DPA extended support to R2P after its initial opposition. A DPA official shared that the concept of 'unbridled sovereignty' is most often a problem that his colleagues encounter in their work. R2P provides DPA an *entry point* to discuss democratic issues:

> It is important for us at the UN to have the concept because it provides an entry point. When the UN was established, the primary focus was on international peace and security. And then you have this concept of sovereignty— big wall that the UN is not allowed to penetrate. The R2P language, that the international community has a responsibility to react, provides us with some legitimacy to at least ask some questions, to voice our opinions on things that are happening inside. (Anonymous DPA official Interview 2013)

However, the regime change in Libya following the NATO-led military intervention cast doubt about whether R2P is a measure—with the moral intent— to protect the local population. The Libya case gives credence to the Global South's fears of R2P as a new imperial ruse—bereft of any moral intention—to interfere in the domestic affairs of weaker countries by violating the latter's sovereignty. 'Sovereignty is also an equalizer, and it is seen by the weak as a protection against the powerful' (Jean-Marie Guehenno Interview August 2013).[15] R2P's endorsement of military intervention—albeit as a last resort—makes mobilization of a political

[15] Jean-Marie Guehenno served as the United Nations' Under-Secretary-General for Peacekeeping Operations (2000–2008). He was also Director, Center for International

consensus to operationalize it difficult since it is seen as a violation of the Westphalian notion of sovereignty. R2P's adoption of Deng's 'sovereignty as responsibility' is an intelligent rhetorical—not necessarily a deceptive—defence as this formulation unlike that of Westphalia cannot be read as a dilution of sovereignty. Deng's redefinition allows sovereignty to be seen as a *spectrum* whereby the degree of a country's sovereignty is contingent on its power and behaviour that in turn determine whether and the extent to which the external agents can lay claim to the former's sovereignty. This implies two things: (a) the breach of the Westphalian principle is only temporary but necessary for the immediate protection of the local population; (b) the country will regain its lost sovereignty i.e., the Westphalian version, when its domestic political situation is congenial. Both non-consensual intervention and its accompanying violation or dilution of sovereignty (depending upon the context) get justified on moral grounds. The issue of morality is a key component in the conceptualization of R2P. The quest for legitimacy for R2P is made on political, legal, *and* moral grounds.

Morality and R2P

The fundamental justification of R2P is that atrocity crimes are cause enough for UN action as human life must be saved (UNOGCR2P 2014: 2). The moral dimension manifests in the form of imputing responsibilities to actors to do their bit to stop atrocity crimes, that is, such responsibilities require action not passive observation. The ICISS suggested that making a '*moral* appeal' is useful to end apathy regarding the suffering of those in remote distant lands (ICISS 2001: 8.13). This positive framing creates a 'normative context' that demands 'saving strangers' who are subjected to 'appalling cruelty by their governments' (Wheeler 2000: 1). It is this moral obligation that Kofi Annan invoked in his exhortation to the UN Member States that they must ensure that the UN lives up to the expectation of being the 'collective conscience of humanity' (Orford 2011: 102).

Through this morality play, there is a construction of categories and meanings that are then identified as legitimate. Thus, any reference to an atrocity crime in a UNSC resolution is projected as an endorsement of

Conflict Resolution, School of International and Public Affairs, Columbia University. Currently, he is President and Chief Executive Officer, International Crisis Group.

the R2P principle by R2P advocates. For instance, the mention of 'crimes against humanity' in resolutions on Cote d'Ivoire (S/RES/1975/2011) and DRC (S/RES/1925/2010)[16] is taken as evidence by a DPA official to argue that the moral lens of R2P, has brought about 'a *psychological shift*, and therefore, the action in Cote d'Ivoire, DRC, Libya and now Syria even though it is a messy example. There is an expectation that it is not okay watching people being killed' (Anonymous DPA official Interview August 2013). Simon Adams contrasts the international community's reactions to the killings under 'Assad Senior' with those under 'Assad Junior,' 'while in the former there was not even a murmur, in Bashar al' Assad's case there is widespread condemnation' (Interview August 2013). Edward Luck credits R2P with saving lives in Kenya, Kyrgyzstan, Guinea, Cote d'Ivoire, and Libya by discouraging 'further violence against populations' (2011: 393). In the aforementioned DPA official's views, although 'R2P is not a generator that you can pick up and put in each office and say now you have R2P,' as a moral discourse R2P facilitates the DPA agenda and empowers local people and prevents their victimization.

However, there is a flip side of raising the moral pitch to a level of naming and shaming a particular leader or group in conflict situations. Such contexts handicap the SAR2P's intervention to address the issue. Such 'moral' construction of categories could possibly turn out to be alienating as this adds hurdles to the political resolution of the problem:

> Societies are not like human beings, human beings if they have cancer would go to a doctor for check-up. But a society has a different outlook. If a country is fragile and you say that it needs to cut and break away a part, most leaders will not like it. If a country is shown as sick, then the person with the UN hat, with a special mandate to deal with the greatest disease is not going to be welcomed in most states. It complicates his work. It immediately elevates things, elevating an issue may be good from an advocacy standpoint – oh now he has gone to this country therefore now the international community is seized with the issue good. But if we agree that in R2P there are less intrusive measures like political, developmental, and diplomatic that can be used to stabilize and prevent deterioration of a situation that could lead to mass killings and human suffering, then those instruments and actions are difficult to develop when

[16] The resolution on DRC also speaks of a second atrocity crime—war crime—(S/RES/1925/2010).

> linked to a high-profile issue. It could go terribly wrong. Therefore, for practical considerations I am not too keen on having a Mr. or Ms. R2P. (Jean-Marie Guehenno Interview August 2013)

Thus there are limits to the advantages that can accrue to R2P's operationalization when R2P is *broadcast* in a moral tone. There is another dimension to the limits of moral discourse on its own spurring R2P action, which stems from the logic of realpolitik whereby national interest may trump the moral voice. This is the paradoxical state of being for R2P: 'Though its political clout stems from moral angst, channeling moral rectitude into effective policy remedies is a formidable challenge' (Luck 2011: 395).

The moral pitch by R2P advocates does not impress OCHA, a persistent sceptic if not detractor of R2P at the UN. The R2P morality narrative, according to OCHA official 1, is destined to be problematic 'as moral values are subjective, difficult to define and are therefore not shared by everybody.' Even though OCHA's work of humanitarian assistance is based on the moral idea, it has strong 'legal foundations, legal acceptability. We adhere to these legislations very seriously as we need state consent, without which we cannot manage humanitarian assistance' (Anonymous OCHA official 1 Interview August 2013).

Responsibility and R2P

R2P renews attention on responsibility, a key attribute of modern politics and state. The question of responsibility is an old or rather a persisting one because the boundaries of its answer are prone to amendment. Changing historical circumstances expand or shrink the range of state responsibilities, and add or subtract the number of actors who must bear political responsibility. The actors could be communities, groups, individuals, and—with the emergence of the international—international organizations. The Peace of Westphalia spelt out this responsibility by demarcating the boundaries of the inside/outside via the concept of sovereignty (see Walker 1993). History of the world post-1648 is witness to the contestation of these boundaries; the irony is that despite being a highly acclaimed and enduring concept—sovereignty—and its enumerated responsibilities have not been stable. So, Francis Deng's casting of sovereignty as responsibility is both at one level tautological and at another level radical because it purports to *officially* make porous and if need be, erase, albeit temporarily, the inside/outside boundary of the nation-state nestled in the interstate system.

The conspicuous display of the concept of responsibility in the R2P framework is simply the reiteration of a historical imperative. At the end of the Second World War, the international community had to grapple with the issue of responsibility. In 1948, the International Law Commission (ILC) began to work on the codification of state responsibility. Coincidentally, it was in 2001, the year of the ICISS Report submission that ILC's codification effort culminated in the adoption of the *Articles on Responsibility of States* (International Law Commission 2001). The ILC is now working on Draft Articles on the Responsibility of International Organizations, whereby international organizations are recognized 'as subjects of international law and as possible perpetrators of particularly serious wrongful acts' (Jorgensen 2012: 126). The millennium began for the UN on several notes of responsibility, that is, in addition to the above, the United Nations Global Compact (UNGC)[17] was founded in 2000 to promote corporate social responsibility (Rasche 2009; Rasche and Waddock 2014; Voegtlin and Pless 2014; Williams 2014a, b). Besides state responsibility being underlined, other entities were identified as new agents of responsibility in different arenas of the international system.

Not surprisingly, the onuses of responsibility to protect that emerge from the concept of R2P range from the specific institutions of the state, regional, and international organizations to the general entities of civil societies/NGOs/INGOs and (*all*) individuals. The post-Second World War order was inaugurated by a certain view about the responsibilities of the entities of the individual (soldier/bureaucrat) and the state. The Nuremberg trials judgement segued state responsibility into individual responsibility so Nazi officers could not take refuge in the argument of merely following state orders and had to bear the responsibility for acts of genocide. The International Military Tribunal at Nuremberg ruled that the individual must transgress state laws if these come into conflict with international rules that protect basic humanitarian values (Antonio Cassese in Held 1989: 234).

Responsibility, tied to the good governance discourse since the 1980s, serves amongst other purposes, as the legitimizing trope of

[17] The UN Global Compact is the 'largest voluntary global governance initiative that addresses the social and ecological responsibilities of multinational corporations' (Voegtlin and Pless 2014: 181).

powerful nation-states' foreign policy initiatives that regards intervention in domestic affairs of states as necessary to build them as responsible members of the international system: The United States and its partners who are 'on the right side of freedom's divide have a responsibility to help all people who find themselves on the wrong side of the divide' (Condoleezza Rice in Reinold 2013: 5). Inspired by a similar belief in the good intentions of R2P, a UN Under-Secretary-General, underlined R2P as a reminder to 'third world states' to be responsible members of the international community and not create the circumstances that invite external intervention (Interview June 2012).

The accenting argument to legitimize R2P evokes the idea of our responsibility to fellow human beings resulting from our membership in the universal category of humanity that transcends national, race, ethnic, and such ascriptive identities. This view gains no small traction from those who see solutions to contemporary global economic, ecological, and political crisis in cosmopolitanism. Cosmopolitanism as the new realism proposes an expansive generous understanding of responsibility that will jettison realpolitik (of the domestic and international levels) (Held 2010; Brown and Held 2010).

The moral basis of the responsibility in R2P is also tied to a particular idea of the community, however, this concept of the community is not communitarian (Etzioni 2004; MacIntyre 1984; Sandel 1982), but a liberal/neoliberal one rooted in individualism.[18] Synchronizing the logic of these two concepts is not easy since idea(s) of community, germane to the concept of R2P, create a slippery slope for the concept of responsibility resulting in the moral hazard dilemma:

> I would say that there is often a moral hazard in intervening in the lives of others, because you cannot fully anticipate all the consequences of your actions. Therefore, one should always act with caution, and make sure intervention will do no harm. (Jean-Marie Guehenno Interview 29 August 2013)

[18] See Chapter 6 for the individualization of responsibility under liberal/neoliberal governmentality.

Protection Mandate

This question of moral hazard is also made in the context of the protection mandate of R2P (Belloni 2006; Crawford 2005; Crawford and Kuperman 2005; Kuperman 2008a, b, 2009). Though the 2005 SOD marks the official entry of R2P into the UN, R2P can be said to have made an earlier *entry of sorts* in 1999 through the Security Council's Protection of Civilians (POC) resolution (S/RES/1265/1999). Both OCHA[19] and OSAPG officials underline the differences between R2P and POC—mainly that R2P is activated when atrocity crimes are (or are likely to be) committed, while POC is limited to protection of civilians in situations of armed conflict. The OCHA officials distance themselves from any conversation about military intervention, as they perceive it as undermining or delegitimizing their humanitarian work of protection:

> We at OCHA work in the protection of civilians which is a concept derived from international humanitarian law. It is a legal norm- protection of civilians in armed conflict while R2P is a political norm. (Anonymous OCHA official 2 Interview August 2013)

Not surprisingly unlike R2P, POC does not make an explicit (or implicit) connection between a state's responsibility to protect and its sovereignty. However, the twinning of R2P and POC mandates in the Security Council resolutions is possible as both R2P and POC underline protection as the responsibility of the government and echo the protection component of the humanitarian agenda of the 1990s. By the 1990s, the UN's understanding had moved away from its earlier 'austere ethics of the 'humanitarian imperative' and towards a commitment to prosecuting evil' (Orford 2011: 102). This necessitated 'political decisions 'about rightness and just causes'' (Nicholas Leader in Orford 2011: 102).

Despite the moral underpinnings of the imperative to protect fellow human beings in distress, the protection mandate raises some ethical

[19] OCHA—The Office for the Coordination of Humanitarian Affairs—describes its protection mandate as the full range of activities that seek to obtain 'full respect for the rights of all individuals in accordance with international law.' In general, protection refers to: protection of civilians in armed conflict (POC), whereby all parties to the conflict are responsible for ensuring that the civilian population is respected and protected; protection in contexts of natural disasters or civil unrest, whereby national authorities have the primary responsibility for the well-being of those affected. (http://www.unocha.org/what-we-do/policy/thematic-areas/protection).

concerns. It involves the identification and classification of fragile/sick/rogue states that are reminiscent of the colonial discourse of infantilizing the native/colonized. The protection agenda of R2P is not merely non-empowering but can lead to the disempowerment of local agency. R2P is in a very bad shape because the concept has not been thought through. A UNDPKO official pointed out that the conceptual problem with R2P is that it posits the people as a sort of disempowered group in need of protection rather than as a group that needs to be organized, that is empowered and capable of protecting itself: 'The best form of protection for people is to make people responsible for their destiny and to empower them rather than protect them' (Anonymous UNDPKO official August 2013). It is argued that R2P's focus on the international community's role in protection ignores history where atrocities have been averted because of the resistance and struggle of the victims. International intervention driven by R2P's 'salvation paradigm' can potentially demobilize or radicalize local resistance (Megret 2009: 576, 588). The promise or possibility of international intervention may embolden rebellion but not 'prevent the state's genocidal retaliation' (Kuperman 2011: 128). R2P advocates do not give credence to the moral hazard argument as it is premised on a 'reductionist' 'deterrence theory' that does not understand the complex historical factors that make genocide possible (Bellamy and Williams 2011a: 557).

In addition to conceptual pitfalls, R2P's protection mandate lacks clarity in terms of its operationalization on the ground. Julia Hoffmann and Andre Nollkaemper ask whether in a situation of conflict, the objective of protection is achieved with a 'semi-permanent ceasefire' or does it require a regime change? But since conflicts are often cyclical can the duty of protection ever end? (2012a: 362). The answer to these questions requires a reminder that in view of the R2P pillars, the meaning of protection cannot be restricted to just a part of pillar three mandate of 'timely and decisive action.' Through pillars one and two, R2P has taken over the broad human security agenda of protecting the 'freedom from want,' 'freedom from fear' and 'freedom to live in dignity.' So, the protection agenda, in the *true,* i.e., the latest official, R2P rendition, cannot be an event, it is likely to be about the *longue duree.* The consequences of compressing R2P's protection agenda to swift surgical-like air strikes as in Libya, not surprisingly, embarrass the R2P advocates.

R2P's re-invention post-2005 as a prevention measure with emphasis on the non-military aspects of its protection mandate has facilitated its non-forced entry into other departments. After all, it is difficult to dispute that the UN's work is about protection, proactive protection in myriad forms where several entities including public–private partners, and individuals have the onus of protection. There are no passive roles in this protection game—though power equations could be different, therefore the decision-making about the form and content of protection rests with some and not all protectors—neither the protector nor the protected can be passive. The latter must allow themselves to be guided in certain ways so that they are protected.

Conclusion

This chapter shows that the 'presence' of R2P at the UN is seen not just in its *office*—OSAPG, but in other UN entitities too. However, R2P's presence, even an officially certified one, does not automatically or immediately translate into its unequivocal incorporation at the UN. R2P has its detractors who oppose it on grounds that it pollutes or comes into conflict, or marginalizes the principles of their respective domains (i.e., departments).[20] Importantly, R2P's uneven incorporation indicates that it is not a political untouchable in all UN quarters. Indeed, resistance to R2P is seen as evidence of its success:

> This opposition to R2P is a counterintuitive attestation to its success as it is the growing traction of R2P that is compelling its critics to raise their voices louder. The fact that they are so on the defensive would be one of the things for me to measure whether the R2P discourse is making a difference because they must have a rationalization as to why it is important for them to dissociate themselves from R2P. For me this is an indication that there is traction in the norm. In this regard one of the interesting ways to measure whether R2P matters is to see whether it is abused. (Thomas Weiss Interview August 2013)

The following chapter discusses how this has become possible. The SG's annual reports on R2P play a key role here, whereby R2P emerges as too ambitious or big an idea to be confined to a specialized office OSAPG.

[20] The role of conflicts or synergies amongst the three UN organs, General Assembly, Security Council, and the Secretariat, in the promotion of R2P is not the subject of a detailed analysis in my research. For an exploration of the same in the context of human security, see Busumtwi-Sam and Kashyap (2015).

The discourse of R2P's three pillars has appropriated, encroached, or laid claim to ownership, or to put it politely embedded itself in the *entirety* of the UN security/development dispositif. R2P advocates see R2P as a catalyst for UN entities to do their respective work (Anonymous OSAPG official 2 Interview August 2012). Such a discourse casts R2P as the UN's overseer, monitor, and conscience keeper that will propel the UN to action so as to realize the Charter's promise and goals of security and development, which this book identifies as those of the liberal/neoliberal security/development dispositif.[21]

Chapter 6 takes this analysis of the nature of incorporation of R2P at the UN further to argue that R2P is not a *discursive shift* but a *discursive rearticulation* within the UN's security/development dispositif.

References

Bellamy, Alex J. 2008. The Responsibility to Protect and the Problem of Military Intervention. *International Affairs* 84 (4): 615–639.

Bellamy, Alex J., and Paul D. Williams. 2011a. On the Limits of Moral Hazard: The 'Responsibility to Protect', Armed Conflict and Mass Atrocities. *European Journal of International Relations* 18 (3): 539–571.

Bellamy, Alex, and Paul D. Williams. 2011b. The New Politics of Protection: Cote d'Ivoire, Libya and the Responsibility to Protect. *International Affairs* 87 (4): 825–850.

Benhabib, Seyla. 1997. Review of 'Between Facts and Norms: Contributions to a Discourse Theory of Law and Democracy. By Jurgen Habermas.' *The American Political Science Review* 91 (3): 725–726.

Breakey, Hugh, Angus Francis, Vesselin Popovski, Charles Sampford, Michael G. Smith, and Ramesh Thakur. 2012. *Enhancing Protection Capacity: A Policy Guide to the Responsibility to Protect and the Protection of Civilians in Armed Conflicts.* Institute for Ethics, Governance and Law.

Brown, Garrett Wallace, and David Held. eds. 2010. *The Cosmopolitan Reader*. Cambridge: Polity Press.

Busumtwi-Sam, James, and Rina Kashyap. 2015. The UN and the 'Mainstreaming' of Human Security: An Institutional Perspective. Paper presented at the British Columbia Political Studies Association Annual Conference, Vancouver May 7-8, 2015.

[21] The liberal/neoliberal aspects of the dispositif are discussed in Chapter 6.

Chigas, Diana, Elizabeth McClintock, and Christophe Kamp. 1996. Preventive Diplomacy and the Organization for Security and Cooperation in Europe: Creating Incentives for Dialogue and Cooperation. In *Preventing Conflict in the Post-Communist World: Mobilizing International and Regional Organizations*, ed. Abram Chayes and Antonia Handler Chayes. Washington, D.C.: Brookings Institution.

Crawford, Timothy W. 2005. Moral Hazard, Intervention and Internal War: A Conceptual Analysis. *Ethnopolitics* 4 (2): 175–193.

Crawford, Timothy, and Alan J. Kuperman. 2005. Introduction: Debating the Hazards of Intervention. *Ethnopolitics* 4 (2): 143–147.

Deng, Francis. 2010. JISB Interview: The Responsibility to Protect. *Journal of Prevention and Statebuilding* 4 (1): 83–89.

Etzioni, Amitai. 2004. *The Common Good*. London: Polity Press.

Evans, Gareth, and Mohamed Sahnoun. 2001. "Foreword." In *The Responsibility to Protect. International Commission on Intervention and State Sovereignty*. Ottawa: International Development Research Centre.

Ferrara, Antonio. 2015. Beyond Genocide and Ethnic Cleansing: Demographic Surgery as A New Way to Understand Mass Violence. *Journal of Genocide Research* 17 (1): 1–20.

Garwood-Gowers, Andrew. 2015. China's "Responsible Protection" Concept: Reinterpreting the Responsibility to Protect (R2P) and Military Intervention for Humanitarian Purposes. *Asian Journal of International Law* 6(1): 1–30.

Guehenno, Jean-Marie. August 2013. *Former Under-Secretary-General UN Peacekeeping Operations*. New York: Personal Interview.

Held, David. 1989. Political Theory and the State: Essays on State, Power and Democracy. Cambridge: Polity.

Held, David. 2010. *Cosmopolitanism: Ideals and Realities*. Cambridge: Polity.

Hoffmann, Julia, and Andre Nollkaemper. 2012a. "Concluding Observations." In *Responsibility to Protect: From Principle to Practice*, ed. Julia Hoffmann and Andre Nollkaemper. Amsterdam: Pallas Publication.

Hoffmann, Julia, and Andre Nollkaemper. 2012b. Introduction. In *Responsibility to Protect: From Principle to Practice*, ed. Julia Hoffmann and Andre Nollkaemper. Amsterdam: Pallas Publication.

ICR2P. 2010. What Did Governments from Your Region Say at the General Assembly Debate on the Responsibility to Protect? Accessed on September 25, 2015. Available at http://www.responsibilitytoprotect.org/index.php/component/content/article/35-r2pcs-topics/2672-what-did-governments-from-your-region-say-at-the-ga-debate.

ICR2P. 2011. National Endorsements of Responsibility to Protect: Policy Papers, Strategy Documents and Focal Points. Accessed on September 25, 2015. Available at http://responsibilitytoprotect.org/Dec%2021%202011%20Revision%20RtoP%20National%20level%20endorsements.pdf.

International Commission on Intervention and State Sovereignty. 2001. *The Responsibility to Protect*. Ottawa: International Development Research Centre.

International Law Commission. 2001. *Articles on Responsibility of States for Internationally Wrongful Acts (2001)*. UN Doc A/56/83 Annex.

Jorgensen, Nina H.B. 2012. Responsibility to Protect and the Obligations of States and Organizations. In *Responsibility to Protect: From Principle to Practice*, ed. Julia Hoffmann and Andre Nollkaemper. Amsterdam: Pallas Publication.

Keck, Margaret, and Kathryn Sikkink. 1998. *Activists Beyond Borders: Advocacy Networks in International Politics*. Ithaca: Cornell University Press.

Kuperman, Alan J. 2008a. Mitigating the Moral Hazard of Humanitarian Intervention: Lessons from Economics. *Global Governance* 14 (2): 219–240.

Kuperman, Alan J. 2008b. The Moral Hazard of Humanitarian Intervention: Lessons from the Balkans. *International Studies Quarterly* 52 (1): 49–80.

Kuperman, Alan J. 2009. Rethinking the Responsibility to Protect. *Whitehead Journal of Diplomacy and International Relations* 10 (1): 33–43.

Kuperman, Alan J. 2011. R2P: Catchy Name for a Fading Norm. *Ethnopolitics: Formerly Global Review of Ethnopolitics* 10 (1): 125–128.

Luck, Edward. 2011. The Responsibility to Protect: The First Decade. *Global Responsibility to Protect* 3 (4): 387–399.

Luck, Edward. 2012. The Responsibility to Protect: The Journey. In *Responsibility to Protect: From Principle to Practice*, ed. Julia Hoffmann and Andre Nollkaemper. Amsterdam: Pallas Publication.

MacIntyre, Alasdair. 1984. *After Virtue: A Study in Moral Theory*. Notre Dame: University of Notre Dame Press.

Megret, Fredric. 2009. Beyond the 'Salvation' Paradigm: Responsibility to Protect (Others) vs the Power of Protecting Oneself. *Security Dialogue* 40 (6): 575–595.

Morris, Justin. 2013. Libya and Syria: R2P and the Spectre of the Swinging Pendulum. *International Affairs* 89 (5): 1265–1283.

Orford, Anne. 2011. *International Authority and the Responsibility to Protect*. Cambridge: Cambridge University Press.

Peck, Connie. 2001. The Role of Regional Organizations in Preventing and Resolving Conflict. In *Turbulent Peace: The Challenges of Managing International Conflict*, ed. Chester A. Crocker, Fen Osler Hampson, and Pamela Aall. Washington, DC: United States Institute of Peace Press.

Pegorier, Clotilde. 2013. *Ethnic Cleansing: A Legal Qualification*. New York: Routledge.

Peters, Anne. 2012. The Responsibility to Protect and the Permanent Five: The Obligation to Give Reason for a Veto. In *Responsibility to Protect: From Principle to Practice*, ed. Julia Hoffmann and Andre Nollkaemper. Amsterdam: Pallas Publication.

Pinder, John. 1996. Community against Conflict: The European Community's Contribution to Ethno-National Peace in Europe. In *Preventing Conflict in the Post-Communist World: Mobilizing International and Regional Organizations*, ed. Abram Chayes and Antonia Handler Chayes. Washington, DC: Brookings Institution.

Rasche, Andreas. 2009. A Necessary Supplement: What the United Nations Global Compact is and is Not. *Business and Society* 48 (4): 511–537.

Rasche, Andreas, and Sandra Waddock. 2014. Global Sustainability Governance and the UN Global Compact: A Rejoinder to Critics. *Journal of Business Ethics* 122: 209–216.

Reinold, Theresa. 2013. *Sovereignty and the Responsibility to Protect: The Power of Norms and the Norms of the Powerful*. New York: Routlegde.

Risse-Kappen, Thomas, ed. 1995. *Bringing the Transnational Back In: Non-State Actors, Domestic Structures and International Institutions.* Cambridge: Cambridge University Press.

Risse, Thomas. 2002. Transnational Actors and World Politics. In *Handbook of International Relations*, ed. Walter Carlsnaes, Thomas Risse, and Beth A. Simmons. London: Sage.

Roberto, Belloni. 2006. The Tragedy of Darfur and the Limits of the 'Responsibility to Protect.' *Ethnopolitics* 5 (4): 327–346.

Sandel, Michael. 1982. *Liberalism and the Limits of Justice*. Cambridge: Cambridge University Press.

Slaughter, Anne-Marie, Andrew Tullumello and Stepan Wood. 1998. International Law and International Relations Theory: A New Generation of Interdisciplinary Scholarship. *The American Journal of International Law* 92 (3): 367–397.

Thakur, Ramesh. 2012. Emerging Powers and the Responsibility to Protect after Libya. *Policy Brief 15*. Oslo: Norwegian Institute of International Affairs.

United Nations General Assembly. 2009a. *The Responsibility to Protect*. UN Doc. A/RES/63/308, 7 October 2009a.

United Nations General Assembly. 2009b. 63rd Session, 97th Plenary Meeting. UN Doc. A/63/PV.101/2009b.

United Nations Office on Genocide Prevention and the Responsibility to Protect. 2014. *Framework of Analysis for Atrocity Crimes: A Tool for Prevention*. New York.

United Nations Secretary-General. 2009. *Implementing the Responsibility to Protect*. Report of the Secretary-General. UN Doc. A/63/677/2009, 12 January.

United Nations Secretary-General. 2013. *Responsibility to Protect: State Responsibility and Prevention*. Report of the Secretary-General. UN Doc. A/67/929-S/2013/399. 9 July 2013.

United Nations Security Council. 1999. UN Doc. S/RES/1265. 17 September 1999.
United Nations Security Council. 2006a. *Responsibility to Protect*. UN Doc. S/RES/1674, 28 April 2006a.
United Nations Security Council. 2006b. UN Doc. S/RES/1674. 28 April 2006b.
United Nations Security Council. 2010b. UN Doc. S/RES/1925. 28 May 2010b.
United Nations Security Council. 2011a. UN Doc. S/RES/1973. 17 March 2011a.
United Nations Security Council. 2011b. UN Doc. S/RES/1975. 30 March 2011b.
United Nations Security Council. 2011c. UN Doc. S/RES/1970. 25 February 2011c.
United Nations Security Council. 2011d. UN Doc. S/RES/1996. 8 July 2011d.
United Nations Security Council. 2011. UN Doc. S/RES/2016. 27 October 2011.
United Nations Security Council. 2012b. UN Doc. S/RES/2040. 12 March 2012b.
United Nations Security Council. 2012c. UN Doc. S/RES/2085. 20 December 2012c.
United Nations Security Council. 2013a. UN Doc. S/RES/2093. 6 March 2013a.
United Nations Security Council. 2013b. UN Doc. S/RES/2095. 14 March 2013b.
United Nations Security Council. 2013. UN Doc. S/RES/2100. 25 April 2013.
United Nations Security Council. 2014. UN Doc. S/RES/2155. 27 May 2014.
United Nations Security Council. 2014. UN Doc. S/RES/2187. 25 November 2014.
United Nations Security Council. 2015a. UN Doc. S/RES/2211. 26 March 2015a.
United Nations Security Council. 2015b. UN Doc. S/RES/2206. 3 March 2015b.
United Nations Security Council. 2015c. UN Doc. S/RES/2196. 22 January 2015c.
Voegtlin, Christian, and Nicola M. Pless. 2014. Global Governance: CSR and the Role of the UN Global Compact. *Journal of Business Ethics* 122: 179–191.
Walker, R.B.J. 1993. *Inside/Outside: International Relations as Political Theory*. New York: Cambridge University Press.
Waltz, Kenneth Neal. 1959. *Man, the State, and War: A Theoretical Analysis*. New York: Columbia University Press.

Weiss, Thomas G. 2007. *Humanitarian Intervention: Ideas in Action*. Cambridge, Massachusetts: Polity Press.

Weiss, Thomas G., Research Director, ICISS, Personal Interview, New York. August 2013.

Welsh, Jennifer. 2012. The Responsibility to Protect an Humanitarian Intervention. In *Responsibility to Protect: From Principle to Practice*, ed. Julia Hoffmann and Andre Nollkaemper. Amsterdam: Pallas Publication.

Wheeler, Nicholas J. 2000. *Saving Strangers: Humanitarian Intervention in International Society*. New York: Oxford University Press.

Williams, Oliver F., ed. 2014a. *Sustainable Development: The UN Millennium Development Goals, the UN Global Compact, and the Common Good*. Notre Dame: University of Notre Dame Press.

Williams, Oliver F. 2014b. The United Nations Global Compact: What did it Promise? *Journal of Business Ethics* 122: 241–251.

Zifcak, Spencer. 2012. The Responsibility to Protect After Libya and Syria. *Melbourne Journal of International Law* 13 (1): 59–93.

CHAPTER 6

Understanding the Map: R2P as Discursive Rearticulation Within the Liberal/Neoliberal Security/Development Dispositif

Introduction

This chapter analyzes the patterns of R2P's incorporation into the UN in order to analyze—whether R2P represents a significant change in the way the UN has approached the relationship between security and development and concludes that R2P represents not a ***discursive shift*** but a ***discursive rearticulation*** of the UN's liberal/neoliberal security/development dispositif. While a discursive shift would indicate a radical structural change in the dispositif, discursive rearticulation denotes that there is no significant change, perhaps only an appearance of change, whereby there is only a rearrangement of elements in the discourse and practice of the dispositif. The lenses of governmentality and biopolitics reveal R2P as an element of the liberal/neoliberal security/development dispositif, but point out that as a ***package deal*** of three pillars, R2P lays claim to the entirety of this dispositif. This is so because the measures to prevent (pillars one, two, and three), react (pillar three), and rebuild (pillars one and two) encompass the range of responses, means, and procedures available in this security/development dispositif. This understanding of R2P's discursive terrain draws on the historical context of R2P (Chapter 3) and the empirical mapping and analysis of R2P at the UN (in Chapters 4 and 5 respectively).

R. Kashyap, *The Political Economy of Security/Development in the Neoliberal Age*, International Political Economy Series,
https://doi.org/10.1007/978-3-031-37279-7_6

This chapter is divided into six sections. Section 'Introduction' summarizes the analysis of the earlier chapters. This is done with three purposes in mind. The first is to bring to the fore the reality of the interweaving of the ostensibly discrete domains of security and development. The second is to show that this interweaving is best understood not simply as a security-development nexus (Stern and Ojendal 2010: 6; DAC 2004) or as a phenomenon of securitization of development (Copenhagen School) but as a security/development dispositif. This is necessary so as to make visible the liberal/neoliberal underpinnings of the UN's security/development dispositif that have manifested as embedded liberalism (1945- to the late 1970s) and neoliberalism (post 1980s). The third purpose is to highlight how despite the addition of *new* offices (e.g., OSAPG) and *different* and *new* articulations of security/development, such as collective security, comprehensive security, and human security, at the UN, there is a fundamental continuity within the UN's security/development dispositif.

Section 'Security/Development Dispositif' discusses the embeddedness of R2P in the UN's liberal/neoliberal security/development dispositif. The argument, using the lenses of governmentality and biopolitics, is that R2P's key themes—legality, sovereignty, protection, morality, and responsibility—are also the themes of the UN's liberal/neoliberal security/development dispositif. Section 'Embedding R2P in the UN's Liberal/Neoliberal Security/Development Dispositif' is a summary that distils certain aspects of R2P from the discussion so far through concepts of governmentality and biopolitics. Section 'R2P's Act of Debris Collector: A Discursive Rearticulation of the Liberal/Neoliberal Security/Development Dispositif' analyzes how R2P and neoliberalism represent a discursive rearticulation within the liberal/neoliberal security/development dispositif. Building on the conclusion of Chapter 2, that the UN through new articulations of security/development such as human security is collecting the debris of responsibilities left behind by the receded embedded liberalism—it is argued that R2P is one of the mechanisms to collect this debris. It also points out that the singularity of the R2P discursive is in it being a context to 'put into words'[1] the reality of the practices through which a fundamental tension, contradiction, or problem of the security/development dispositif's putative premise is often

[1] Orford (2011) argues that R2P puts into words the UN deeds of executive action.

controversially played out (e.g., the NATO interventions in Bosnia and Kosovo [1990s] and Libya [2011]). The source of that tension is the clash between the UN Charter's two principles—sovereignty (regarded as a foundational principle of the international system since the Treaty of Westphalia 1648) and collective security (which makes possible military intervention in a state). Section 'R2P: A Discursive Shift?' is a venture into the realm of speculation to visualize what R2P as a discursive shift *may* look like. With that goal in mind, it is suggested that pillars 1 and 2 be strengthened so that prevention and rebuilding responsibilities are realized in practice and not in mere rhetoric. This suggestion, it needs underlining, is not necessarily the fated destination of R2P's discursive shift. Discursive shift could be a result of movement in *any* direction, it could be regressive or progressive. The last section is the 'Conclusion.'

Security/Development Dispositif

The fact that the UN system includes not just the General Assembly, Security Council, and the Secretariat but also the World Bank and the IMF, is evidence of the UN's dispositif as being constituted by security and development concerns. It is misleading and simplistic to view security and development as discrete domains and functions of the UN[2] and the Bretton Woods system respectively. It would be more accurate to say that the framers of the post-war international institutions regarded the security component of the security/development assemblage as the *primary* responsibility of the UN's three key organs while the UN's two specialized agencies, the International Monetary Fund (IMF) and the World Bank—the Bretton Woods institutions—would be *chiefly* responsible for the development component. Having a primary or chief function does not preclude an institution's other or supplementary responsibilities. The point that matters here is that the architects of these institutions acknowledged the link between security and development. The creation of the International Bank for Reconstruction and Development (IBRD)[3]

[2] From here onwards, the term United Nations (UN) would be used to denote the six UN organs and not include the IMF and the World Bank.

[3] The World Bank is comprised of four institutions: the International Bank for Reconstruction and Development (IBRD, 1944), the International Finance Corporation (IFC, 1956), the International Development Association (IDA, 1960), and the Multilateral Investment Guarantee Agency (MIGA, 1986).

in 1945 was 'part of a strategy to build and sustain peace in the aftermath of World War Two. The intention at the Bretton Woods conference in 1944 was to integrate the IBRD and IMF into a global economic system that would help prevent another hegemonic war by promoting economic growth and stability' (Busumtwi-Sam 2004: 335–336).

However, between the two sets of institutions, it is the UN that has asserted ownership of both the components of the security/development assemblage. The UN expansion into the domain of development began with the formation of United Nations Conference on Trade and Development (UNCTAD) in 1964 and United Nations Development Programme (UNDP) in 1965. The 1960s, christened as *UN Development Decade,* witnessed the changing profile of UN membership as newly decolonized 'third world' countries acquired a numerical majority in the General Assembly. The radical/socialist/left of centre leaders, that included Jawaharlal Nehru, Kwame Nkrumah, and Julius Kambarage Nyerere, sought to engage international politics on terms that would be equitable to these newly independent countries. Forums such as the Non-Aligned Movement drew attention to the skewed notions of security resulting from bipolar militarization and the neglect of the third world's development needs by the Bretton Woods System. In the immediate aftermath of World War II the prime beneficiaries of the 'IBRD loans and the Marshall Plan' were not the developing countries but West European states and Japan (Busumtwi-Sam 2004: 336). The Bretton Woods idea of development was exposed as being a shrunken concept of development, focused on rebuilding infrastructure and economic growth sans any social assessment and indicators. The creation of the UNDP and UNCTAD was followed by the demand for a New International Order (NIEO) in 1974. The oil crises of 1973 and 1979 only heightened the tensions about the international economic order within and between the developed and the developing worlds; the 1970s also saw a rise in third world debt, which culminated in the 1982 debt crisis. Beginning in the 1980s the IMF and the World Bank responded to these problems through neoliberal policies in the form of the structural adjustment programme(s) that would also end the 'rent-seeking'[4] politics of the third world countries; thus neoliberal policies were seemingly directed at changing both the economic and

[4] Anne O. Krueger coined the term, rent-seeking, and she argued that in some contexts of third world economies, rent-seeking took the form of 'bribery, corruption, smuggling, and black markets' (1974: 291).

political behaviour and policies of a state and its population. The UN on the other hand supported the creation of commissions on the subjects of security and development from a social-democratic perspective (or embedded liberalism).[5]

It is not to suggest that the World Bank/IMF and the UN are working at cross-purposes by subscribing to the policies of neoliberalism and (re)-embedded liberalism respectively. To re-state briefly the argument made in the earlier chapters: embedded liberalism and neoliberalism are part of the liberal continuum. It is misleading to view the turf battles resulting from the division of labour between these three institutions of the UN system (i.e., the key UN organs, IMF, and World Bank) as reflective of radically antagonistic philosophies. In fact, the turf fights between the IMF and the World Bank are legendary (Woods 2006: 6). The two sets of institutions—World Bank/IMF and the UN viewed the problem from the vantage point of liberalism, only the spectacles change from embedded liberalism to neoliberalism. Indeed, embedded liberalism informed the creation of the IMF and the World Bank (Ruggie 1982). It is because there is no polarity between liberalism (UN) and neoliberalism (World Bank/IMF) that the Brandt Commission initiated by Robert McNamara (World Bank President) could submit its report to the UN Secretary-General (Cooper and English 2005: 13). As argued in Chapters 2 and 3 that to maintain order, stability, and security, the debris of responsibilities left behind by the receded embedded liberalism had to be picked up by the expansive notions of security and development—'comprehensive understanding of security' (Brandt Commission), 'common security' (Palme Commission) and 'human security' (Human Security Now) in the era of neoliberalism:

> The wider view of security advocated in the late 1970s by the *development*-oriented Brandt Commission, was taken up explicitly by the *security*-oriented Palme Commission in the early 1980s, and further developed by the *environment*-and *development*- oriented Brundtland Commission in the late 1980s. Taken together, the Brandt, Palme, and Brundtland Commissions consolidated acceptance of a broader approach to security and contributed to the emergence of the 1990s human security movement. (Wiseman 2005: 62)

[5] These commissions are discussed in Chapter 3.

The discussion of NIEO initiated by the UNGA in 1972 had gathered momentum so the Brandt Commission's intervention to reframe the terms of debate of the international economic order, could very well be the first world's bid to reclaim the power of agenda setting in this context. Not only is there seamlessness between the ostensibly discrete domains of security and development but also this security/development dispositif has liberal/neoliberal underpinnings. This is evident in the increasing role of non-state actors like civil society organizations. The template for civil society's expanding role is determined by the liberal/neoliberal agenda, premised on the belief that the best form of state is that which governs the least. In this scenario a range of private actors such as private military security companies step in to perform functions that were once regarded as the exclusive domain of the state (O'Hanlon and Singer 2004; Pattison 2010; Singer 2003).

Understanding how the incorporation of R2P, albeit uneven, occurred at the UN requires contextualizing R2P in the UN's liberal/neoliberal security/development dispositif. Viewing the UN as a dispositif, as an assembly of knowledge/power, allows us to see how it enables and constrains agency. The support or resistance to R2P by different UN agencies and departments takes place *within* the framework of the UN Charter. This framework formulated in 1945 continues to provide the template for *new* ideas of security/development. The novelty of the new idea is limited by the liberal horizon of the UN Charter, therefore, all attempts at change have to conform to some version of liberalism such as embedded liberalism, neoliberalism, or re-embedded liberalism. For example, the 2001 ICISS report embedded R2P in the UN's human security discourse which itself is embedded in the UN Charter. Similarly, the recommendations of the international commissions on security/development sponsored by the UN and World Bank did not deviate from the UN Charter. The concept of dispositif helps us understand how this is possible. The R2P discourse must be seen in the context of the *evolving* security/development discourse that deems legitimate certain issues and actors in situations of conflict.

Security and development are not discrete but related domains, their relationship is best understood as security/development on the lines of Foucault's conceptualization of power/knowledge that denotes the circularity of the theory and practice of the two concepts. This aspect is neither captured by the security-development nexus argument nor by the Copenhagen School's theory of securitization. While the nexus argument refers to *some* overlap between the security and development concerns, the securitization theory views the boundaries of the field of security expanding and encroaching upon the non-security fields—including that of development—and securitizing them. Foucault's concepts of governmentality, biopolitics, and thanatopolitics reveal as congenital the twinning of security and development in the liberal dispositif. In this regard, the purpose of security is to defend a particular form of development of the economy, the rationality of which then informs the social domain.

Embedding R2P in the UN's Liberal/Neoliberal Security/Development Dispositif

R2P is a rearticulation of the rationality of the existing liberal/neoliberal security/development dispositif, that is, R2P is a measure of the liberal/neoliberal governmentality. This is evident from an analysis of how the key themes—*legality, sovereignty, morality, protection, and responsibility*—emerging from R2P resonate with the themes of the liberal/neoliberal security/development dispositif such as conflict prevention/resolution/transformation, peacekeeping and peacebuilding, and negotiation, arbitration, adjudication, and reconciliation.[6] Indeed, R2P is not just similar to these measures but subscribes to all of them through its three pillars: R2P consolidates and streamlines 'the existing practices of protection that have developed and been institutionalized since the late 1950s' (Orford 2011: 103).

R2P as the Moral Imperative in the Humanitarian Age

The characterization of R2P as a moral measure is unmistakable in the R2P discourse. Indeed today 'humanitarian militarism' is not oxymoronic but only tautological as humanitarianism is used to legitimize 'the politics of international condemnation, sanctions, and bombings' (Chandler 2001: 698, 700). The context of the challenge for the ICISS was that despite the rich positive connotations of the word humanitarian, humanitarian intervention, particularly in the wake of Rwanda and Kosovo, *had received bad press* and was largely viewed as a military measure aimed

[6] These are mentioned in the Secretary-General's Annual Reports on R2P and the Security Council Resolutions that reference R2P.

at realizing not humanitarian goals but the interests of the powerful Western states (Le Houerou 2014: v). Clearly while the idea of humanitarianism was still regarded as legitimate, military intervention in the name of humanitarianism was suspect. Since the 1990s the West has been engaged with an unsuccessful bid to impose new global norms on issues related to intervention, R2P represents that failure (McCormack 2010a: 69). The ICISS had to retrieve the lost legitimacy of humanitarian intervention, it did so by adding the responsibilities to prevent and rebuild to reaction i.e. military intervention aimed at protection and saving human beings including 'strangers' (Wheeler 2000). The trope of human security's broad agenda (freedom from fear and want) was used by adding responsibilities of prevention and rebuilding into that of protection.

The casting of R2P as 'rectitude' (Luck 2011: 9) also fits in with a trend in both the policy and academic world which had since the 1990s begun to emphasize ethical approaches to international affairs and foreign policy (Bulley 2010; McCormack 2010b: 70; Powers 2002). Humanitarian issues had assumed centre-stage in the international arena (Barnett 2010; Scott 2011; Weiss 1999, 2000; Yamashita 2015), and humanitarianism was being increasingly used 'to legitimize emergency measures' (Scott 2011: 3) and soon covered the domains of 'military action, governance and development':

> Humanitarianism is now conceived as a movement that offers justifications for military interventions in order to halt human rights abuses and humanitarian crises in intrastate and regional conflicts (humanitarian intervention); demands improvements in the quality and capabilities of governance because bad governance constitutes one of the 'root causes' of such crises; and works with and contributes to development assistance in an integrated effort to remove the socio-economic root causes (Yamashita 2015: 413. Also see Barnett 2010; Gibbons and Heintze 2015; Hoffman and Weiss 2006; Macrae 2002; Pattison 2014).

In this moral trope of saving lives, wherein 'neutrality, impartiality, and consent are second order principles' (Weiss 1999: 12), Francis Deng's proposition of 'sovereignty as responsibility' (1996) became morally persuasive. Though questions of moral hazard remained (Anderson 1999; Bulley 2010; Kuperman 2009), these were sidelined for the imperative of protecting lives and the international community was exhorted to assume responsibility and not look the other way. The environment of international politics in terms of policy and discourse was thus congenial for the 2001 ICISS Report on R2P. Given the scale of the humanitarian crises in Africa in the 1990s (Rwanda, Sudan, Somalia, DRC, Sierra Leone, Liberia, etc.) it is not surprising that the lineage of the R2P idea is traced to Africa. R2P received its earliest official endorsements through the 2002 African Union's Constitutive Act's embrace of 'a spirit of non-indifference towards war crimes and crimes against humanity' (Murithi 2009: 95).[7]

R2P as the Imperative of Responsible Protection in the Humanitarian Age

Protection mandate is a chief characteristic of the liberal/neoliberal security/development dispositif and R2P is amongst a host of measures that aim at protection. This protection takes place across a spectrum of security/development activities in which the act of saving lives is just one component. Human lives are saved so that they can live a *particular* way which liberal/neoliberal governmentality initiates them into. States and their populations are educated about the art of 'good governance,' which includes reform of political (democratization, freedom of press, human rights, and civil society actors) and economic institutions (free market principles and reform of labour laws). The protection mandate entails teaching and building the capacity of the *disabled* state to assume responsibility while simultaneously assisting the state in inculcating a similar ethos of responsibility in its population.

Education about good governance (and statebuilding) takes place through multiple modes—World Bank/IMF diktats (e.g., Structural Adjustment Programmes), lectures/power points by international experts and 'organized mentoring' (Rosén 2011: 151). In addition to the World Bank and the IMF various other UN agencies and departments are involved in the propagation of the good governance model in the developing countries. For example, the UNDP is involved in assisting the drafting of national constitutions, setting up of parliament buildings, and initiating the local leadership into the ethos of a parliamentary democracy:

[7] Indeed, the decade of 2000 saw a high profile endorsement for an activist international community that included Romeo Dallaire (2004), Samantha Powers (2002), George Clooney, and Bono who drew attention to dimensions problem of human insecurity in Africa.

> Our work on governance in Afghanistan involves strengthening the parliament—we set up the parliament that includes making the building, putting the chairs and mikes, helping formulate rules and training the parliamentarians on the legislative processes. We ensure national ownership, therefore, all this was done in consultation with the Afghanis, and it came through from the Bonn Conference. The UN is supporting the drafting of the constitution in Nepal, which is an extremely sensitive thing because there cannot be anything more sovereign than the drafting of the constitution so it has to be done by the concerned country. Our role, well we bring together the good, the bad, and the ugly, it is a delicate balance. We have been involved in the constitution making process in parts of Africa, Latin America. We have access to experts, we know what worked what did not. Our job is to put it out on the table. (Anonymous UNDP official 1 Interview July 2012)

Although, other UN officials expressed similar efforts in ensuring local involvement and ownership in security/development projects, there is no denying that there is a normative assumption about the goodness of the liberal/neoliberal governance model. With the involvement of international organizations like the UN, the recommended governance framework is that of liberalism/neoliberalism. Governmentality, we must note, is 'ontologically prior to the individuals who may enact it' as they rely on and draw from 'existing practices, strategies and institutions' (Joseph 2010: 232). The UN is a practioner of, what Larner and Walters (2004) have described as, 'global governmentality.'

Liberal/neoliberal governmentality's notions of protection and responsibility further construct categories of the protector, protected, and also of those who are outside the purview of protection. This process (as argued in Chapter 1) involves: (1) The identification of the conflict-ridden, civil war striven, 'failed states,' politically unstable, poor third world states as Objects of Knowledge; (2) The construction of vulnerable individuals/groups, communities, and states i.e., victims (the protected), and states, regional organizations, international organizations i.e., security providers (the protectors) as Subjects of Power; (3) The use of responsibilities of prevention and rebuilding (that are common to three R2P pillars) and the responsibility to react (though primarily a pillar three concern can also be a duty of pillar two) as Technologies of Power (governance). Classification is a political act, that is, subjectivization entails both inclusion and exclusion. The identification of some groups/entities as legitimate protectors and the (deserving to be) protected is a default disqualification of others from these categories. Under liberal/neoliberal governmentality the construction of these categories is in accordance with the truth of the free market. Through biopolitics liberal/neoliberal governmentality ensures that the prosperity of free market strives to 'make live,' that is, ensure the health and prosperity of the population. Biopolitics, however, is accompanied by thanatopolitics i.e., politics of death. There are limits to the free market's capacity to deliver prosperity to all so it cannot '*make all live*.' So the liberal/neoliberal governmentality's imperative to 'make live' is accompanied by that of 'let die' (*thanatos*). Those on the margins of society, bracketed as the dispensable such as the poor, the lazy, and the 'impure race,' have to be either left to die (through acts of omission) or to be killed (via acts of commission); biopolitics and thanatopolitics are two sides of the liberal/neoliberal governmentality. That is, *legitimate* death in this context can occur by the *non-action* of 'letting die' and by the action of killing. The 'let die' ethic is applied to those who, according to the liberal/neoliberal 'regime of truth' do not qualify for protection i.e., they are responsible for themselves and are not the responsibility of an external agent—the state. The poor individuals within the domestic society and the poor states in the international system are *not entitled* to protection but can be recipients of charity which is contingent on (a) the benevolence of the giver or (b) the pragmatism of the giver if the death of the poor (individuals and states) is or may become a source of disorder. The givers—the state and international organizations in such a case subscribe to principles of embedded liberalism, thus the adoption of welfare measures by the liberal state and also by its neoliberal avatar (though in lesser degrees). It is no surprise that in the wake of mounting criticisms of structural adjustment programmes increasing poverty in Africa and elsewhere, the IMF and World Bank began emphasizing 'poverty alleviation' and initiated the Poverty Reduction Growth Facility (PRGF) in 1999, designed to accommodate higher pro-poor public expenditure (Craig and Porter 2006; Busumtwi-Sam 2008). Until they become a political problem, the poor can be treated by the policy of 'do the least harm' (Astri Suhrke and Kathleen Newland in Weiss 1999: 15) or by the 'governing of indifference' (Basaran 2015: 205). The cultivation of indifference is a technique whereby citizens in liberal societies are made 'indifferent to the lives and sufferings of particular populations.' This is often justified on grounds of security and entails measures like sanctions and letting people die at borders (Basaran 2015: 205). The attitude of indifference, to look the other way has to be actively produced through a discourse that casts the victims as the undeserving population, not entitled to being saved as they would be a drain on state and society's resources, in addition to being a security risk. Thus the rationale for the attitude of indifference to the plight of victims lies not just in security but security/development concerns.

The ethic of thanatopolitics is also visible in how the security dispositif is expanding to include as legitimate the killings that were hitherto not regarded so. Susanne Krasmann discusses the transmutation of illegal political assassinations into legal and legitimate 'targeted killings' of leaders of terrorist organizations (2012: 682, 678). We may recall and underline that such killings are done in the name of the defence of the life of a threatened population. The biopolitical imperative 'to make live' is also evident in the R2P regime's segmentation of nation-states as 'sovereign states whose citizens have political rights, and de facto trusteeship territories whose populations are seen as wards in need of external protection.' This regime legalizes 'certain types of violence (such as Western counterinsurgency efforts), while arbitrarily criminalizing the violence of other states as "genocide"' (Mamdani 2010: 53). R2P in such a context is a replay of an old story—colonialism as a civilizing mission.

The liberal/neoliberal underpinnings of these notions of responsibility and protection are also seen in the privatization of some sectors of defence and security that had until now been deemed as the exclusive domain of the state. The Private Military & Security Companies (PMSC) are regarded as an example of the free market ingenuity that found employment for the '6 million' soldiers forced into retirement by the 'global military downsizing' following the end of the cold war. Great powers use PMSCs 'in violent, but less strategically significant, conflicts around the world' (Singer 2003). The argument for the relevance of PMSC finds takers even amongst the UN peacekeeping supporters like the former UN Under-Secretary-General for Special Political Affairs, Brian Urquhart, as the PMSC present 'twenty-first century business solution to the world's twenty-first century human security problems' (O'Hanlon & Singer 2004: 91). Since PMSCs are already being hired to provide 'training and logistical support' and 'armed guarding of personnel and infrastructure,'[8]

[8] The use of PMSCs 'has been most documented in Iraq, where the UK and US governments have employed companies such as Aegis, Blackwater…Control Risks Group, Erinys, KBR and Vinnell…PMSCs have been hired throughout the world by a multitude

James Pattison proposes that it would be 'morally justifiable' to outsource R2P 'to the private sector' (2010: 3, 27).

The recession of state responsibilities in the economy is also encouraged by the donor funding of civil society organizations, thus weakening the state capacity in countries like Somalia (Jayne S. Docherty[9] interview August 2013). Though bypassing the 'corrupt' and 'fragile' state institutions and instead using non-governmental organizations to reach the local people may appear as the only viable option to donors, there is no denying that such an act is a double edged sword which may further *entrench* the fragile state phenomenon; in such a situation the relative capacity of the state to fulfil its responsibility is further debilitated. The liberal/neoliberal dispositif accords a privileged position to civil society vis-à-vis the state in the Global South. Civil society organizations are a significant part of the R2P paraphernalia to help it realize the goals of the pillars, especially one and two. Besides operationalization, civil society is seen as the fountain of R2P since the latter is 'a bottom-up, not top-down, enterprise' created in no small measure by 'movements for human rights, humanitarian affairs and human security' and efforts of 'norm entrepreneurs—Bernard Kouchner, Francis Deng, Gareth Evans and Kofi Annan' (Luck 2012: 39–40). The foregrounding of civil society is inevitable in the R2P regime as the state's sovereignty is under scrutiny, some *sort of* responsibilities of governance need to be temporarily transferred to non-state surrogates. Thus, in addition to civil society actors other non-state entities like regional organizations (e.g., the Economic Community of West African States [ECOWAS] and the African Union [AU]) are expected to be proactive in the promotion and operationalization of R2P.

R2P as the Imperative to Redefine Sovereignty for Responsible Protection in the Humanitarian Age

The ICISS's casting of the R2P premise as 'sovereignty as responsibility,' is the most discussed aspect of R2P. Though this principle was introduced as a reprimand to an errant state that it can then be legitimately stripped of its sovereign robes, but subsequently R2P advocates

of actors, including states, multinational companies, NGOs, and the UN' (Pattison 2010: 3).

[9] Jayne S. Docherty is former Professor of Leadership and Public Policy, Centre for Justice and Peacebuilding, Easter Mennonite University.

promoted R2P as an affirmation and strengthening of the principle of sovereignty. This latter reassurance is key in increasing of R2P's support base amongst nation-states. This reassurance has had to be constantly reiterated by the Secretary-General in his annual reports on R2P. Despite this the likelihood of R2P being misused by the powerful states for their own ends continues to be a concern of many countries of the Global South. As a result, the General Assembly's endorsement of R2P, during its annual debates on R2P, is accompanied with the insistence of the inviolability of the principle of sovereignty.[10]

The fear of R2P being a Trojan horse of twenty-first-century imperialism gained credence after the 2011 intervention in Libya when some Security Council members expressed a 'buyer's remorse' at the way R2P was used (Luck 2011: 392). Advocates of R2P do not dismiss these concerns but point out that today certain humanitarian crises make intervention inevitable. In this scenario R2P is an invite for the international community to prepare itself 'normatively, organizationally, and operationally' and choose whether intervention is 'ad hoc or rules-based, unilateral or multilateral, and divisive or consensual' (Thakur 2013: 62). R2P as a 'multilateral' response can circumvent its misuse by powerful countries (Luck 2011: 396). What is, therefore, being suggested is that instead of withdrawing, the Global South states should take ownership of the concept through the multilateral forum of the UN. It is perhaps for this reason that the OSAPG, ICR2P, and GCR2P put equal emphasis on working to mobilize Member States both at the UN headquarters and at the national capitals. Working through the capitals is necessary, as R2P must be integrated 'into notions of national interests and hierarchies of national security priorities' (Luck 2011: 395). Indeed, it is argued that mainstreaming R2P at the UN itself requires mobilization of national governments who have the capacity 'to take on the concept and run with it. Therefore, a network of states like the "Group of Friends of R2P"[11] championing R2P will help the Secretariat to be more forceful

[10] This paradox of the simultaneous affirmation and undermining of the concept of sovereignty is an acknowledgement of the power of the *sovereignty discourse*. R.B.J. Walker's writings are a helpful guide in this context: The story of transcendence of sovereignty 'is itself produced by sovereignty, largely by rescripting a number of other stories through which sovereignty is itself constituted' (2002: 10; also see Walker 1993, 2010, 2015).

[11] The Group of Friends of R2P is an informal cross regional group of UN Member-States that seek to advance R2P within the UN system. It is co-chaired by the Netherlands

in that area' (Andrea Bartoli in interview August 2013). Acknowledging the limitations of the bureaucratic progress with which he has been so closely involved, Edward Luck says that reports and resolutions are only instruments for the end of 'changed behavior.' Therefore, the final test for the success of R2P lies in the 'capitals and in fields, not in the UN conference halls' (2012: 39). The OSAPG work gives special attention to working (i.e. advocacy and lobbying) at the national capitals. Clearly these national capitals are not just some geographical points but multiple nodes in the international power network. The UN's 'executive action'(s) such as R2P (Orford 2011) have to take this strategic power field into account.

Sovereignty's continuing significance is evident from the fact that even the theoretical dilution or redefinition of sovereignty cannot take place without the consent of the states. If the overwhelming number of states wants to hold on to the Westphalian notion of sovereignty, then a question needs to be answered: How did R2P, premised on conceptualization of sovereignty—as conditional and not absolute—which does not *precisely* adhere to the Westphalian notion, emerge and receive support from a large number of *sovereign* states at the 2005 World Summit? This issue must be discussed from various dimensions. The Westphalian notion of sovereignty is only a Weberian 'ideal type,'—wherein the states as territorial units enjoy complete juridical autonomy in domestic affairs and are not subservient to any external authority (see Krasner 2001: 230)—the reality of sovereignty has not always or strictly conformed to this model. The theory and practice of sovereignty have yielded an understanding of sovereignty in its two forms: sovereignty as authority/legitimacy/recognition (i.e., the Westphalian notion), and sovereignty as capability/power. This enables us to understand how sovereignty, depending upon the context, is accompanied by a reciprocal norm of non-intervention—the earliest example of this being the states agreeing to tolerate foreign 'islands' of sovereignty within their territories (i.e., diplomatic representation and immunity) and the norm of intervention—justified by the

and the Republic of Rwanda. Its members include: Argentina, Australia, Bangladesh, Belgium, Botswana, Canada, Chile, Costa Rica, Côte d'Ivoire, Czech Republic, Denmark, European Union, Finland, France, Germany, Ghana, Guatemala, Hungary, Italy, Liberia, Liechtenstein, Luxembourg, Mali, Mexico, Morocco, Mozambique, New Zealand, Nigeria, Norway, Panama, Republic of Korea, Senegal, Sierra Leone, Singapore, Slovakia, Slovenia, South Sudan, Sweden, Switzerland, Tanzania, United Kingdom, United States and Uruguay (see GCR2P 2014).

'laws of marque and reprisal, the medieval practice of capitulations...doctrine of the just war, the justification of colonialism' (D'Amato 2010: 1). Indeed '(B)reaches of the Westphalian model' are an abiding feature of international relations (Krasner 1995: 115). Great powers have often transgressed the sovereign boundaries of weak states as is evident from the phenomena of colonialism and neocolonialism. Decolonization, democracy, and human rights movements in the twentieth century delegitimized colonial style interventions (military, economic, and cultural), which were then replaced by the relatively subtle form of neocolonialism. The fact is that in the Westphalian notion of sovereignty, 'domestic jurisdiction' is a malleable concept and the scope of states' domestic jurisdiction has progressively shrunk, while the scope for external intervention has widened.

R2P advocates emphasize that the international situation today makes intervention necessary and unavoidable, so the more useful discussion would be how to ensure that military intervention is a multilateral and not unilateral act (Luck 2011; Thakur 2015; Weiss 2011). It is the aspect of multilateral support that was the ground for Jurgen Habermas to defend US action in the Gulf War—which from no angle is humanitarian intervention—since it had the UNSC backing (Edgar 2005). Military intervention's legitimacy is contingent on the 'intended moral and political goals,' and its adherence to 'procedural legal rationality,' that is it must be in accordance with international law (Hohendahl 1994: xviii). Notably Habermas was critical of the 2003 US action in Iraq as it was without the support of the UN Security Council (McCormack 2010b: 16; also see Edgar 2005). The reason for bringing in Habermas's viewpoint into the discussion is because this putative *critical voice* echoes here a liberal argument. This distinction 'between power that is based on relations of domination and force, and power that is legitimate because it is predicated on shared norms' (Wheeler 2000: 2) is similar to the liberal rationale that seeks to give legitimacy to the principle of R2P by making its operationalization a multilateral act.

This is the lineage in which the Francis Deng conceived 'sovereignty as responsibility' was delivered, the new born was accompanied by a legitimizing trope: it was a public declaration of consent to be administered the bitter pill, in case of 'bad behaviour' (read 'bad governance'). This conceptualization of 'sovereignty as responsibility' was by a global–local (Deng as a Sudanese UN diplomat) who saw it as an apt template of conflict management for his continent's political and economic problems.

This local patronage was as immaculate a conception as it could be of 'good governance'—self confession following self surveillance. A state on the brink of being errant can invite and host external interveners! (see Deng et al. 1996).

Morality, protection, responsibility, and sovereignty are key themes of R2P that find resonance as themes of the liberal/neoliberal security/development dispositif. The next section is a brief summary that distils aspects of R2P from the discussion so far through the concepts of governmentality and biopolitics.

R2P Through the Lenses of Governmentality and Biopolitics

Using the concepts of governmentality and biopolitics, this section delineates aspects of R2P that emerge from the discussion so far. *First*, it follows that R2P is not just a measure to be employed in the future but also a normative condition that must always be present in sovereign states because the states and the international community are fulfilling their respective responsibilities (to protect). Sovereignty as a responsibility requires that state actions and policies (long term and short term) lead to and ensure protection of the population from atrocity crimes (pillar one). The international community through organizations like the UN must aid in building the capacity of the state to do so (pillar two). The normative expectation in the notion of R2P is that its pillars one and two are always in the operational mode, they are in a perpetual state of being as they prevent atrocity crimes. R2P and its premise, sovereignty as responsibility, expect the *normative normal* national condition to be a robust and continuous exercise of pillars one and two measures. The invocation of R2P's pillar three is necessitated by an *abnormal* national condition that is a consequence of the failure of pillars one and two; pillar three is an exceptional measure.

To summarize, in the R2P postulation pillars one and two must be eternally present in the *normal* national condition, indeed these two pillars make the normal possible; their absence results in an *abnormal* national condition which in order to be *normalized* must be re-infused with R2P (pillars one and two) through pillar three: The three pillars 'must be ready to be utilized at any point, as there is no set sequence for moving from one to another, especially in a strategy of early and flexible response' (A/63/677/2009/para12).

Second the UN's early warning and surveillance mechanisms are important components in the operationalization of R2P (UNOGPR2P 2014). The ontological premise of surveillance mechanisms, including assessment of *risk* situations undertaken by the UN, is that the threat (of atrocity crimes) is ever present in the conditions that prevail in certain countries. Though not named, it is obvious that the reference is primarily to countries of the Global South. The assumption is that efficient surveillance and risk assessment can lead to the termination of plans of atrocity crimes. The significance and need of surveillance mechanisms is an admission that other preventive measures of pillars one and two have not yet been able to expunge structural causes of atrocity crimes: 'Effective action under pillars one and two may make action under pillar three unnecessary. Pillar three action should also contribute to the future achievement of pillar one goals' (A/66/874-S/2012/578/para15). It can be argued in defence of these other measures that while prevention and rebuilding are projects of long periods of gestation, surveillance, and risk assessment exercises are important in the short-term. The *Framework of Analysis for Atrocity Crimes* and the OSAPG organized training workshops[12] based on it, serve as the discursive panopticon of R2P. Timely preventive action is made contingent on the routinization of surveillance (see A/67/929/2013/para13).

Third, the notion of responsibility under R2P is almost all encompassing of the international, national, and local domains, the entities of which are expected and exhorted to not be mute spectators but active stoppers of atrocity crimes. R2P's *responsible* actors include macro entities of state (pillar one), regional organizations (pillars two and three), and international organizations (pillars two and three), and the micro entities of individuals including both the leader and the ordinary citizen.[13] In addition to the multiple actors, the expansive nature of R2P's concept of responsibility manifests in wide-ranging forms and content of responsibilities expected of these actors. Despite the segregation of responsibilities,

[12] See http://www.un.org/en/preventgenocide/adviser/training.shtml.

[13] Individual responsibility must be fostered as 'even in the worst genocide, there are ordinary people who refuse to be complicit in the collective evil, who display the values, the independence and the will to say no to those who would plunge their societies into cauldrons of cruelty, injustice, hatred and violence. We need to do more to recognize their courage and to learn from their actions' (A/63/677/2009/para27). The responsibilities of individual leaders and citizens by implication are present under all three pillars.

there is an overlap in both the content and temporality of the transaction of these responsibilities; there is no 'rigidly sequenced strategy' of the three pillars (A/63/677/2009/para50).

Regarding the content of the three pillars' respective responsibilities, each contains slices of both prevention and rebuilding. The responsibility of the state under pillar one requires preventive measures that include the establishment and strengthening of political institutions (good governance), addressing the root causes of atrocity crimes that exist in economic and social structures. Responsibilities of regional and international organizations involve similar preventive measures so as to assist the state in building its capacity in the aforementioned tasks. These preventive measures involve what the peacebuilding literature (including that of the UN) calls rebuilding or peacebuilding tasks undertaken in *post*-conflict situations (Lederach 2003, 2005a, b; *Agenda for Peace* 1992; A/RES/60/2005; S/RES/1645/2005; also see 2001 ICISS Report). The application of *post*-conflict measures as preventive devices should not surprise us since the *normal* conditions (of fragile economies and unstable political regimes) in some countries of the Global South is understood as being equivalent to that of situations of violent conflict. If such is the normal condition of a country then it is close to defaulting on its responsibility to protect. Preventive measures of rebuilding—lively and robust civil society, independent press, independent judiciary, strengthening national institutions that make possible good governance (A/67/929/2013/para47; A/63/677/2009/para17), promotion of economic development and prosperity, reduction of corruption (A/67/929/2013/para45) must be undertaken to avoid the state reneging on its sovereign promise of R2P.

Under the pillar two stipulation regional organizations and the international community must expand development assistance to the 'bottom billion' that 'enhances equality and social justice' thereby contributing in the prevention of atrocity crimes (A/63/677/2009/para43). The third pillar of 'timely and decisive response' from the international community is comprised of not just the Security Council-sanctioned military action but also 'a wide range of non-coercive and non-violent responses under Chapters VI and VIII of the Charter' (A/63/677/2009/para51). Preventive deployment option is also available under pillar two (A/63/677/2009/para41). Thus 'the three pillars relate to and reinforce each other' (A/66/874-S/2012/578/para20).

Fourth, R2P is also about educating, guiding, and disciplining errant states and their populations so as to generate good governance for good behaviour. This education cannot always be conducted in a deliberative mode because a pathologized entity (the errant state) is not easily persuaded through reason alone; therefore, a promise or fear of punishment is required. To explain this further, for example in order to ensure that a State fulfils its responsibility under pillar one, it may need to be educated, trained, or be persuaded (publicly or confidentially) by other States or international[14] and regional organizations (see A/63/677/2009/para24). This latter action requires activation of pillar two (A/63/677/2009/para30). When a State is too weak to stop the commission of atrocity crimes by an armed opposition, the international community could provide military assistance to the 'beleaguered State.' Pillar two's military assistance, persuasive measures, and positive incentives 'supplement the policy tools under pillar one and complement those under pillar three because none of the pillars is designed to work in isolation from the others' (A/63/677/2009/para30). *Therefore,* these three pillars are not just evidence of R2P's embeddedness in the UN's security/development dispositif but its imbrication in the entirety of the dispositif.

Fifth a liberal/neoliberal argument of 'veridiction by the market' (Foucault 2008: 32) informs the articulations and practices of R2P. The good governance discourse that prevails in pillars one (state responsibility) and two (international assistance and capacity building) is a liberal/neoliberal one. Pillar three (timely and decisive action) includes the mechanism of coercive intervention not just to save lives but also to bring order in a polity and society that is unable to bear the costs of neoliberal economic policies. That is the harsh economic consequences of these policies lead to the play of zero sum politics in an economy of scarcity in which refuge in ascriptive identities ensures relatively greater chances of accessing a slice of natural resources.[15] R2P advocates' defence of R2P is

[14] This would include the services of the 'United Nations High Commissioner for Human Rights, the United Nations High Commissioner for Refugees, the Emergency Relief Coordinator, the Special Adviser on the Prevention of Genocide, other special advisers, special representatives and envoys of the Secretary-General, and ranking officials of the United Nations, its development agencies and the Bretton Woods institutions' (A/63/677/2009/para 30, also see para 33).

[15] Atul Kohli makes this argument as an explanation of populist politics and democracy in developing countries (1994).

often within the liberal/neoliberal trope. For example, a UN official criticized those who apportioned the blame for economic underdevelopment and political crisis in the Global South states on the legacy of colonial exploitation:

> These states need to get out of their trade union mentality and take responsibility to put their own house in order, admit the indigenous, inherent flaws of their societies and not just blame their colonial past. R2P can be about prevention if there is self-scrutiny or self-monitoring by the third world states. This will ensure R2P does not become an instrument of imperialism's backdoor entry. (Anonymous USG Interview June 2012)

Clearly what is being privileged here is the liberal/neoliberal ethos of individualism that decries the collective. Self-monitoring and individual responsibility are technologies of liberal/neoliberal governmentality. Foucault observes that neoliberals do not conceive *homo economicus* as the subject of exchange and the market but as an entrepreneur (of the self). In neoliberal times each individual human being and individual state is an entrepreneur who takes responsibility for self care and for the consequences of risks that are taken in self care. This way the moral opprobrium that accompanied the structural adjustment programmes is avoided.[16]

R2P's Act of Debris Collector: A Discursive Rearticulation of the Liberal/Neoliberal Security/Development Dispositif

This section argues that R2P is a measure to collect the debris of responsibilities left behind by the receded embedded liberalism in the neoliberal era. Indeed, the criticisms of the neoliberal economic consequences have

[16] Since the 1980s 'Third World' debt crisis which saw the imposition of punitive measures of the IMF's structural adjustment programmes, the political question of 'legitimate and illegitimate indebtedness' was raised. Subsequently, the World Social Forum campaigned for cancellation of debts that are a form of neocolonialism. The debts result from the uneven relationship between the North and the South: 'The Global South (already exploited as a source of mining and agricultural raw materials) is really trading promises of development against an accumulation of obligations. Underdeveloped ex-colonial countries are serving a continuous flow of interest to the North, whose sum total largely overcomes whatever they have received: so that in fact they repay their debts not once or twice, but indefinitely' (Balibar 2013).

compelled its advocates to inject some degree of (re)-embedded liberalism so as to mitigate the harsh effects of neoliberalism (see Abdelal and Ruggie 2009; Craig and Porter 2006). Not surprisingly, those identified as neoliberals have for long denied the phenomenon of neoliberalism. However, in 2016 IMF economists finally acknowledged 'a strong and widespread global trend toward neoliberalism since the 1980s' that had promoted austerity measures resulting in increasing income inequality and reduced economic growth. So, they suggested that policymakers be 'more open to redistribution' (Ostry et al. 2016: 38–41). What is being recommended here is the anaemic implementation of, in the parlance of this book, debris of responsibilities left behind by receded embedded liberalism. The UN, World Bank, IMF, and other international bodies along with national actors are aware that the context of globalization has made national borders more porous whereby the domino effects are fast tracked. The 'global governmentality' (Larner and Walters 2004) of these international institutions aims to quarantine the *dangerous* condition of the *local* through measures such as R2P. This instrumentality of R2P like responses goes beyond the altruistic impulses of an international people who come together ephemerally to voice ethical and moral concerns about famine and genocides in different parts of the world. R2P clearly is not a form of charity but governments often tap into their citizens' emotional impulses and bleeding hearts for the faraway unfortunate innocent fellow human beings to legitimize coercive intervention under R2P (see Chandler 2003). R2P wrapped in this moral discourse gets reduced to a constricted view of pillar three as military intervention. R2P operationalized as such provides to the affected population only temporary relief of freedom from fear while its freedom from want remains a distant dream. This lens of *abridged* morality does not see the problem as a manifestation of a systemic flaw and therefore does not provide a long-term solution that requires preventive and rebuilding measures promised by pillars one and two. Upscaling governmentality to the global level reveals how the global financial institutions project the neoliberal economy as a panacea not the cause of global economic problems. Questioning this benign *disposition* of neoliberalism are critics who point out the deleterious effects of neoliberalism—'emergence of a 'debt economy'[17] (Balibar 2013; Lazzarato 2012), the increasing economic inequalities within and between states (Harvey 2004, 2006b; ICISS 2001: 3.8[18]; Mazur 2000; Picketty 2014; Stiglitz 2002), emergence of the 'precariat as the new dangerous class'[19] (Standing 2011; also see Munck 2013); the political and economic instability, 'new wars' and violent conflict (Bond 2004; Demmers et al. 2005; Duffield 2001; Saad-Filho 2004). Understanding neoliberalism, imperialism, and globalization as part of a continuum (Saad-Filho and Johnston 2004: 2) reveals measures like R2P as liberal/neoliberal technologies.

To explain this further, the simultaneity of the timing of the neoliberal discourse and good governance discourse is not a coincidence; indeed, they are tautological in content and intent. The World Bank and the IMF's good governance prescription recommends the adoption of free market, democratic and transparent governance, and human rights as instruments to help the South achieve economic prosperity, reduction of poverty, rule of law, an accountable and corruption free public

[17] Maurizio Lazzarato discusses how in the late 1970s neoliberalism changed the structure of the creditor-debtor relationship that can be traced to the history of Christianity. Neoliberalism's debt economy creates the subject—the '*homo debitor*'—who has the moral responsibility to repay debt and carry guilt (Charbonneau and Hansen 2014: 1040).

[18] Indeed, the ICISS Report points out the necessity for robust development assistance so that the international community fulfils the prevention responsibility beyond mere espousal of rhetoric. It criticizes the trade policies of rich industrialized states that impose unfair restrictions on the developing countries making it difficult for the latter to repay debts or 'meet the social and economic needs of their populations' (2001: 3.8). There is in this a hint about global structural inequalities.

[19] Precariat, a neologism, combining the words precarious and proletariat denotes a new class, which according to Guy Standing (2011) is a result of the second phase of proletariatization. This class lacks traditional labour security (i.e., 'adequate income-earning opportunities' and secure social income and work-based *identity*) (12). It is dangerous as it often uses its feelings of 'anger, anomie, anxiety and alienation' (19) to demonize vulnerable social groups e.g., immigrants who are then blamed for poaching jobs and resources over which the precariat claims rightful entitlement. They fail to see 'that the social and economic structure is producing their common set of vulnerabilities. Many will be attracted by populist politicians and neo-fascist messages, a development already clearly visible across Europe, the United States and elsewhere' (25). This view is criticized for seeking to universalize an argument that ignores the experience of the South. Also, though Standing distances the precariat from Marx's concept of the lumpen proletariat, it is considered as essentially being in the same genealogy (Munck 2013: 758–759).

sector (Demmers et al. 2005: vii–viii). The good governance discourse introduces and enables operationalization of the neoliberal agenda, plus by default lends further legitimacy to neoliberal principles. This legitimacy is made possible by the very nomenclature of good governance, the adoption of good governance measures by a state implies an acknowledgement of its past practices as a manifestation of bad governance. Having made this implied admission, the local (state and its population) must dutifully take ownership of the 'failures' that plague their economy and polity. If post the adoption of good governance, the old problems persist or new ones emerge, then they can be blamed on the congenital traits of bad governance that have not yet been fully exorcised from the country. The aphorisms—Old habits die hard; Rome was not built in a day—could serve as pithy neoliberal explanations! The good governance template also informs conflict resolution/transformation/peacebuilding discourse of the liberal/neoliberal security/development dispositif sans the military option (which is however always present, albeit, in the background as a last resort) (see Carothers 2006; Chandler 2009; Cousens et al. 2001; Duffield 2001; Paris 2004; Suhrke and Buckmaster 2006; Woodward 2002). It is also present, as the above sections have shown, in R2P's pillars one and two that encompass a range of measures to fulfil the responsibilities of prevention and rebuilding: 'Democratization and marketization' are key elements in post-conflict peacebuilding missions (Paris 2004: ix).

R2P's accent on the primacy of responsibility of the state is in consonance with the neoliberal and good governance discourse that engineers states and their populations to be good neoliberal cadets. The good governance approach is an attempt to depoliticize governance but such sanitized notions of politics cannot empower people (Demmers et al. 2005: viii). The creation of neoliberal subjectivities of the responsible *and* guilty state (and most often its population or a section of it) has implications for the principle of sovereignty.

These workings of the international economy reveal the disjunction between the theory and practice or reality of sovereignty, that is, the principle is not sacrosanct and is diluted of its Westphalian normative omnipotence. R2P's advocacy of sovereignty as responsibility merely echoes the practice of sovereignty in the liberal/neoliberal security/development dispositif. One of the most prevalent manifestations of neoliberal economic crisis is in the form of debt which 'constitutes the most deterritorialized and the most general power relations' of the neoliberal power bloc. Through this latest form of neocolonialism, neoliberal institutions act 'at the global level, affecting entire populations, calling for and contributing to the ethical construction of the indebted man' (Lazzarato 2012: 89). The state's 'regal prerogative' of monetary sovereignty is neutralized by the neoliberal international financial institutions (IFI) (Lazzarato 2012: 99). The conditionalities imposed by the IFIs necessitate the withdrawal of social spending (Lazzarato 2012: 103) by the states in the Global South, example, food subsidies. Privatization of public sector institutions, particularly those of education and health, has an immediate effect of increasing the economic burden of the least well off in society.[20] The IFI conditionalities create conditions for resistance to it forcing neoliberalism to develop a 'human face' (Arestis and Sawyer 2001: 275; Cornia et al. 1987).

The improvisation of neoliberal economic policies was also driven by the domestic compulsions of states in the North. The introduction of 'Third Way'[21] politics and economics in the US, UK, and Germany in the 1990s represented a new or rather revised version of Keynesianism. The 'Third Way' admits the necessity of the free market but tempers it with state interventions to ensure that the economy 'remains cohesive, inclusive, and egalitarian' (Anthony Giddens in Arestis and Sawyer 2004: 181). At the international level the 'third way' arguments were found in the proposal for a post-Washington Consensus where policies would be '"sustainable", "egalitarian", and "democratic"' and the state was no longer regarded antagonistic to the market but as an entity that could learn to be 'market friendly.' Despite these evocative terms of social justice the post-Washington Consensus is not a radical departure from its predecessor in terms of 'methodology and policy recommendations' which remain loyal to the principles of 'free trade and economic openness'

[20] 'The transformation of social rights into debts and beneficiaries into debtors is part of a program of "patrimonial individualism"...whose basis is the assertion of individual rights, but according to a completely financial conception of these rights, rights understood as "securities" ...the beneficiary as "debtor" is not expected to reimburse in actual money but rather in conduct, attitudes, ways of behaving, plans, subjective commitments, the time devoted to finding a job, the time used for conforming oneself to the criteria dictated by the market and business itself....in other words, debt reconfigures biopolitical power by demanding a production of subjectivity specific to the indebted man' (Lazzarato 2012: 104).

[21] The 'Third Way' approach is associated with UK Prime Minister, Tony Blair, US President, Bill Clinton, and German Chancellor, and Gerhard Fritz Kurt Schroeder.

(Lesay 2012: 185–190). The terms 'embedded liberalism,' 're-embedded liberalism,' 'third way,' 'new Keynesianism' and 'post-Washington consensus' may be regarded as synonyms as they all play notes in a strain not very different from another collection of synonyms—neoliberalism, free market, and Washington Consensus.

The humanizing of neoliberalism is aimed at recovering the legitimacy of the free market economy, it is not directed at regaining the nation-state's omnipotent sovereignty. Contrary to this *march of history* the political discourse in the nation-states regards sovereignty as an inviolable feature. R2P advocates reassure that recognition of sovereignty as responsibility, strengthens the principle of sovereignty since external military intervention is only the very last resort and is undertaken only under exceptional circumstances. Most countries of the Global South view the threat to sovereignty emerging mainly from great power military intervention, in the process non-military sites like monetary and finance are viewed from the point of view of domestic economic stability and not as a compromise on principles of sovereignty. States, today, are active participants along with global forces to 'partially' disassemble their respective national structures (Saskia Sassen in Abrahamsen and Williams 2009: 5).[22] Therefore, R2P's pillars one and two find endorsement in the General Assembly even though they merely re-state principles of good governance which as discussed above is an accompaniment of neoliberal economic policies that create neoliberal subjectivities of states and their populations. These paradoxes help us understand that while states of the Global South continue to be suspicious of R2P as humanitarian intervention in disguise, the philosophical roots[23] of R2P are traced to Africa i.e., the

[22] '"We generally use terms such as deregulation, financial and trade liberalization, and privatization to describe the changed authority of the state when it comes to the economy. The problem with such terms is that they only capture the withdrawal of the state from regulating its economy. They neither register all the ways in which the state participates in setting up the new frameworks through which globalization is furthered, nor do they capture the associated transformations inside the state…"' (Sassia Sasken in Abrahamsen and Williams 2009: 5).

[23] Edward Luck points out two distinct intellectual traditions from which R2P originates: 'The humanitarian intervention track, associated with Bernard Kouchner's advocacy of the right to interfere (intervene) in the 1980s, led to a series of speeches by Secretary-General Kofi Annan and in the late 1990s, culminating in his well-crafted but ill-fated speech to the GA in Sept 1999. On a less heralded track, Francis Deng and others developed the notion of sovereignty as responsibility in the mid-1990s. It was embraced first by ECOWAS and then the AU in Article 4(h) of its 2002 Constitutive Act.' The OAU's

Sudanese Diplomat, Francis Deng's conceptualization of sovereignty as responsibility and the African Union's (AU) Constitutive Act's adoption of the principle of non-indifference replacing the Organization of African Union's Charter's principle of non-intervention.[24]

Regional organizations along with civil society organizations are important actors in the neoliberal regime as the state's functions are trimmed because of the logic of free market principles that want minimal interference by the state in the economy. There is another reason why the non-state entities are more important in some parts of the Global South. As discussed earlier in the chapter, donor agencies tend to bypass most states in the Global South and reach directly to civil society organizations as the states are deemed as *failed/failing/fragile* and corrupt and lacking administrative capacity. Keeping this faith in the virtue of civil society organizations are the Secretary-General's[25] assertions of their role in operationalizing R2P's pillars one and two.

To summarize the arguments of this section: The post-Second World War order was marked by a philosophy of expansive political and economic responsibilities whereby development had connotations other than economic growth and capital accumulation. The UN, World Bank, and the IMF's assumption of these responsibilities were described as embedded liberalism (Ruggie 1982) while at the domestic level the welfare state model pledged a similar promise. In this context issues of social benefits (such as health and education), human well-being, and equality were on the political agenda as a matter of rights. On the other hand, the neoliberal state—with a shrunken social expenditure—doles out *reduced* social benefits not as rights but as social policy of a benevolent state (or leader). This 'benevolent' trope is more evident since the second decade of the millennium that has seen the rise of authoritarian populism across the world. Such humanitarianism doesn't bode well for those hoping that the march of history is towards a democratic and egalitarian

'credo of non-interference was replaced by the AU's emphasis on non-indifference. All of this...preceded the coining of the phrase "responsibility to protect" by the farsighted' ICISS (2012: 40).

[24] Article 4(h) of the AU Constitutive Act states 'the right of the Union to intervene in a member State pursuant to a decision of the Assembly in respect of grave circumstances, namely: war crimes, genocide and crimes against humanity.'

[25] See Secretary-General's annual reports on R2P.

horizon. Though the era of neoliberalism began by truncating the responsibilities of the international organizations and the states, economic and political crisis (e.g., debt, intrastate wars, and mass killings as in Bosnia, Srebrenica, and Rwanda) forced these entities to (re)pick up the discarded responsibilities (although, in smaller measures). At the international level, this assumption of responsibilities took the form of measures such as human security, protection of civilians, Peacebuilding Commission, and R2P. At the domestic level the discarded responsibilities were resumed partly by states but mainly by civil society organizations. Sophie Harman and David Williams in their study of international development detect a 'shift in thinking' amongst the development actors (donor and recipient countries, international organizations like the World Bank) that questions 'the utility of market-based policy prescriptions and re-emphasizes the role of the state in the development process' (2014: 926). Understanding the complexity of the neoliberal economy requires taking into account its constant improvisations, since neoliberalism is 'as much a journey of mistakes and unintended consequences as one of intentional domination over the developing world' (Beardsworth 2011: 159). Liberal governmentality is always a work in progress, constantly evolving and adapting (Foucault 2008). It is this ability to improvise in response to challenges that even in its moment of crisis of legitimacy liberalism springs up in a new avatar. Avatars[26] are not exact replicas and therefore may *appear* different but they embody the same spirit. Re-embedded liberalism is not simply a return to embedded liberalism. The liberal *mentality* is now improvising on neoliberal policies so that it can incorporate what Brian Burgoon terms as the 'causal harmony between' the two components of embedded liberalism—'economic openness and social protection' (2013: 5).

The argument regarding the role of international institutions in creating a humanitarian crisis including that of atrocity crimes in 'fragile' and 'failing' states is also the concern of Robin Dunford and Michael Neu (2019). While Dunford and Neu do point out how socio-economic problems such as hunger, poverty, underdevelopment, and unemployment stoke ethnic tensions—leading to an atrocity crime—they put an accent on the third R2P pillar. In this regard they are echoing the popular perception of R2P as being primarily about military intervention. This

[26] In Hindu epics the avatar of a God assumes different forms (without any facial likeness) to right the wrongs of the corresponding ages.

book notes the perception and argues that prevention can be a game changer for R2P on the ground and can be the discursive shift.

R2P Enterprise as Reinventing the Wheel

The analysis of R2P so far has shown that even though it has been projected as a new way of thinking about an old problem (i.e., of humanitarian intervention), advocates of R2P emphasize its embeddedness in the UN Charter and the existing international law:

> The RtoP is an important innovation not a radical departure. It is based on the existing body of law, not on novel theories. To the extent possible, the Secretary-General's implementation strategy seeks to use the existing tools, procedures and institutions, rather than invent new ones. By combining established elements in fresh combinations, the whole has the potential to be much more than the sum of its parts. (Luck 2012: 39)

R2P is seen as: a catalyst for the other UN agencies to do their job (Anonymous OSAPG Officer 3 Interview 2012), an indicator of the poor or non-implementation of the existing duties in this field (Hoffmann and Nollkaemper 2012b: 359), 'a facilitating norm for harnessing political will and buttressing the legitimacy and credibility of contemporary peace operations' (Hunt and Bellamy 2010: 5). For Simon Adams R2P's relevance lies in being a corpus or framework that includes conceptualization of sovereignty as responsibility, global responsibility to protect populations from mass atrocity, and the three pillars: 'If R2P is about prevention, it is about development, peacekeeping, rule of law, tolerant and stable societies. This requires a whole and not part-system wide approach' (Interview August 2013). The template of R2P thus lays claim to the entire UN security/development dispositif. But if R2P is omnipresent in the UN does it not make redundant or superfluous the office of the SAR2P? Francis Deng admits that although R2P has not added anything new in the UN's tools to respond to conflict and crisis, it has sharpened 'our consciousness of the problem' whereby mobilization of the relevant tools and actors can be undertaken (2010: 86).

R2P's claim to the generic goals and tools of the UN security/development dispositif do not go uncontested. For example, the General Assembly noted that the notion of human security is distinct from the responsibility to protect and its implementation (A/RES/66/290/

2012/para3d). The irony is that the General Assembly's endorsement of R2P emphasizes the prevention and capacity building goals of pillars one and two that echo the human security agenda. It is the foregrounding of these two pillars and the relative recession of the third pillar that speeded up the incorporation of R2P at the General Assembly. The General Assembly endorsed R2P—with an encaged pillar 3—then becomes just another version of human security; on one hand the General Assembly views R2P and human security as distinct and yet on the other hand reimagines R2P as a version of human security by downplaying pillar three. The General Assembly can be flawed for the contradictions in its avowals or it can be pardoned for being tempted by the protection mandate of R2P. Perhaps the observation of a UN official would help understand the General Assembly's dilemma: 'Having pointed out what is wrong with R2P, I must admit that it has some good points…As you can see, I am quite schizophrenic about the concept' (Anonymous UNDPKO Official Interview August 2013). This predicament informed the views of several other UN officials and academics interviewed who acknowledged their frequent dilemma in classifying R2P either as the virtuous elixir or as the forbidden fruit.

This difficulty can be understood by noting that the UN Charter aspired to be a panacea for social, political, and economic ills that plagued the world (see the UN Charter's Preamble). Its conceptualization of security (as collective security) aims to not just maintain international peace and security but also to realize the normative promise of human rights, dignity of human beings, 'equal rights of men and women,' 'social progress and better standards of life in larger freedom.'[27] The Charter recognizes the relationship between security and development and its promise is premised on expansive notions of security and development.[28] The Human Security Unit (HSU)—tasked with mainstreaming human security in UN activities—was a fulfilment of this foundational commitment of the Charter (HSU 2014: 7). The interlude (1945–2004) particularly the 1980s saw the UN-sponsored international commissions

[27] See Preamble of the UN Charter.

[28] More recently, the Security Council, has used its powers to identify not just military but also non-military issues as threats to international peace and security, examples- HIV/AIDS (S/Res1308 (2000), root causes of armed conflict and political and social crisis (S/Res/1625 (2005), climate change (Security Council debate April 17, 2007), and Ebola virus (Resolution S/Res/2177 (2014).

make articulations of security and development on similar lines. These *new* articulations have not led to the erasure of collective security, they push for reform not the dismantlement of collective security's operator, the Security Council. This is because the concept of collective security in the UN Charter's chapter VII appears as a mechanism, an instrument aimed at confronting military aggression that threatens international peace and security. The expansive or broad articulations of security since the decade of the 1980s are a push for an interventionary UN role in the case of non-military threats. To overcome the limitation of great power politics and agenda that tends to determine Security Council decisions, the Commissions proposed the reform of Security Council and the, creation of an Economic and Social Security Council at par with the Security Council. The debate is about the form and structure of collective security and not about the content of security. However, it is not to deny that the advocates of broad notions of security do seek to bring about some changes in the structure and instruments of collective security to make its decision-making more democratic and reflective of the reality of a post decolonized international order.[29] There is no principled opposition or fundamental incompatibility between collective security and human security at the UN. R2P's pillar three relies on the mechanism of collective security to realize a *sub-category* of human security the goal of freedom from fear, that is, of protecting populations from the four atrocity crimes. R2P's pillars one and two aim to achieve the broad human security agenda so as to prevent atrocity crimes.

The above discussion shows that the fundamental or core ideas of R2P reflect the security/development mandate of the UN Charter. The blue ribbon international commissions are similarly placed vis-à-vis the Charter. Some themes are common to the commissions and UN reports post 1980s: (a) the issue of questioning the notion of absolute sovereignty; (b) the relative devaluing of the state and the promotion of civil society actors as more reliable agents of good governance in the domains of politics, security, and development.

The institutional manifestations[30] of R2P at the UN and its emerging legal, normative, and ideational dimensions show that R2P has been incorporated into the UN, and different departments (elements of the

[29] For example, Security Council reforms.

[30] See this chapter.

dispositif) adopt different aspects of R2P and interpret R2P in accordance with their respective agenda or mandate. This at first glance could lead to the conclusion that various versions of R2P exist within the UN itself. However, on closer scrutiny R2P comes across as a package deal whereby the so-called versions appear only as disputants in regards to its *pillar accent* (i.e., the question about which amongst the three pillars must be emphasized). This insight allows us to appreciate the various facets of R2P as well as the mutations they undergo, thereby locating R2P beyond the confines of its small office (OSAPG) in other parts of the UN and outside the UN. The INGOs—ICR2P, GCR2P, and the APR2P have played a crucial role in R2P's incorporation at the UN and its growing awareness outside the UN.

The R2P advocacy discourse is so constructed that it retains enough fluidity to not be a conversation stopper. This characteristic of flexibility in R2P as a concept allows its advocates to negotiate its meaning(s) and agenda in the context of new questions and challenges; some of its former detractors like the UN Department of Political Affairs are its current supporters. This apparent[31] malleability of R2P has allowed different meanings to be imputed to it. The preventive aspects promoted by the Secretary-General's annual reports made possible its acceptance by the GA. Pillar three is where the Security Council has a near exclusive hold of the R2P agenda but since it wants to retain the freedom or option to take or not take military action, it finds it useful to also endorse R2P's prevention aspects (of pillars one and two and non-military actions under pillar three).

The legal, ideational and normative dimensions of R2P reveal that in addition to the specificities like 'sovereignty as responsibility,' R2P also lays claim to generalities of the security/development dispositif including the idea of protection and the accompanying notion of responsibility. The dominant themes of the liberal/neoliberal security/development dispositif are the responsibility and protection mandates. R2P is in sync with this protection mandate and this is what gives it a *staying power*. Critics of R2P who term it as an imperial design put a mistaken weight behind the *intentions* of the ICISS. The ICISS report was candid in its admission that it was seized with the problem of humanitarian intervention and it had found a solution by reinventing it as a responsibility—a

[31] I use the word, apparent, deliberately as I am arguing that R2P is a package deal and this is what gives it the strength to withstand conceptual challenges.

duty, an obligation, and not as a right. The extant literature mostly overlooks the fact that the ICISS bowed down to the logic of the security/development dispositif as it was compelled to include the responsibilities of prevention and rebuilding in addition to that of reaction. The additional responsibilities, if we go by the intention argument, may have been a tactical window dressing. However, this has been the selling point and most actively endorsed and legitimizing aspect of R2P. Responsibilities of prevention and rebuilding (ICISS) and pillars one and two (Secretary-General reports) have been criticized on count of being ill conceived or too vague and broad to be implemented. Supporters like Gareth Evans, Thomas Weiss, Alex Bellamy, Madeline K. Albright, and Richard S. Williamson consider the third pillar's feature—military intervention—to be most important, and advocate its robust application in atrocity crime situations. These criticisms have not led to the erasure of these responsibilities. R2P, thus, despite criticism and attempted dilution of the concept continues to be a package deal. This embeddedness of R2P in the themes of the existing security/development dispositif enables the incorporation of R2P in the UN even by those actors in the UN who do not like the package, but are compelled to do so by the structural logic of the liberal/neoliberal security/development dispositif.

R2P: A Discursive Shift?

Having analyzed how R2P is a discursive rearticulation, this section reviews the arguments and aspects of R2P that are put forth as evidence of R2P breaking the earlier mould of security(/development) measures. After discussing these and giving reasons as to why these *changes* do not qualify as discursive shift, suggestions are made as to how R2P can be a discursive shift.

Since a discursive field is constituted by relationships between language, institutions, subjectivity, and power, discursive rearticulation can be understood as taking place *within* the existing dispositif, while a discursive shift indicates a *moving out* of it. Discursive shift is bound to have elements of continuity, whereby the rearrangement of the old elements is not cosmetic but indicates a change in the 'order of things'—for example, old entities could be differently related to each other even as they get connected to new ones, that is, their raison d'etre could change wherein they perform new roles with different mandates. From a Foucauldian lens R2P as a discursive shift would require fundamental changes that ultimately result in its liberation *from* the governmentality of the existing liberal/neoliberal security/development dispositif. The *official* discourse of R2P highlights its embeddedness in the *existing* regime of international law (including the UN Charter). Also, R2P's ideational/normative and institutional/operational incorporation into the UN conforms to the *existing* practices of the liberal/neoliberal security/development dispositif. As of now R2P is only rearticulating the rationality of the existing security/development dispositif.

Ideationally/normatively within the circumscribed field of humanitarian intervention—that until recently was hostage to Cold War dynamics of unilateral military action—R2P can be credited with offering an alternative and compelling narrative of the moral imperative to save people. R2P's three pillars strategy employs a 'wider spectrum of responses' and veers the decision-making regarding the action to a multilateral forum i.e., the UNSC (Ramsbotham et al. 2011: 327; also see Thakur 2015). As evident from the above discussion this does not qualify as discursive shift because R2P does not propose or employ any *new* instrument; it only seeks to reactivate the existing panoply of instruments of collective security available under the UN Charter's Chapter VI and VII.

R2P in the ICISS version may be commended for endorsing Francis Deng's envisioning of 'sovereignty as responsibility' (see Deng et al. 1996). The concept of 'sovereignty as responsibility' entails a sovereign state's submission to normative and legal constraints—on the commission of atrocity crimes in its domestic jurisdiction—imposed by an external (if not higher) authority i.e., the international community of states. Since sovereignty has never been absolute, Deng's synonymizing of sovereignty with responsibility—as the above discussion indicates—is not by itself radical as it is the duty of the sovereign to protect. But the conceptual breakthrough in Deng's move is the assertion of the duty as opposed to the right and power of the sovereign. *This* duty was not merely unfulfilled by the concerned state but this neglect was also selectively ignored by the international community whose recall and amnesia regarding the same were often hostage to the game of realpolitik—best exemplified by the UNSC's veto power. This reassertion of the responsibility aspect of sovereignty—one of the founding principles of international law—is a discursive shift if fate of the potential victims would not be captive to great power politics.

Institutionally and operationally, the principle of 'sovereignty as responsibility' could be tested primarily in the context of responsibility to react i.e. pillar 3.[32] To qualify as a discursive shift, this pillar of 'timely and decisive action' would have to be on autopilot so that those who intend to commit atrocity crime are stopped at the threshold. This was the ICISS attempt or goal as proposed in the report's Chapter 4, 'The Responsibility to React'—how to ensure humanitarian military intervention, how to actualize the 'never again' refrain of the international community post the genocides in Rwanda and Srebrenica (A/63/677/2009/para5). From the ICISS's perspective R2P would be a discursive shift if the international community's[33] *reaction* (including military) were to be certain and immediate; this would also assure R2P's effectiveness as a deterrent. Ironically R2P itself is being deterred not just by *realpolitik* but also by the principle of sovereignty—the very principle it was expecting to revamp.

R2P could be a discursive shift if pillars 1 and 2 prevent the very commission of atrocity crimes. R2P's pillars 1 and 2 seek to reactivate the ICISS Report's responsibilities to prevent (and rebuild).[34] These two pillars are important as their premise dictates that R2P is not merely geared for action to stop atrocity crimes in the future but must be in constant operation so that even the initial stages of occurrence of such crimes are prevented.[35] An effective art of governance, would then involve the quotidian employment of the techniques of prevention. Prevention can manifest in various ways:

[32] This is not to deny that intervention takes place not just under pillar 3, but also occurs under the other two pillars in military and non-military forms.

[33] Though like during the Cold War, unilateral military action continues, e.g., the French intensifying their military attack on the ISIS in Syria following the Paris attacks in November 2015.

[34] The 2013 Secretary-General's Annual Report on R2P underlines R2P's preventive action to address structural and operational factors that would build state capacity to prevent atrocity crimes (A/67/929-S/2013/399/para31), build national resilience (A/67/929-S/2013/399/para35); establish transitional justice mechanisms (A/67/929-S/2013/399/para42); implementation of security sector reform (A/67/929-S/2013/399/para44). While promotion of economic equality receives mention in paragraphs (A/67/929-S/2013/399/paras45-46), the structural issue gets diluted as corruption and favouritism are pointed out as the major problems. This puts the emphasis back on the need for political institutions reforms i.e. statebuilding.

[35] See the agendaof pillars 1 (A/67/929-S/2013/399) and 2 (A/68/947-S/2014/449).

a. A permanent coercive machinery/police/military force[36] that deters violent perpetrators (of atrocity crimes). At the domestic level this role of the protector is performed by the state that could also seek assistance in capacity building from other sovereign states, regional organizations, and the international community (see A/67/929-S/2013/399; A/69/981-S/2015/500). But if the state itself is a perpetrator and not merely a weak incapacitated failing/failed state then the international community's promise of military force must be credible enough to act as a deterrent. From the perspective of governmentality and biopolitics what is significant in this scenario is the prevalence of conflict and the division of population into enemy camps, and the task of R2P is to constrain or keep in check the genocidal tendencies;
b. Prevention could mean forestalling the division of the population into enemy camps which would require addressing the root causes of the enmity. The identification of enemies on the basis of religion, caste, race, ethnicity, nation etc., is not merely a psychological or cultural assertion of identity but an exercise in power relations to access or restrict claims to political and economic resources. The concept of biopolitics uncovers modern racism as the bid by those in power to deal with the problem of surplus population created by the free market (Foucault 2008; also see Duffield 2007). Addressing root causes would require equitable distribution of resources so that grievances do not remain. Recommendations of this nature were made in the ICISS Report (2001: 3.22) and the subsequent annual Secretary-General's reports (A/68/947-S/2014/449).[37] *If* an equitable distribution of resources at the global and local levels were to take place, a conceptual wrinkle still remains un-ironed in this hypothetical solution: what is the guarantee that some will not try to avert this situation of equality on grounds of justice (and liberty). This is the classic problem of liberty upsetting patterned

[36] Therefore, the significance of security sector reforms (see A/67/929-S/2013/399/para44; ICISS 2001: 3.24).

[37] There is a need to address 'horizontal inequality in society, which frequently results from the systematic exclusion of particular groups from civil, political, economic, social and cultural rights' (A/68/947-S/2014/449para41).

principles of justice (Nozick 1999: 160–164).[38] In the context of R2P this problem (i.e., the possibility that the act of distributive justice—a prevention measure to address economic inequality, the structural root cause of atrocity crime—would be undone in the name of liberty; the premise here is that the yearning for liberty is paramount amongst people and they are bound to feel stifled by acts of distributive justice). This problem can be possibly dealt in two ways:

(i) By establishing a smart coercive apparatus (panoptican) that is vigilant and acts as an effective deterrent for any attempt to overturn the act of distribution of economic resources. This would include the range of measures under the third pillar including early warning mechanisms. However, such an apparatus would lack legitimacy because of its compromise or attack on liberty. Also, the subtext of the adoption of the panoptican as a solution is an implicit admission that the *will to genocide* amongst the population cannot be exterminated, it can only be kept in check through effective surveillance and credible threats of punishment; genocidal tendencies remain, albeit below the surface. From this perspective, the panoptican is a crucial element in the solution to the problem of atrocity crime, but it comes with a high cost i.e., the death of liberty; or.

(ii) Have a diluted version of equal distribution of resources that accommodates the principle of liberty so that the distribution is not challenged as unjust. This could be achieved through operationalizing the distribution on the basis of John Rawls' (1999) 'difference principle' whereby inequalities benefit the least advantaged and they have no stake in changing the national/international unequal order. Versions of this principle already exist—as the welfare state at the domestic level and

[38] Robert Nozick argues that the 'entitlement conception of justice' cannot be successfully rivalled by 'alternative conceptions of distributive justice.' This is so because a desired distribution (which he calls D1) in accordance with any of the latter conceptions is likely to be overturned by the play of free will of individuals. Individuals for reasons such as pleasure or services may voluntarily transfer their respective share of property to another. This act of transfer(s) consequently creates a new distribution of resources in society (which he labels D2) that is clearly an unequal allocation of resources. The only way D2 can be prevented is if individuals' liberty is interfered with and they are forbidden from exercising their free will regarding their resources (private property) (1999: 160–162).

embedded liberalism/re-embedded liberalism at the international level. Aid and development assistance to the developing world is an example of the same. Since these measures are part of the UN's security/development the Rawlsian solution too is not a discursive shift. Also, such economic measures do not always[39] yield the desired end of violence aversion, necessitating the reliance on the coercive element as a preventive mechanism—either as a deterrent or as a punisher that may put the atrocity crime perpetrator away to death or seek to rehabilitate the perpetrator. The International Criminal Court and the UN-assisted tribunals are essential R2P tools for the purpose of punishment (A/63/677/2009/para18). The perpetrator's rehabilitation (particularly in the case of child soldiers), an example of responsibility to rebuild, involves measures like demobilization, education, truth commissions, and other transitional justice mechanisms (A/63/677/2009/para25 and 33; A/67/929-S/2013/399/2013/para42 and 43; A/69/981-S/2015/500/para35). Thus, currently prevention under pillars 1 and 2 becomes a matter of avoidance or minimizing of killings and does not focus on the root causes.

This discursive rearticulation is so persistent because of a key trait of liberal/neoliberal governmentality. Liberal/neoliberal governmentality's ability to improvise ensures that it appropriates the language of its own criticism. The quality of this self-critique is such that its core principle (i.e., market as a site of truth veridiction) is retained even as it conceptually expands to address new tasks (e.g., poverty, distribution of resources) pointed out by critics. An equitable distribution of resources is a goal contradictory to the principles of the free market—that has been declared, albeit under the pseudonym of liberal democracy, as the untrammelled victor post the 'fall of communism' (Fukuyama 1992). Issues of equity in this context take the 'trickle down' route whereby a weak degree of nominal equality is achieved with the promise of greater equality in the

[39] The experience of welfare state policies has not been homogeneous across countries; historical context, institutional structures, and political culture play an important role in determining the success of these policies. For example, Francine Frankel (1978) credits the success of the odd antipoverty programme of India's mixed economy for *postponing* a violent revolution.

distant future. Reaching that destination is made the primary responsibility of the concerned sovereign state, while the international community is seen as having fulfilled its bit of responsibility by directing the former to the path of good governance—the putative route that had been taken by the developed states of the North *yesterday*.

Reforming R2P is possible and laudable and probably the only pragmatic possibility to save if not the entire, at least some of the population from atrocity crimes. Efforts on these lines are being made by the UN (e.g., Secretary-General annual reports on R2P) and the UN's civil society accompaniments (e.g., APR2P's Policy Briefs on R2P[40] and Research Programs[41]). However, they all remain susceptible to charges of being mechanisms of liberal/neoliberal governmentality and biopolitics. Foucault himself said that he had not yet seen a viable alternative practice to liberal governmentality (2008: 92), therefore, to perfect R2P is to admit to the continuity of circumstances that necessitate governmentality measures like R2P.

Two observations serve to clarify the meaning and context of discursive rearticulation. *First* the contention that R2P is a discursive rearticulation should be read as a description of the R2P *condition*. This description, *in itself*, is not a criticism of R2P. That is, it does not automatically follow from this description that (a) R2P *should or should not* be a discursive rearticulation; or (b) R2P *should or should not* be a discursive shift. *Second* the characteristic of discursive rearticulation does not in itself suffice as a reason for success or failure of R2P. This book aims to understand the phenomenon of R2P and its finding is that R2P's incorporation since 2001 has been such that it has conformed to the principles and agenda of the UN's liberal/neoliberal security/development dispositif. How should one read the fact that despite R2P there is the continuation of violence and atrocity crimes—e.g., the agenda of organizations such as the ISIS, Boko Haram, Syrian crisis, and the Russian attack on Ukraine? One reading could be that R2P's prevention responsibilities (pillars 1 and 2) have not been fulfilled and there is also a similar retraction from the promise of the responsibility to rebuild (pillars 1 and 2) e.g., Libya,[42]

[40] See http://www.r2pasiapacific.org/r2p-ideas-in-brief.

[41] See http://www.r2pasiapacific.org/research-programs.

[42] The March 2011 UNSC authorized military intervention in Libya is an example of the Western powers 'fight from flight' (only aerial strikes and 'no boots on the ground') followed by 'flight' (i.e., exit) from responsibility to rebuild the Libyan conflict zone.

therefore pillars 1 and 2 must be operationalized more efficiently and robustly. A second reading, a biopolitical one, could be that the task of prevention (in this dispositif) is not to create order but to manage disorder (Agamben 2001) given the fact that civil wars—a background for most atrocity crimes—have been on the rise since 1945 (Fearon 2004: 275). It could be argued that R2P is a success, not just on counterfactual basis,[43] but because it fulfils its dispositif's security/development agenda.

This positing of R2P as a discursive shift is not aimed at mere efficient management of disorder, the purpose is to end atrocity crimes. In this task there is an implicit recognition of the inevitability of the occurrence of atrocity crimes, the issue is only of the number of victims and the duration of the crime, and importantly the geographical circumscription of the crime. This venture to propose what a R2P discursive shift would look like must be preceded by two qualifications. *First*, Foucauldian framework aims at a critique that *follows* description, Foucault did not set up the analysis to make policy recommendations. Critique can alert the policymakers to the problematique of R2P, but it does not easily translate into a policy blueprint. Theoretically a discursive shift could move in any direction—e.g., progressive or regressive. *Second*, the question of R2P's discursive shift is different from those such as: Is R2P a success? How can R2P be an effective strategy to end atrocity crimes? To say that R2P is a discursive rearticulation is not to mean that it has failed, or is much ado about nothing. The R2P discourse has certainly been a useful peg for drawing attention to atrocity crimes, and the perils of the international community's action and inaction (Libya and Syria respectively).[44]

My visualization of R2P as a discursive shift is made with the acknowledgement that there are possibly other forms that a discursive shift could take. My philosophical bias would conceptualize that change as not a *more*

[43] Pillars one and two's prevention agenda is a slippery terrain to as it easily lends itself to counterfactual claims. It can be argued that potential commission of atrocity crimes in various parts have been averted because of R2P's preventive measures of diplomacy, negotiations as in Kenyan elections, advocacy, and training. Two interviewees (one each from ICR2P and GCR2P) contended that R2P is a success as its discourse has further stigmatized atrocity crimes and deterred potential perpetrators. The package of three pillars leads to an 'elastic' interpretation of R2P that allows its advocates to arbitrarily 'associate it with successes and dissociate it from failures' (Pingeot and Obenland 2014: 33).

[44] In Libya, there was both action and inaction, that is, the inaction (on the responsibility to rebuild) following the military action (responsibility to react).

(as in relative terms) egalitarian and just international order but as an egalitarian and just international order that would make R2P redundant or, to borrow Friedrich Engels phrase, make it just 'wither away.' The direction of my proposed discursive shift requires further strengthening and robust application of pillars 1 and 2.

That is, the first two pillars must *walk the talk* and the content of the talk has to change. These two pillars should cease to be window dressing for pillar three (timely and decisive response). If the measures under (pillars 1 and 2) responsibility to prevent were able to prevent the commission of crimes it would be a discursive shift. If measures under pillars 1 and 2 could rebuild post-conflict societies it would be a discursive shift. If pillars 1 and 2 could make pillar 3 redundant it would be a discursive shift. But post WSOD 2005 commission of atrocity crimes has not stopped. Notably the content of rebuilding and prevention responsibilities stands diluted from even the ICISS Report's version which put a relative accent on its recommendation of a 'fair distribution of resources' as a necessary preventive measure (2001: 3.2).

> Root cause prevention may also mean tackling *economic* deprivation and the lack of economic opportunities. This might involve development assistance and cooperation to address inequities in the distribution of resources or opportunities; promotion of economic growth and opportunity; better terms of trade and permitting greater access to external markets for developing economies; encouraging necessary economic and structural reform; and technical assistance for strengthening regulatory instruments and institutions. (ICISS 2001: 3.22)

For the states, regional/international organizations to effectively fulfil their responsibilities of prevention and rebuilding under pillars one and two changes need to move beyond the realm of state and politics to the economy at both the local and global levels. For example, if tasks of education, employment, and poverty elimination are to move beyond mere rhetoric then the issue of redistributive justice becomes important and involves thinking about how global resources can be shared in a more egalitarian way by states. The institutional/operational manifestation of this discursive shift would be the creation within the UN of an 'Economic Security Council' (CGG 1995: 341–342; UNDP 1994: 6). This Council would be as powerful as or more powerful than the Security Council and its members would not be the same as the latter's. The seats in the Economic Security Council (ESC) would have a fixed term of five years. The General Assembly could through consensus choose the Member States for the ESC seats. This Council would work towards the creation of a global economic order where social and economic rights of individuals, communities, and nation-states are respected. The focus of the context of atrocity crimes would shift from 'international humanitarian law to international economic law' so that the hitherto vulnerable states could reject the 'imposition of draconian international economic agreements (on trade, patents, finances, loans, and so on)—agreements which often have devastating effects upon the most vulnerable populations within weak states' (Lafont 2015: 7). The IMF and the World Bank have been the implementers of such policies that have transformed 'social rights into debts and beneficiaries into debtors' (Lazzarato 2012: 104). It has been suggested that the UN's Post-2015 Development Agenda must ensure that the global trade and finance must be in consonance with the ecosystem and equitable social development so as to break the 'donor-beneficiary or partners dynamic' (Pingeot and Obenland 2014: 49–50). The ESC's interventions would be of a different nature as not the market but social and economic rights (concerns and needs) of the population(s) will be the site for *truth veridiction.* ESC's policies would go beyond the cosmetic homage paid to social justice by the UN in its *UN Global Compact* and the *UN Guiding Principles on Business and Human Rights.* These documents have so far ended up endorsing a version of corporate social responsibility.

Casting R2P as such would be a discursive shift as it would bring about changes in the normative/ideational dimensions of R2P. The moral imperative in this conceptualization of the international community's responsibility to protect would privilege the removal of the very conditions that create the need for protection and create the responsibility to do so. Robust pillars 1 and 2 would make pillar three redundant in the long run. Even in the short run where pillar 3's 'timely and decisive action' may be necessary, it is R2P's promise of prevention and rebuilding that will act as a restraint: 'Without the R2P acting as a shackle the military intervention is much less accountable and tactically flexible' (Chandler 2015: 3). Thus, the radicalness of R2P lies in its guarantee for the Global North's responsibility for outcomes (see Chandler 2015). If the international community were to honour its pledge to prevent atrocity crimes, it indicates a normative discursive shift in the conceptualization of sovereignty. R2P then becomes a recognition of a new aspect of sovereignty which is that the 'international community has a "backup" responsibility to protect human rights whenever states are unwilling to do so' (Lafont 2015: 1). So implemented, R2P as discursive shift introduces a new actor as the *additional* holder of responsibility but continues to respect and expect the sovereign state to fulfil its primary responsibility of protection. In this conceptualization the military powers of the Global North cannot get away with a 'fly by night operator's' attitude. The moral expectation will be to ensure prevention (including capacity building of a weak state) and if unable to do so, then make certain the rebuilding of society, economy and polity of the state so that its sovereign capacity is revitalized.

Unless this approach is adopted R2P's three pillars will continue to be practices defined by liberal/neoliberal governmentality that create subjectivities to manage the disorder. In their current form the pillars are restricted by the good governance discourse (or liberal/neoliberal governmentality). The aim instead should be to end the subjectivization created by the neoliberal governmentality of biopolitics, a point eloquently made by Giorgio Agamben:

> Nothing is therefore more important than a revision of the concept of security as the basic principle of state politics. European and American politicians finally have to consider the catastrophic consequences of uncritical use of this figure of thought. It is not that democracies should cease to defend themselves, but the defense of democracy demands today a change of political paradigms and not a world civil war which is just the institutionalization of terror. Maybe the time has come to work towards the prevention of disorder and catastrophe, and not merely towards their control. Today, there are plans for all kinds of emergencies (ecological, medical, military), but there is no politics to prevent them. On the contrary, we can say that politics secretly works towards the production of emergencies. It is the task of democratic politics to prevent the development of conditions which lead to hatred, terror, and destruction -- and not to reduce itself to attempts to control them once they occur. (Agamben 2001: para 5)

With the serious operationalization of the first two pillars R2P would cease to be an ad hoc or knee jerk reaction to crisis. As of now R2P in *practice* or action is essentially a response to an ongoing conflict where acts of violence have reached the level of atrocity crimes. R2P as discursive rearticulation focuses 'on people once they begin to starve or kill each other. It is less concerned with what happens to these people when their land is taken away from them, their environment is destroyed, or they lose their means of subsistence' (Pingeot and Obenland 2014: 55).

Conclusion

At the moment pillars one and two are mere palliatives, an ensemble of ad hoc responses. If in the process of making these pillars strong, atrocity crimes are about to take place then 'decisive and timely action' under pillar three should be undertaken irrespective of the strategic interests of the P5. So far, the wisdom (knowledge) of even pillars one and two is hostage to the power of the liberal/neoliberal governmentality.

> The doctrine of the "responsibility to protect" (R2P) has suffused the language and institutions of international diplomacy'...R2P has become the framework through which the international community's commitment to, and involvement in, crisis and conflict is mediated and understood. (Cunliffe 2010: 35)

The UN security/development dispositif is informed by a liberal/neoliberal governmentality that employs biopolitical measures. Since liberal development concerns arise or are rooted in the free market, biopolitics aims to ensure the flourishing of a prosperous life so that *healthy* labour and consumers are possible. Those who are neither will lose claim to protection, and in addition this 'unprotected status' identifies them as the potential challengers to the prosperous (who enjoy the first right, and therefore, the *legitimate* claim to protection). Each perceives the other as a threat to its survival; thus, these battle lines—the congenital and quotidian features of liberal/neoliberal governmentality—confirm this *scenario* of politics as a pursuit of war by other means. R2P as a measure of this politics responds to and strengthens this governmentality's creation of these subjectivities. The Foucauldian lenses problematize these categories and reveal their construction in power/knowledge that has both material and discursive basis.

The journey of R2P since the 2001 ICISS Report is described variously as: 'from principle to practice' (Hoffmann and Nollkaemper 2012a), 'from words to deeds' (Ban 2008) 'from deeds to words' (Orford 2012). This travel of R2P is also one of the conceptual mutations although not in a linear sense. Depending upon the context the R2P meaning changes since it ranges from the very 'narrow' scope of military intervention to the 'broad' expectation of prevention and rebuilding. The latter requires a host of operational measures of social, economic, and political nature. R2P's conceptual development has cast it simultaneously as a specific act and as a continuous and continuing process.

> Neoliberalism 'blurs the boundaries between state and civil society'. Neoliberalism is also a rationality and a certain way of seeing things. It is more than just the dominant ideology of a particular set of agents, more than just the imposition of the power of the dominant states on the world stage, more than just a leading group's conception of the world, but is a framework, a set of practices, a way of seeing and doing things that transcends such boundaries. (Joseph 2010: 232)

R2P is not a radical break with the past, it merely gives additional weightage to the existing security/development measures. R2P has not invented any new measures nor discovered new 'causes,' cause celebre or new crimes. Then what is R2P's value? Well, it has added alacrity and urgency to the need to use the existing measures and called for a more frequent deployment of the same. R2P is a reminder and exhortation to the elements of the security/development dispositif to do their respective duties. R2P is also an attempt to fine-tune the measures, coordinate them better, shepherd them in synchronous acts so that they are not individually wasted; R2P is a guide, a technique to transact the liberal/neoliberal security/development agenda more efficiently. This is in consonance with Foucault's insight about liberal governmentality being in a perpetual mode of change and adaptation. The resilience of the system lies in its dynamism that results from its congenital trait to improvise and evolve. R2P embodies this spirit, its mandate of protection can be read as an effort to plug the loopholes in the liberal/neoliberal security/development dispositif and improve it.

Thus, efforts to transform R2P into a discursive shift are fraught with challenges and problems if not impossibilities. Clearly, R2P is a 'product' (or proposal) of the ICISS which itself is a part of the liberal/neoliberal security-development dispositif. Detectable in its very composition and mandate is the scent of continuity, however irrespective of these *intentions* the ICISS planted seeds of possibilities of the 'otherwise' by leaning in on Francis Deng's idea of 'sovereignty as responsibility' which deceptively at first glance appears to be only an admonishment to failed states of the Global South. Yet as the R2P details were fleshed out by the ICISS and subsequently, by the Secretary-General's reports, the sword of admonishment has come to cut both ways. That is along with the *failed* (or perpetrator) state the international community emerged as a defaulter from its responsibilities. R2P provides an opportunity for those who believe in addressing structural root causes to seize this moment of 'logic of unintended consequences' before it is completely appropriated by liberal/neoliberal governmentality.

References

Abdelal, Rawi, and John G. Ruggie. 2009. The Principles of Embedded Liberalism: Social Legitimacy and Global Capitalism. In *New Perspectives on Regulation*, ed. David Moss and John Cisternino. Cambridge, MA: The Tobin Project, One Mifflin Place.

Abrahamsen, Rita, and Michael C. Williams. 2009. Security Beyond the State: Global Security Assemblages in International Politics. *International Political Sociology* 3 (1): 1–17.

Adams, Simon, Director, Global Centre for Responsibility to Protect, Personal Interview, New York, USA, August 2013.

Agamben, Giorgio. 2001. Security and Terror. *Theory and Event* 5 (4). http://muse.jhu.edu.proxy.lib.sfu.ca/journals/theory_and_event/v005/5.4agamben.html.

Anderson, Mary B. 1999. *Do No Harm: How Aid Can Support Peace—Or War.* Boulder, CO: Lynne Rienner.

Arestis, Philip, and Malcolm Sawyer. 2001. *The Economics of the Third Way: Experiences from Around the World*. Northampton, MA: Edward Elgar.

Arestis, Philip, and Malcolm Sawyer. 2004. *Neo-liberal Economic Policy: Critical Essays.* Cheltonham, UK: Edward Elgar.

Balibar, Etienne. 2013. Politics of the Debt. *Postmodern Culture* 23 (3). http://muse.jhu.edu/journals/postmodern_culture/v023/23.3.balibar.html.

Ban, Ki-moon, 2008, July 15. Secretary-General Defends, Clarifies "Responsibility to Protect" at Berlin Event. https://press.un.org/en/2008/sgsm11701.doc.htm

Barnett, Michael N. 2010. *The International Humanitarian Order*. New York: Routledge.

Bartoli, Andrea, Dean, School of Diplomacy and International Relations, Seton Hall University, New Jersey, USA, Personal Interview, New Jersey, August 2013.

Basaran, Tugba. 2015. The Saved and the Drowned: Governing Indifference in the Name of Security. *Security Dialogue* 46 (3): 205–220.

Beardsworth, Richard. 2011. *Cosmopolitanism and International Relations Theory*. Cambridge: Polity Press.

Bond, Patrick. 2004. Neoliberalism in Sub-Saharan Africa: From Structural Adjustment to NEPAD. In *Neoliberalism: A Critical Reader*, ed. Alfredo Saad-Filho and Deborah Johnston. London: Pluto Press.

Bulley, Dan. 2010. The Politics of Ethical Foreign Policy: A Responsibility to Protect Whom? *European Journal of International Relations* 16 (3): 441–461.

Burgoon, Brian. 2013. Political Economy of Re-embedding Liberalism. *Inaugural Lecture 482*. Amsterdam: University of Amsterdam. www.uva.nl/binaries/content/documents/.../b/u/b...burgoon/.../asset? Accessed 16 Sept 2015.

Busumtwi-Sam, James. 2004. Development and Peacebuilding: Conceptual and Operational Deficits in International Assistance. In *Durable Peace: Challenges for Peacebuilding in Africa*, ed. Taisier M. Ali and Robert O. Mathews. Toronto: University of Toronto Press.

Busumtwi-Sam, James. 2008. Contextualizing Human Security: A 'Deprivation-Vulnerability' Approach. *Policy and Society* 27 (1): 15–28.

Carothers, Thomas. 2006. *Promoting the Rule of Law Abroad: In Search of Knowledge*. Washington, DC: Carnegie Endowment of International Peace.

Chandler, David. 2001. The Road to Military Humanitarianism: How the Human Rights NGOs Shaped a New Humanitarian Agenda. *Human Rights Quarterly* 23 (3): 678–700.

Chandler, David. 2003. Rhetoric without Responsibility: The Attraction of 'Ethical' Foreign Policy. *The British Journal of Politics and International Relations* 5 (3): 295–316.

Chandler, David, ed. 2009. *Statebuilding and Intervention: Policies, Practices and Paradigms*. New York: Routledge.

Chandler, David. 2015. The R2P Is Dead, Long Live the R2P: The Successful Separation of Military Intervention from the Responsibility to Protect. *International Peacekeeping* 22 (1): 1–5.

Charbonneau, Mathieu, and Magnus Paulsen Hansen. 2014. Debt, Neoliberalism and Crisis: Interview with Maurizio Lazzarato on the Indebted Condition. *Sociology* 48 (5): 1039–1047.

Cooper, Andrew F., and John English. 2005. International Commissions and the Mind of Global Governance. In *International Commissions and the Power of Ideas*, ed. Ramesh Thakur, Andrew F. Cooper and John English. Tokyo: United Nations University.

Cornia, Andrea Giovanni, Richard Jolly, and Frances Stewert. 1987. *Adjustment with a Human Face: Protecting the Vulnerable and Promoting Growth*. Oxford: Oxford University Press.

Cousens, Elizabeth M., Chetan Kumar, with Karin Wermester, eds. 2001. *Peacebuilding as Politics: Cultivating Peace in Fragile Societies*. Boulder, CO: Lynne Rienner.

Craig, David, and Doug Porter. 2006. *Development beyond Neoliberalism? Governance, Poverty Reduction, and Political Economy*. New York: Routledge.

Cunliffe, Philip. 2010. Introduction: Critical Perspectives on R2P. *Journal of Intervention and Peacebuilding* 4 (1): 35–37.

DCD/DAC. 2004. The Security and Development: Challenges for Aid. *Organisation for Economic Cooperation and Development, Development Assistance Committee High Level Meeting*. April 15–16 (DCD/DAC(2004)9/REV2). http://www.peacepalacelibrary.nl/ebooks/files/31785359.pdf. Accessed 24 Oct 2014.

Dallaire, Romeo. 2004. *Shake Hands with the Devil: The Failure of Humanity in Rwanda*. Toronto: Vintage Canada.

D'Amato, Anthony. 2010. There is No Norm of Intervention or Non-Intervention in International Law. *FacultyWorking Papers*. Paper 80. (pp. 1–4). Northwestern University School of Law. https://scholarlycommons.law.northwestern.edu/cgi/viewcontent.cgi?article=1079%26context=facultyworkingpapers

Demmers, Jolle, Alex E. Fernandez Jilberto, and Barbara Hogenboom, eds. 2005. *Global Governance in the Era of Global Neoliberalism: Conflict and Depoliticization in Latin America, Eastern Europe, Asia and Africa*. New York: Routledge.

Deng, Francis. 2010. JISB Interview: The Responsibility to Protect. *Journal of Prevention and Statebuilding* 4 (1): 83–89.

Deng, Francis, Sadikiel Kimaro, Terrence Lyons, Donald Rothchild, and William I. Zartman. 1996. *Sovereignty as Responsibility: Conflict Management in Africa*. Washington, DC: Brookings Institute.

Duffield, Mark. 2001. *Global Governance and the New Wars: The Merging of Security and Development*. London: Zed Books.

Duffield, Mark. 2007. *Development, Security and Unending War: Governing the World of Peoples*. Cambridge: Polity Press.

Dunford, Robin and Michael Neu. 2019. *Just War and the Responsibility to Protect: A Critique*. London: Zed Books.

Edgar, Andrew. 2005. *The Philosophy of Habermas*. Acumen Publishing.

Fearon, James D. 2004. Why Do Dome Civil Wars Last so Much Longer than Others. *Journal of Peace Research* 41 (3): 275–301.

Foucault, Michel. 2008. *The Birth of Biopolitics: Lectures at the College de France, 1978–79*. New York: Palgrave Macmillan.

Frankel, Francine. 1978. *India's Political Economy*. Princeton, NJ: Princeton University Press.

Fukuyama, Francis. 1992. *The End of History and the Last Man*. New York: Avon Books.

Gibbons, Pat, and Hans-Joachim. Heintze, eds. 2015. *The Humanitarian Challenge: 20 Years European Network on Humanitarian Action (NOHA)*. Cham: Springer International Publishing.

Global Centre for the Responsibility to Protect. 2014. *Summary of the Sixth Informal Interactive Dialogue of the UN General Assembly on the Responsibility to Protect held on 8 September 2014*. http://www.globalr2p.org/media/files/summary-of-the-r2p-dialogue-2014.pdf.

Harman, Sophie, and David Williams. 2014. International Development in Transition. *International Affairs* 90 (4): 925–941.

Harvey, David. 2004. The New Imperialism: Accumulation by Dispossession. *Socialist Register* 40: 63–87.

Harvey, David. 2006a. *Spaces of Global Capitalism: Towards a Theory of Uneven Geographical Development*. New York: Verso.

Harvey, David. 2006b. A Conversation with David Harvey. http://www.logosjournal.com/issue_5.1/harvey.htm. Accessed 16 Sept 2015.

Hoffman, Peter J., and Thomas G. Weiss. 2006. *Sword and Salve: Confronting New Wars and Humanitarian Crises*. Lanham, MD: Rowman & Littlefield.

Hoffmann, Julia, and Andre Nollkaemper. 2012a. Introduction. In *Responsibility to Protect: From Principle to Practice*, ed. Julia Hoffmann and Andre Nollkaemper. Amsterdam: Pallas Publication.

Hoffmann, Julia, and Andre Nollkaemper. 2012b. Concluding Observations. In *Responsibility to Protect: From Principle to Practice*, ed. Julia Hoffmann and Andre Nollkaemper. Amsterdam: Pallas Publication.

Hohendahl, Peter. 1994. Foreword. In Jurgen Habermas (interviewed by M. Haller), *The Past as Future*. Trans. and ed. Michael Pensky. Lincoln: University of Nebraska Press.

Human Security Unit. 2014. Strategic Plan 2014–2017. New York: United Nations. Available at http://www.un.org/humansecurity/sites/www.un.org.humansecurity/files/HSU%20Strategic%20Plan%202014-2017%20Web%20Version.pdf. Accessed 21 Sept.

Hunt, Charles T., and Alex Bellamy. 2010. *Mainstreaming the Responsibility to Protect in Peace Operations*. Working Paper No. 3. Program on the Protection of Civilians. St. Lucia. Asia-Pacific Centre for the Responsibility to Protect.

International Commission on Intervention and State Sovereignty. 2001. *The Responsibility to Protect*. Ottawa: International Development Research Centre.

Joseph, Jonathan. 2010. The Limits of Governmentality: Social Theory and the International. *European Journal of International Relations* 16 (2): 223–246.

Kohli, Atul. 1994. Centralization and Powerlessness: Indian Democracy in a Comparative Perspective. In *State Power and Social Forces: Domination and*

Transformation in the Third World, ed. Joel Samuel Migdal, Atul Kohli, and Vivienne Shue. New York: Cambridge University Press.
Krasmann, Susanne. 2012. Targeted Killing and Its Law: On a Mutually Constitutive Relationship. *Leiden Journal of International Law* 25: 665–682.
Krasner, Stephen. D. 1995. Compromising Westphalia. *International Security* 20 (3): 115–151.
Krasner, Stephen D. 2001. Abiding Sovereignty. *International Political Science Review* 22 (3): 229–251.
Krueger, Anne O. 1974. The Political Economy of the Rent-Seeking Society. *American Economic Review* 64 (3): 291–303.
Kuperman, Alan J. 2009. Rethinking the Responsibility to Protect. *Whitehead Journal of Diplomacy and International Relations* 10 (1): 33–43.
Lafont, Cristina. 2015. Sovereignty and the International Protection of Human Rights. *The Journal of Political Philosophy* 1–19.
Larner, Wendy, and William Walters 2004. Introduction: Global Governmentality. In *Global Governmentality: Governing International Spaces*, ed. Wendy Larner and William Walters. London: Routledge.
Lazzarato, Maurizio. 2012. *The Making of the Indebted Man: An Essay on the Neoliberal Condition*. Amsterdam: Semiotext(e).
Le Houerou, Fabienne. 2014. *Humanitarian Crisis and International Relations (1959–2013)*. Oak Park, IL: Bentham Science Publishers.
Lederach, John Paul. 2003. *The Little Book of Conflict Transformation*. Intercourse, PA: Good Books.
Lederach, John Paul. 2005a. *The Moral Imagination: The Art and Soul of Peacebuilding*. New York: Oxford University Press.
Lederach, John Paul. 2005b. *Building Peace: Sustainable Reconciliation in Divided Societies*. Washington, DC: United Services Institute of Peace Press.
Lesay, Ivan. 2012. How 'Post' Is the Post-Washington Consensus? *Journal of Third World Studies* 29 (2): 183–198.
Luck, Edward. 2011. The Responsibility to Protect: The First Decade. *Global Responsibility to Protect* 3 (4): 387–399.
Luck, Edward. 2012. The Responsibility to Protect: The Journey. In *Responsibility to Protect: From Principle to Practice*, ed. Julia Hoffmann and Andre Nollkaemper. Amsterdam: Pallas Publication.
Macrae, Joanna. 2002. Analysis and Synthesis. In *HPG Report: The New Humanitarianisms: A Review of Trends in Global Humanitarian Action*, ed. Joanna Macrae. London: Humanitarian Policy Group.
Mamdani, Mahmood. 2010. Responsibility to Protect or Right to Punish. *Journal of Intervention and Peacebuilding* 4 (1): 53–67.
Mazur, Jay. 2000. Labor's New Internationalism. *Foreign Affairs* 79 (1): 79–93.
McCormack, Tara. 2010a. The Responsibility to Protect and the End of the Western Century. *Journal of Intervention and Peacebuilding* 4 (1): 69–82.

McCormack, Tara. 2010b. *Critique, Security and Power: The Political Limits to Emancipatory Approaches*. New York: Routledge.

Munck, Ronaldo. 2013. The Precariat: A View from the South. *Third World Quarterly* 34 (5): 747–762.

Murithi, Tim. 2009. The African Union's Transition from Non-Intervention to Non-Indifference: An Ad Hoc Approach to the Responsibility to Protect? 90–106. http://library.fes.de/pdf-files/ipg/ipg-2009-1/08_a_murithi_us.pdf. Accessed 5 July 2015.

Nozick, Robert. 1999. *Anarchy, State, and Utopia*. Oxford: Blackwell.

O'Hanlon, Michael, and Peter Warren Singer. 2004. The Humanitarian Transformation: Expanding Global Intervention Capacity. *Survival* 46 (1): 77–100.

Orford, Anne. 2011. *International Authority and the Responsibility to Protect*. Cambridge: Cambridge University Press.

Orford, Anne. 2012. In Praise of Description. *Leiden Journal of International Law* 25: 609–625.

Ostry, Jonathan D., Prakash Loungani, and Davide Furceri. 2016. *Neoliberalism: Oversold*, 38–41. Finance and Development. Washington, DC: IMF.

Paris, Roland. 2004. *At War's End: Building Peace after Conflict*. Cambridge: Cambridge University Press.

Pattison, James. 2010. Outsourcing the Responsibility to Protect: Humanitarian Intervention and Private Military Security Companies. *International Theory* 2 (1): 1–31.

Pattison, James, ed. 2014. *Humanitarian Intervention*. Thousand Oaks, CA: Sage Publications.

Picketty, Thomas. 2014. *Capital in the Twenty-First Century*. Cambridge: Harvard University Press.

Pingeot, Lou, and Wolfgang Obenland. 2014. *In Whose Name?: A Critical View of the Responsibility to Protect*. Bonn: Global Policy Forum.

Powers, Samantha. 2002. *A Problem from Hell: America and the Age of Genocide*. New York: Basic Books.

Ramsbotham, Oliver, Tom Woodhouse, and Hugh Miall. 2011. *Contemporary Conflict Resolution: The Prevention, Management and Transformation of Deadly Conflicts*. Cambridge, UK: Polity.

Rawls, John. 1999. *A Theory of Justice*. Cambridge, MA: Belknap Press of Harvard University Press.

Rosén, Frederik Ferdinand. 2011. No Words will Deliver Anything: Coaching and Mentoring as Neoliberal Governance Strategy in the Afghan State Administration. *Journal of Intervention and Statebuilding* 5 (2): 151–173.

Ruggie, John G. 1982. International Regimes, Transactions, and Change: Embedded Liberalism in the Postwar Economic Order. *International Organization* 36 (2): 379–415.

Saad-Filho, Alfredo. 2004. The Political Economy of Neoliberalism in Latin America. In *Neoliberalism: A Critical Reader*, ed. Alfredo Saad-Filho and Deborah Johnston. London: Pluto Press.

Saad-Filho, Alfredo, and Deborah Johnston, eds. 2004. *Neoliberalism: A Critical Reader*. London: Pluto Press.

Scott, Watson. 2011. The 'Human' as Referent Object?: Humanitarianism as Securitization. *Security Dialogue* 42 (1): 3–20.

Singer, Peter W. 2003. Peacekeepers, Inc. http://www.brookings.edu/research/articles/2003/06/usmilitary-singer.

Standing, Guy. 2011. *The Precariat: The New Dangerous Class*. London: Bloomsbury Academic.

Stern, Maria, and Joakim Ojendal. 2010. Mapping the Security–Development Nexus: Conflict, Complexity, Cacophony, Convergence? *Security Dialogue* 41 (1): 5–30.

Stiglitz, Joseph. 2002. *Globalization and Its Discontents*. New York: W. W. Norton.

Suhrke, Astri, and Julia Buckmaster. 2006. Aid, Growth and Peace: A Comparative Analysis. *Conflict, Security & Development* 6 (3): 337–363.

Thakur, Ramesh. 2013. R2P after Libya and Syria: Engaging Emerging Powers. *The Washington Quarterly* 36 (2): 61–76.

Thakur, Ramesh. 2015. The Development and Evolution of R2P as International Policy. *Global Policy* 6 (3): 190–200. https://doi.org/10.1111/1758-5899.12258.

The Commission on Global Governance. 1995. *Our Global Neighbourhood*. Oxford: Oxford University Press.

United Nations Development Program. 1994. *Human Development Report–1994*. New York: Oxford University Press.

United Nations General Assembly. 2005. *The Peacebuilding Commission*. UN Doc. A/RES/60/2005. 20 December 2005.

United Nations General Assembly. 2012. *Follow-up to Paragraph 143 on Security of the 2005 World Summit Outcome*. UN Doc. A/RES/66/290. 25 October 2012.

United Nations Office on Genocide Prevention and the Responsibility to Protect. 2014. *Framework of Analysis for Atrocity Crimes: A Tool for Prevention*. New York.

United Nations Secretary-General. 1992. *An Agenda for Peace: Preventive Diplomacy, Peacemaking and Peace-keeping*. Report of the Secretary-General. UN Doc. A/47/277—S/241111, 17 June 1992. New York: Department of Public Information, United Nations. http://www.un.org/documents/ga/res/47/a47r120.htm.

United Nations Secretary-General. 2009. *Implementing the Responsibility to Protect*. Report of the Secretary-General. UN Doc. A/63/677/2009, January 12.

United Nations Secretary-General. 2012. *Responsibility to Protect: Timely and Decisive Response*. Report of the Secretary-General. UN Doc. A/66/874-S/2012/578. 25 July 2012.

United Nations Secretary-General. 2013. *Responsibility to Protect: State Responsibility and Prevention*. Report of the Secretary-General. UN Doc. A/67/929-S/2013/399. 9 July 2013.

United Nations Secretary-General. 2014. *Fulfilling Our Collective Responsibility: International Assistance and the Responsibility to Protect*. Report of the Secretary-General. UN Doc. A/68/947-S/2014/449. 11July 2014.

United Nations Secretary-General. 2015. *A Vital and Enduring Commitment: Implementing the Responsibility to Protect*. Report of the Secretary-General. UN Doc. A/69/981-S/2015/500. 13 July 2015.

United Nations Security Council. 2005. UN Doc. S/RES/1645. 20 December 2005.

Walker, R.B.J. 1993. *Inside/Outside: International Relations as Political Theory*. New York: Cambridge University Press.

Walker, R.B.J. 2002. After the Future: Enclosures, Connections, Politics. In *Reframing the International: Law, Culture, Politics*, ed. Richard A. Falk, Lester Edwin J. Ruiz, R. B. J. Walker. New York: Routledge.

Walker, R.B.J. 2010. *After the Globe, Before the World*. New York: Routledge.

Walker, R.B.J. 2015. *Out of Line: Essays on the Politics of Boundaries and the Limits of Politics*. Abingdon: Routledge.

Weiss, Thomas G. 1999. Principles, Politics and Humanitarian Action. *Ethics and International Affairs* 31 (1): 1–22.

Weiss, Thomas G. 2000. The Politics of Humanitarian Ideas. *Security Dialogue* 31 (1): 11–23.

Weiss, Thomas G. 2011. RtoP Alive and Well after Libya. *Ethics & International Affairs* 25 (3): 287–292.

Wheeler, Nicholas J. 2000. *Saving Strangers: Humanitarian Intervention in International Society*. New York: Oxford University Press.

Wiseman, Geoffrey. 2005. The Palme Commission: New Thinking about Security. In *International Commissions and the Power of Ideas*, ed. Ramesh Thakur, Andrew F. Cooper and John English. Tokyo: United Nations University.

Woods, Ngaire. 2006. *The Globalizers: The IMF, the World Bank and Their Borrowers*. Ithaca: Cornell University Press.

Woodward, Susan L. 2002. *Local Governance Approach to Social Reintegration and Economic Recovery in Post-Conflict Countries: The Political Context for Programs of UNDP/UNCDF Assistance*. Discussion paper for Institute of Public Administration Workshop 'A Local Governance Approach to Post Conflict Recovery', New York, October 8.

Yamashita, Hikaru. 2015. New Humanitarianism and Changing Logics of the Political in International Relations. *Millennium—Journal of International Studies* 43 (2): 411–428.

CHAPTER 7

R2P: The Journey So Far

Introduction

R2P's being and aspirations are in sync with a state of paradox—R2P is about noble aspirations (and at times deeds) and the guilt of mute spectatorship practices (such as genocide in Rwanda). It is about the simultaneity of the sovereign will to 'make live and to let die,' it is about 'saving strangers' and killing 'intimate enemies,'[1] it is about protection and atrocity crimes. R2P is as much a discourse and practice about abdicating responsibility as it is about taking responsibility.

R2P continues to be an emerging field twenty years after it was first officially proposed by the ICISS in 2001. Since it was adopted by the UN General Assembly in 2005, R2P has been conceptually *refined*, militarily operationalized in Libya (2011) and credited with preventing the escalation of violence, thereby saving and protecting lives in Cote d'Ivoire and Kenya (Serrano 2011: 11; Thakur 2015: 7). The academic and policy worlds' interest in the subject continues to increase (Aneja 2014; Basaran 2014; Bellamy 2014, 2021, 2022; Bellamy and Dunne 2016; Cairns 2014; Chesterman 2021; Dunne and Wheeler 2012, Falk 2015; Gallagher et al 2021; Glanville 2021; Hunt and Bellamy 2010; Illingworth 2023;

[1] I borrow this phrase from Ashis Nandy's book titled *The Intimate Enemies: Loss and Recovery of Self Under Colonialism*.

R. Kashyap, *The Political Economy of Security/Development in the Neoliberal Age*, International Political Economy Series,
https://doi.org/10.1007/978-3-031-37279-7_7

Kolmasova 2023; Glanville 2016, 2021; Thakur 2015, 2020; Weiss and Serrano 2014). Representatives of national governments, the UN, and civil society (national and international non governmental organizations, think tanks, and academia) are involved with R2P from the vantage points of their respective mandates—national interest, goals of international peace and security, moral considerations, and the humanitarian imperative. R2P advocates or more specifically R2P norm entrepreneurs, e.g., UN Secretary-Generals (Kofi Annan and Ban Ki-moon), ICISS Commissioners (Lloyd Axworthy, Gareth Evans, Thomas Weiss, and Ramesh Thakur), SAR2Ps (Edward Luck and Jennifer Welsh) seek to underline the compatibility of these different interests. The proliferating manifestations of R2P have not been without controversy and contestation, which include charges of imperial designs (Chomsky 2009) and regime change (Breakey 2012). Lest these controversies consume R2P or seal its fate, these advocates remain proactive in their defence, responding to criticisms by further improvising R2P. Individual support for R2P from the various UN quarters (i.e., different departments/offices), as shown in Chapters 5 and 6, is partial and not necessarily in full measure (i.e., inclusive of all three pillars). R2P by necessity continues to be a work in progress.

In view of this unfolding story and this book's examination of R2P's genesis and evolution, the following pages present the concluding arguments that are organized into four sections: 'The Relevance of R2P', 'Summarizing the Book,' 'Research Contribution'—outlining certain significant aspects of this study—and 'Conclusion' concludes the book with suggestions about possible directions for future research on R2P.

The Relevance of R2P

What is the relevance of R2P? A seemingly straightforward question, comfortably answered but not so easily explained, so this book. The book's raison d'etre is to explain how the *answer* came to ascribe an eternity of relevance to a concept that existed even before its official birth and christening as R2P and one that will live on even when or if it is officially declared dead: 'the R2P is dead, long live the R2P.'[2] R2P will survive under another name.

[2] The phrase is part of the title of an article by David Chandler who uses this to discuss how the R2P doctrine was used to separate 'military intervention' from 'legal and normative concerns of sovereignty and intervention' (2015: 4).

A prime contention of this book is that though R2P was hailed as a new paradigm—R2P is 'a wholly new vision of international law that is here to stay '(Hilpold 2015: 1)—it is not a discursive shift but a discursive rearticulation since it is primarily transacting the role of a collector of debris of responsibilities left behind by receding embedded liberalism. So as long as the global political economy moves on a continuum of liberalism—embedded and neoliberal liberalism, an R2P-like measure will always find relevance.

As pointed out in the earlier chapters, liberalism and neoliberalism are arts of governing (governmentality), the principles of which are derived from political economy. This political economy as knowledge identifies the market as a site of truth veridiction (a point to which we will come back in a bit). The art of governing involves certain measures of security and development that get intimately related to each other—security secures development, the imperatives of development necessitate certain kinds of security measures to secure itself, one of those imperatives being to secure it from its own consequences. Irrespective of a liberal or a neoliberal economy, the raison d'etre of security remains unchanged, that is, it has to secure development, including at times to save development from itself. While new ways and technologies of security may emerge,[3] the ostensible grounds—state, human, planet—for justification may change but they all have to be secured within the framework of liberal/neoliberal development.

There is at the UN, a repertoire of liberal/neoliberal security/development measures—some get refurbished, others may stay dormant, some get embellished from time to time, and some get look-alike(s), albeit with a different name. R2P employs several of the *pre*-existing measures—of development and security across a range of UN departments and offices.[4] R2P has not accelerated the deployment of these measures, however, R2P's significance lies in providing a new vocabulary for the justification of the operationalization of such measures. The new vocabulary is not just additional synonyms but a new conceptual argument, which questions and seeks to amend if not upend the foundational principle of the international order—sovereignty—the practice of which,

[3] While this change is relevant in itself and worthy of research, the essential purpose of security remains the same.

[4] The UNSG has urged all departments to use R2P along with the FOA (Chapter 4).

Stephen Krasner, describes as 'organized hypocrisy.' Conceptually rich, R2P can be interpreted in a manner that qualifies it for a discursive shift, this is one way to do it. UNSGs and R2P advocates, want to retain the impression of a discursive shift but are simultaneously through UNGA resolutions and UNSG's annual reports, seeking to strip off the radical nature of R2P, so that it doesn't go off the liberal/neoliberal script.

The question then is why is a new conceptual argument being used to justify old action(s)? Well in the 1990s, there was an intersection of 'heading in the same direction' of three *entities*—globalization, the humanitarian agenda, and the UN's human rights agenda. That is, all three are headed in a direction that requires the transcendence of national boundaries—which the UN paradoxically also upholds in the name of the principle of sovereignty. Yet even as we hurl towards globalization with a humanitarian zest (after all the most pernicious acts including atrocity crimes are justified by their perpetrators as necessary to exterminate the evil that resides in the midst of humanity), the idea and the reality of the nation-state is ever stronger. Indeed, the logic of this globalization and the limits of our humanitarian practices necessitate the survival of the nation-state. But this time round the nation-state is *scapegoated*, it is required as a *convenient container* of tensions and problems—economic, political, and social—that are not of its own making but are externally driven global forces that may spill over the borders (e.g., as refugees) into other *peaceful* parts of the world. Indeed, the resurrection of borders is necessary for neoliberals as they don't see global government as a panacea for a global market economy. Hypothetically speaking, in the Hayekian framework of liberty, consent would be sacred, only a sovereign (not a failed) state can legitimately give 'consent' including the consent to be exploited (Slobdian 2018: 6–11). Since power hierarchies continue to be maintained in favour of the Global North enabling it to 'guide,' 'mentor,' and 'dictate' its global counterpart towards compliance with rules and regulations of the neoliberal economic order, there is no need for it to have a formal direct political control *a la* colonialism.[5] The powerful states of the Global North steer clear of political responsibility including that of mundane administrative issues while continuing

[5] This point here is partially a throwback to the neocolonial—another out of fashion term in the neoliberal era—argument—wherein, exploitation and extraction of resources can happen without territorial control—that was popular with the advocates of NIEO. See Chapter 2.

to strongly influence the economic, social, and political policies of the Global South states. Thus, the Global North has a stake in ensuring that the formal political sovereignty of the states of the South is strengthened. The 'capacity building' and 'rebuilding' responsibilities in the R2P doctrine are important so that there is no local—to paraphrase Thomas Hobbes's famous description of the state of nature—'war of all against all,' so that there be enough peace to ensure that if not 'art' or 'culture' then at least 'industry' is possible. The local national boundaries must be strong enough to contain the problem, that is, the physical borders as barriers to the escape (or entry into the European and American shores) of refugees and migrants—emerging from the categories of either victims/survivors of atrocity crimes or those marginalized by development processes. The R2P doctrine thus is an attempt to save not erase sovereignty. However, sovereignty in economic matters was and continues to be undermined but that undercutter and culprit is not R2P but the logic of the liberal/neoliberal dispositif—the contradictions and violent consequences of which manifest as atrocity crimes; measures such as R2P are attempts to save the dispositif from destroying itself. By drawing attention to 'sovereignty as responsibility' R2P is bolstering the tottering sovereignty of a fragile nation-state to be a container, contain and seal its problems within. And when it is unwilling or unable to do so R2P-like measures discipline it into doing so by passing that responsibility to the international community temporarily. R2P is aimed at 'containing' the problem of atrocity crimes, so it supports and aims for the nation state to be the container. For the nation state to be an effective 'container' R2P's first two pillars (post SOD 2005 evolution) through measures like foreign assistance and development aid, capacity building aims at bolstering a country's sovereignty. This book has also argued that the R2P however is not just about an ever-expanding circle of responsibility, it is as much a discourse about abdicating responsibility as it is about taking responsibility. The bid to make the Global South nation state an 'effective container' may require the counterintuitive effort on behalf of the Global North countries to be less nationalistic. The case in point being the ludicrousness of 'vaccine nationalism' during the COVID-19 pandemic years: 'It's a basic premise in public health the population level immunity is a public interest. In a globalized world that population includes every country' (Lee 2021). The dire need to recognize the interdependency of our times and humanity requires the jettisoning of realpolitiks that premises our rational calculations of geopolitics and geoeconomics discussed in the paragraphs below. Underlining the same interdependence in the context of climate change, Dipesh Chakrabarty dismisses the myth of the lifeboat available for the rich to escape the climate crisis (2016: 106). R. B. J Walker proffered a more nuanced view pointing out the commonalities between R2P and the pandemic: 'Both the responses to COVID and R2P are variations on the practice of dividing people … R2P is an inclusion/exclusion practice played out in a conventional international context. COVID works partly that way too, in relation to national differentiations. But it also works in ways that elude nationalisms and states, and reveals a broader structural pattern that is more transversal, contingent, and fluid, in ways that are difficult to confine to conventional cartographies.'[6]

The R2P doctrine doesn't examine or question international practices and institutions that create congenial environments for atrocity crimes, and how a sovereign state is depleted of its sovereignty bit by bit, gradually, over a period of time whereby a country is hurled into economic crisis and the resulting political instability mobilizes anger of a section of population making it believe in the necessity of atrocity crimes. The R2P advocates must take into account Focarelli's concern about the increasing inability of states to protect their populations from 'unemployment, state solvency, hunger, and other economic macro-variables affecting people's daily lives' (2015: 417). The non-addressal of these issues of 'freedom from want' creates grounds for 'freedom from fear' to elude a people who then come to inhabit a political space where the evil of an atrocity crime is always waiting in the shadows, ready to strike. The fact that the liberal peacebuilding project[7]—deploying liberal/neoliberal governmentalities—is riddled with complexities is so dramatically evident in the 2001 American intervention in Afghanistan that lasted for two decades.

Altruistically inclined responsibility—which may involve saving 'strangers'[8] (Wheeler) or perceived hapless groups such as 'Muslim women' (Abu-Lughod 2013)—may have disastrous consequences for the local population, although the face of destruction could be different. Altruism-premised responsibility has a shelf life, as witnessed throughout

[6] R. B. J. Walker shared via email the above as a response to my question on R2P and COVID-19 (18 February 2022).

[7] R2P is a part of this project (See Chapter 2).

[8] The imperatives for intervention are rarely noble, there are geopolitical, economic, and strategic compulsions pushing for intervention.

history, and more recently in Iraq and Afghanistan where interveners exit and leave the local population to their fate and expect them to take responsibility to fend for themselves. In this way the responsibility discourse segues away from altruism and into an individuated notion of responsibility reminiscent of what Iris Marion Young called the *blame model*. The volte-face subscription to the blame model—premised on the idea of individual agency—by the exiting intervener is sought to be justified on grounds of altruism fatigue. The local population's agency is expected to overcome hurdles, including structural ones, via its agency of hard work, human ingenuity, and risk-taking capacity. The reality of the intervener's failure to create enabling conditions for the local population to chart a different route needs to be acknowledged and analysed. For example, post the withdrawal of American troops from Afghanistan, Afghanis pointed out that the beneficiaries of the American aid were the multinational corporations, not the local population. So, intervention is still very much a continuing saga of great powers' interest.

Is there something in the very liberal conceptualization of responsibility that makes this subterfuge, this corruption of meaning likely? The irony being that the premise of sovereignty is being made on a concept—responsibility—that itself has not firm but contingent foundations. That is to say that the liberal conceptualization of responsibility is dynamic enough to be in the service of liberalism's premise—the market (in its various avatars ranging between free market and a welfare state model). Let's recapitulate the various meanings through which the liberal concept of responsibility glides: (a) failure or lapse of the individual state's responsibility to protect its population from atrocity crimes; (b) this is followed by the benevolent adoption of responsibility by the international community to protect the individual state's forsaken population. This responsibility is enacted through intervention and deployment of the resources—human and material—of the respective members of the international community who are intervening. How and where these resources and aid will be used is an important question to ask. Also, as the experience of American intervention in Afghanistan and Iraq shows it is likely that in the long term, the local population will pay for this *altruism* through labour or oil. The liberal/neoliberal notion of charity is flawed, the market sets it up to fail if it aims for something beyond the cosmetic.

Privileges and rights are not free lunches, they entail responsibility. And there are some moments when powerful states will choose to note a state's non-fulfilment of its responsibility—not responsibilit*ies*, but the singular responsibility—to protect its citizens from atrocity crimes. Not all such lapses by states come under the scrutiny of great powers. There are various reasons why the commission of similar atrocity acts in two different countries draws different levels of response such as turning a blind eye, verbal condemnation, economic sanctions, military intervention or all these responses in a sequential manner. This is because *all acts of atrocity crimes are not equal* for various reasons. Perhaps, the scale of the atrocity crime has to be high enough to draw international action or there could be geopolitical, geoeconomic, and geostrategic factors at play which may lead a great power to react or ignore an atrocity crime. Thus, the idea of responsibility to intervene—militarily and humanitarianly—itself is deceptive, that is, the ideas of charity, altruism, and benevolence that seemingly premise this responsibility are for all practical purposes chimerical. So, based on the foregoing paragraphs can we not conclude that intervention plotted anywhere on the liberal peacebuilding spectrum will inevitably turn out to be an example of Rittel and Webber's (1973) 'wicked problem'?

A significant revelation to emerge is that the Global North is not interested, at least for now, (it doesn't make the Global North countries more powerful to add more administrative units to their territory as it comes within today's age with additional responsibility and a set of expectations that enhance responsibility as accountability) in taking away the political sovereignty of small and weak states. The fear of the Global South regarding R2P as a ruse to erase or undermine their respective sovereignties is misplaced or not the complete picture. A pure, untouched, un-meddled with, sovereignty has not been a reality for most countries of the Global South since long. Aid—bilateral or institutional—with strings attached, such as the IMF conditionalities, has oriented a country's economic policies and influenced its political roadmap. Domestic issues on which local governments have complied include laws especially labour laws and tax regimes, while in foreign policy matters, compromise has been made on issues such as alliances, military bases, and regional organization membership.

Summarizing the Book

The analysis of R2P's incorporation in the UN's security/development dispositif was done by using the Foucauldian template of dispositif, governmentality, and biopolitics. The R2P discourse must be understood in the realms of both ideas and practice. Locating R2P in the liberal/neoliberal security/development dispositif creates a framework to make sense of the movement and noise on R2P. Thus located R2P loses the sheen of singularity as its profile is reflected in other measures of this dispositif. The seeming dynamism of R2P is a result of its constant makeover within the framework of the liberal/neoliberal security/development dispositif. R2P is not a discrete phenomenon and it belongs not to the domain of security but to that of security/development.

This conclusion was reached by tracing the genealogy of R2P in the UN's liberal/neoliberal security/development dispositif. Chapter 2 established the seamlessness between the putatively discrete domains of security and development. It proposed instead the concept of security/development to underline the circularity of this relationship.[9] Having established the similarity between the respective premises of embedded liberalism and neoliberalism it proposed the term liberal/neoliberal to describe the UN's security/development dispositif. That is, it demonstrated that the UN's security/development paradigm is informed by a liberal/neoliberal philosophy.

Chapter 3 traced the genealogy of R2P by historicizing it in the mandate of the UN Charter and subsequent UN resolutions/reports and reports of prominent international commissions on the issue of security/development. R2P ideationally coincides with the foundational ideas of the UN and is not a radical departure from the same. The sketch of R2P's lineage to the UN Charter itself underlines this argument and thus points out the limitations in the dominant literature that regards R2P simply as an imperative emerging in the context of intrastate violence, genocide, and ethnic cleansing of the 1990s. Next, using the concept of dispositif, a detailed empirical mapping of R2P in the UN was done in Chapter 4, that is, R2P's manifestations in the UN's institutional structure and discourse were identified. The mapping noted the crucial role played by civil society organizations in R2P's promotion. It also showed how the package deal

[9] This argument is inspired by Foucault's concept of power/knowledge (1980).

of R2P's three pillars makes possible its integration into the UN security/development policies even though some officials from individual departments/agencies are disinclined towards R2P's third pillar. The first two pillars are crucial to the legitimization of R2P and make opposition to it a difficult normative proposition. Disagreement over the goals of prevention and rebuilding, embodied in these two pillars, is a *morally* weak argument to sustain.

The empirical mapping was analysed in Chapters 5 and 6 to understand 'how' R2P came to be incorporated at the UN's security/development dispositif. Protection, responsibility, morality, legality, and sovereignty were identified as themes that resonate with the mandates/agenda of both R2P and the UN's liberal/neoliberal security/development dispositif. These themes are reflected in the UN Charter and have informed the security/development policies of the UN in its phases of embedded liberalism and neoliberalism. Thus, the key argument of the book is that R2P is only a discursive rearticulation of and not a discursive shift of the UN's liberal/neoliberal security/development dispositif. Even, then there is a possibility to extract something more constructive from the same. Developing Anne Orford's excellent point—R2P is a case of 'from deeds to words'—further it must be added that those deeds need to have a greater sincerity, more substance not cosmetic, but guided by the normative promises that premise these measures, realize them in full measure.

Research Contribution

The book is part description[10] (ontological) and part critique that contributes to better understanding (epistemological). It is not tasked to recommend specific solutions or to answer the question, Vladimir Lenin (1963) posed in another context, 'what is to be done?' However, understanding the problem is a prerequisite for exploring solutions, also the book's criticism of the liberal/neoliberal dispositif is not intended as an *implied* endorsement of non-action on our part as members of a community (local, national, or international). For the responsible 'scholar,' making claims to 'international citizenship,' it is obligatory to 'speak out against every abuse of power, whoever its author, whoever, its victims' (Foucault 1994: 474). Thus, while there is a need to interrogate R2P

[10] I borrow this term from Anne Orford's (2012) article on the subject of R2P.

and its advocacy, it is equally imperative to acknowledge and applaud the commitment of R2P's advocates—academics, bureaucrats, political leaders, and workers on the ground (UN and other international aid agencies)—who pursue the task of resistance to atrocity crimes and to practices that inhibit human freedom. This thought is not a ritualistic nod to a concluding chapter that ends on a note of hope; it is simply a reflection of the complexity of reality in which despite leading, mostly, an individuated existence, some of us shrink away from ethical depravity, and agree with Adam Smith's emphasis on 'moral sentiments.'

The emphasis is on 'problem-revealing' rather than 'problem-solving.' While R2P is explored as a discursive shift, the focus is on uncovering the 'facts' about R2P's institutionalization in the UN, to understand how it came about, and to reveal the implications thereof. So, empirical mapping of R2P at the UN was done keeping in mind that the UN's security/development dispositif itself is located in the broader liberal/neoliberal security/development (political economy's) dispositif; the UN certainly is not a discrete organization 'squatting outside the world.'[11] The mapping identifies a panoply of 'R2P similar' measures of the UN's dispositif.

The notion of dispositif unpacks the connections between concepts, policies, and frameworks in the global political economy that at first glance appear discrete and unrelated. The analysis in the book substantiates links between R2P and the notions of 'good governance' and 'ownership' in the discourses on international development aid. Second, dispositif enables problematization of the notion of change and thus steers away from a tendency to associate 'discursive shift' with virtually any type of policy or institutional change. Dispositif contextualizes and historicizes the emergence and incorporation of R2P at the UN and notes how continuity survives surreptitiously in the name of change. Thus, the argument that R2P's incorporation in the UN is a discursive rearticulation rather than a discursive shift.

The ICISS's incorporation of a 'large civil society component within the ongoing structure of its activities' (Cooper and English 2005: 19) is reflective of a trend in neoliberal political economy wherein the state's recession from the economy and welfare activities necessitates and privileges the role of non-state actors. The latter becomes even more

[11] I borrow the phrase from Karl Marx's (1843) *A Contribution to the Critique of Hegel's Philosophy of Right* See https://www.marxists.org/archive/marx/works/1843/critique-hpr/intro.htm.

significant when they deliver surrogate governance in the 'fragile/failed/failing' states of the Global South. The advocacy role of organizations like GCR2P, ICRtoP, and APR2P in R2P's promotion is significant in this light. The UN, along with other international organizations and states are essentially in pursuit of like-minded ideas and engage in practices characterized by the same rationality i.e., liberal/neoliberal governmentality. Dispositif also reveals how even at the UN, power is best understood as a network with multiple points of manifestations that are also sites of resistance (Foucault 1980), therefore, the significance of studying the *smaller* UN offices and departments in addition to the three key organs—General Assembly, Security Council, and the Secretariat.

These proliferating points of power do not bring chaos to the UN since the liberal/neoliberal dispositif provides the template to design limits, create possibilities of action, and identify the criteria of truth and falsehood whereby potential challengers are appropriated and mainstreamed. Recall here that the *truth* of neoliberal political economy is the market, the discursive rules must be in accordance. Thus, for R2P to embody the 'truth' of our times, it must reflect the knowledge of the liberal/neoliberal security/development dispositif. R2P advocates are obeying the rules of *this* discursive formation as they relentlessly pursue the conceptual refinement and development of R2P. The UN is an example of a 'material and informational resource' rich international organization, a gigantic bureaucracy whose pursuit of 'socially valued goals' of peace and human rights' gives it legitimacy (Barnett and Finnemore 2004: 5), but studying the UN *only* as a bureaucracy has analytical limitations. It does not tell us how despite the resistance of some UN officials and departments, R2P was incorporated in the UN. The subjective opinions of individual UN officials, whether supportive or critical of R2P, are mostly made within the framework of the UN's liberal/neoliberal security/development dispositif. R2P advocates underscore its conformity to the UN Charter, and they take this into account in the continuing conceptual refinement of R2P. This refinement is in consonance with the liberal/neoliberal governmentality's rationality that is in a constant mode of *being* and *emergence*. All acts of improvization and improvement are pursued within the same dispositif i.e., within the *existing* framework, its entrenchment is a result of constant makeovers. The rearticulations are a sign of dynamism of a system that is being perfected from within without losing its essential character that hinges on the free market principle. The liberal/neoliberal dispositif responds to challenges of a possible discursive shift by appropriating and domesticating radical ideas; a discursive rearticulation entails claiming new ideas but processing them in a manner that rids them of any critical potential.

Analyzing R2P in this book has also been a context to underline the twinning of the seemingly disparate domains of security and development in this dispositif. The duties of prevention and rebuilding (2001 ICISS Report; A/63/677/2009) involve non-military activities that are best classified as development practices. The consequences of the ostensibly discrete sphere of development, in this case, liberal/neoliberal development, necessitate measures of the ostensibly discrete sphere of security to secure development. The lines between security and development are blurred as they cohabit in a relationship of circularity (a la power/knowledge). Liberal/neoliberal governmentality's accompaniment, biopolitics, discloses the non-military aspects of security that include measures to ensure responsible self-conduct by the population. The premise of this 'conduct of conduct' under liberal/neoliberal governmentality is derived from the market principles since biopolitics is economic in character and is itself a dispositif of security (Dillon 2015: 46). In post-conflict peacebuilding projects development has emerged as a 'civilian technology of counterinsurgency' (Duffield 2007: 215). The segmentation of security and development into separate realms justifies the status quo and helps in the evasion of responsibility for the consequences that result from the security/development measures. This is particularly problematic since these consequences entail the loss of human lives (e.g., genocide and ethnic cleansing that are classified as security issues), deprivation of a humane and dignified life (e.g., famine, internal displacement, and refugees that are classified as development concerns) and an accompanying cultivation of an ethos that encourages and justifies indifference to the loss of lives *and* loss of dignified lives.[12] The root cause of this issue must be taken seriously and not be reduced to radical rhetoric and symbolic acts. The warning that climate change would be the context of the 'next genocide' (Snyder 2015) should have us all worried. The premise of this forecast is the likelihood of the conflict(s) that will ensue from food and water scarcity making 'climate refugees' the new entrants into the categories of 'internally displaced people' and (unwanted and burdensome) migrants. This also extends to the global discourse on

[12] 'Freedom to live in dignity' has been added to the initial human security goals of 'freedom from fear' and 'freedom from want' (HSU 2014: 4–6).

the environment and sustainable development where, for example, the notion of social and ecological 'resilience' (the capacity to absorb shocks and bounce back) has become central in discussions of climate change adaptation.

The biopolitical underpinnings of this liberal/neoliberal art of government reveal how the security/development discourse is engaged in the simultaneous pursuit of two seemingly contradictory goals of preservation of life and the destruction of life. The contradiction is resolved by adding qualifiers to the categories of those who deserve to live and those who deserve to die. Indeed, the preservation of life of some—the deserving—requires the destruction of life of the *others* who are cast as dispensable, and even as evil. These *others*, i.e., the undeserving, could be the poor, a religious, ethnic, or national group. This modern form of *racism*, Foucault observed, is an inversion of Clausewitzian wisdom[13] since politics has now become a pursuit of war by other means (1997: 48). This Foucauldian insight draws attention to two types of killings: (a) those that result from the use of guns, machetes, and bombs; (b) those that are a consequence of liberal/neoliberal governmentality's imperative to 'let die' (1997: 237). For example, in the neoliberal milieu poverty, loss of employment can be blamed on an individual's inefficiency or laziness for which society or state cannot be held responsible even if these conditions (poverty and unemployment) lead to deaths of those who are denied food and healthcare, this is evident from a spate of examples of the countries that have experienced a financial crisis in recent times. Neoliberal policies are selective in the promotion of individualism, the neoliberal state and the World Bank/IMF introduce policies that ensure individualization of profit and 'socialization of losses' (Evans 2015: 754; Engelen et al. 2011: 30). An ethos that reifies individual responsibility and views such consequences as just desert is vulgar (Ramsay 1997; Young 2011).Foucauldian way of seeing allows us to see the war that is carried out in everyday politics; the liberal/neoliberal security/development discourse views it not as a war but merely as a condition that is *just* and inevitable. The liberal/neoliberal security/development discourse appropriates the *noble* purpose of humanism and makes possible killings and counter-killings. The R2P discourse seen through the lenses of governmentality and biopolitics reveals the paradox of the simultaneity

[13] 'But after all war is no more than the continuation of politics' (Carl Von Clausewitz in Foucault 1997: 48).

of two seemingly contrary responses to killings- one of concern and the other of indifference:

> When I say killing, I obviously do not mean simply murder as such, but also every form of indirect murder: the fact of exposing someone to death, increasing the risk of death for some people, or, quite simply, political death, expulsion, rejection and so on. (Foucault in Fishel 2013: 212)

The concurrent pursuit of biopolitics and thanatopolitics aims to secure the surplus population through development that is the 'liberal alternative to extermination or eugenics.' This explains how 'development constitutes a liberal problematic of security' (Duffield 2007: 216). The role of security is to manage the economic crisis—a congenital feature of capitalism—so that the 'self-valorization' of capital is not interrupted (Aradau and Blanke 2008: 11).

Criticism of R2P does not imply that one is making a case for indifference to atrocity crimes. On the contrary, one is arguing for the extension of the concern for the lives lost due to 'structural violence' (Galtung 1969) that is the victims of the 'let die' liberal/neoliberal rationality. The limitation of the R2P lens so far is that it is exhorting the state and international community to action only in response to certain acts of commission, not omission. The R2P doctrine is silent on killings that are not on a massive scale (numbers), killings that are not a result of direct violence, i.e., those that involve the use of guns, machetes, gas chambers, etc. R2P advocates, interviewed, recognize these other contexts (and causes) of deaths as concerns but underline that these are not R2P concerns. Similarly, the argument of 'operational utility' restricts the scope of R2P to the four atrocity crimes and does not extend it to 'calamities, such as HIV/AIDS, climate change or the response to natural disasters' (A/63/677/2009/para 10b). Contesting this endorsement and excuse of a limited R2P mandate, the argument of the book instead proposes that *this* form of thanatopolitics should be an R2P concern. Privileging of or reserving concern and moral outrage for only certain killings is a result of an exclusive focus on the symptoms and overt manifestations of the act. As a consequence, panacea is sought in the removal or incarceration of evil-minded leaders, ideologues or incompetent, and poor leadership but the conditions that facilitated their success are ignored. Those conditions are structural and make the killings possible. Understanding the

R2P discourse as practice that is informed by liberal/neoliberal rationality draws attention to the structural aspect of international relations. The workings and consequences of the liberal/neoliberal economy create conditions of *disorder* that necessitate R2P-like measures to maintain order or put limits on the disorder that is a result of resistance to power.[14]

R2P's key (interrelated) themes—protection, responsibility, sovereignty, morality and legality—were identified and problematized to understand how R2P creates liberal/neoliberal subjects (responsible protectors, protected, and those who fall outside the domain of protection). This subjectivization is compatible with and entails the internalization of good governance alias liberal/neoliberal norms alias free market principles. One of the problems with the good governance discourse is that it expects adherence to practices and institutions imported from a different political, economic, and cultural context. The good governance thesis is in the lineage of the modernization theory[15] (Rostow 1960, 1963, 1971; Huntington 1968) that aspired to be a policy guide to transform the developing countries in the political, economic, and social image of the West. This externally guided path is different from the homespun attempts at telescoping various stages of development by some of the socialist governments in the developing world, e.g., India (Myrdal 1968). While these indigenously designed national projects have had varying degrees of success and failure, the flaws in the projects have not brought further ruin or caused irreparable damage to these countries. The problem with engineering development under the current good governance discourse is that it takes as given the Global South's acquiescence to the harsh neoliberal economic demands of austerity.

Conclusion

Understanding of R2P would be enriched if the World Bank's and the IMF's policies are studied in terms of R2P's prevention and rebuilding template. While two World Bank officials (an economist and a lawyer) in separate interviews stressed that R2P was 'too political' and therefore

[14] 'Where there is power there is resistance' (Foucault 1990: 95).

[15] The lineage of the modernization theory itself can be traced to the colonial claim of the civilizing mission.

'too hot' for the Bank's agenda, the third official (a social development specialist) saw no connection between her organization's work and R2P. Contrary to this view the fact is that the World Bank has begun to factor violent conflicts (causes and impact) in their policies and projects (World Bank 2011; also see Collier et al. 2003). The themes of protection and responsibility in the World Development Reports would further support the argument that R2P is part of the liberal/neoliberal security dispositif. These financial institutions are not unaware of the political challenges to their work but they deal with it through the *apolitical* mechanisms of good governance; also note that even when they recognize an economic condition, e.g., poverty, as a cause of conflict, lack of good governance is seen as the cause of poverty. However, such reading—which regards as benign the linkages between domestic and global economic structures and views the Global North as creating new opportunities of economic and technological growth for the Global South—is flawed as it ignores the ground reality that shows otherwise (see Mazur 2000; Milanovic 2003; Stiglitz 2002).

Flowing from the above two possible directions for future research are suggested. The first avenue of research would be a different level of analysis whereby R2P is studied through the lens of foreign policy. Individual countries' specific responses could be compared in detail and these positions could be contextualized with their respective geostrategic and economic interests. This is important since the UN is a 'membership club of nation-states' (Andrea Bartoli and Thomas Weiss in separate interviews August 2013),successful R2P advocacy requires an articulation that identifies common ground between R2P and the national interest of states. This line of inquiry no doubt touches the paradoxical aspect of the R2P discourse that exhorts nation-states to dilute the traditional/Westphalian notion of sovereignty. Though there is some work on R2P from a country and region-specific perspective (Aneja 2014; Kassim 2014; Kingsbury 2012), there is a need for a rigorous comparative study of individual state policies. The GCR2P's work of developing R2P focal points in national capitals would be a useful input into this inquiry. Foreign policy level of analysis can reveal not just how R2P is used to justify 'imperial designs' (e.g., Russia's justification for intervention in South Ossetia in 2008) but also how states in the Global North claim the moral halo of an 'ethical foreign policy' via the protection of the vulnerable in situations of violent conflict in countries where they have no geoeconomic or strategic interests:

> Ethical foreign policy is ideally suited to buttressing the moral authority of governments, often under question in the domestic context, because policy-makers are less accountable for matching ambitious policy aims with final policy outcomes in the international sphere. The gap between rhetoric and responsibility lies in the fact that policy can be declared a success with little regard for policy outcomes, as there is no formal accountability to non-citizens abroad, while problems can be blamed on the actions of other people or their governments. (Chandler 2003: 295)

Exposing such subterfuge is important if R2P's promise of prevention and rebuilding has to move beyond the realm of mere words. Such exposure may risk non-action by the states in the North which is contrary to the efforts of the advocates of R2P and of 'sovereignty as responsibility,' who exhort states to overcome domestic 'budgetary constraints' and 'pursue activist policies outside their national borders' (Deng et al. 1996: xix). Though research that reveals such truth may discourage states to intervene, it would be an important step in ensuring the 2011 Brazil's cautionary approach of 'responsibility while protecting' (McDougall 2014).

The second research site would be the UN's two influential specialized agencies, the World Bank and the IMF. Officials of UN departments and the World Bank and the IMF, even more so, describe their work as apolitical, a claim that political scientists would disagree with since *politics is everywhere* (Leftwich 2004: 1–22). Research in this area would contextualize R2P's first two pillars with an analysis of the World Bank and the IMF's approach towards issues of security/development. Recent reports of these agencies express concerns about violent conflicts as major hurdles to development projects in countries of the Global South (IMF 2008;World Bank 2011). Relatedly keeping track of the evolving good governance discourse would be useful in order to see how it impacts the tweaking or further conceptual refinement of R2P's first two pillars.

Since R2P is a work in progress, a detailed analysis of the three pillars (as they evolve) in the context of the structures of the global political economy would be the third area of research. While this book premises primary arguments in the political economy via the concept of liberal/neoliberal governmentality, there is scope for further investigation from this perspective. This is especially so as this analysis confirms the role of the neoliberal economy in making possible the modern forms of genocide that necessitate a governmentality of R2P-like measures to maintain order. Since the purpose is not to recommend non-action when atrocity crimes are committed, it is important to explore how R2P can be made to jettison control and oppressive subjectivization so that it clears the way for enhancing freedom. The argument about structures focuses on causes and solutions that remedy the problem and prevent its future occurrence.

Analysis of the three pillars is crucial to both critique and *save* R2P. R2P must be viewed as a package of three pillars since R2P by its own *official* account is not merely about humanitarian military intervention (Secretary-General's annual reports on R2P 2009–2014). Intellectual jujitsu to refine the third pillar of 'timely and decisive action' should continue and the recent writings of the ICISS commissioners—Gareth Evans, Thomas Weiss, and Ramesh Thakur focus on this aspect of R2P. The research projects and literature coming out of the GCR2P, ICRtoP, and APR2P are also concerned about the same. Recommendations made in this regard include—emphasis on diplomatic negotiations and economic sanctions to pressurize the perpetrator state to assume its responsibility to protect; Security Council reforms so as to ensure that the process of decision-making is democratic and the intervention to protect is a multilateral effort and not an individual state's initiative; creation of the UN's own standby military force; accountability of the interveners. The problem or the limitation of these efforts is the premise that intervention today is inevitable (see Bellamy 2014; Fiott and Koops 2015; Thakur 2015; Weiss 2001) and in this worldview the condition that necessitates intervention is taken as a stubborn reality and is therefore not questioned. These R2P advocates concentrate in exploring and strengthening the third pillar to control the violent and inhumane manifestation arising out of these intractable conditions. Although these advocates do not deny that atrocity crimes are a result of structural causes, they consider the solution beyond the scope and mandate of R2P.

This argument is clearly disingenuous in light of R2P's three pillars' promise of responsibilities of prevention and rebuilding. These activities were absent in the 2011 Libyan intervention. The intervention in Libya is problematic from the R2P lens not because there were no grounds for intervention but because it was *not enough intervention*, (Stewart 2011; Pape 2015), it was flawed as it did not fulfil the *spectrum of responsibilities*. The R2P promise requires that having fulfilled its third pillar responsibility to take 'timely and decisive action,' i.e., military intervention, the international community needs to follow it up with the responsibility to rebuild:

> Libya's 'recent turmoil is not a result of too much intervention, but too little. The international community did not do enough to encourage the growth of local political and economic development, resulting in the burgeoning civil war we see in the summer and fall of 2014. (Pape 2015: 10)

While adherence to the first two pillars to fulfil the responsibilities to prevent and rebuild will be an important step, I suggest that like the third pillar, the other two pillars also require additional intellectual rumination. R2P's first two pillars involve activities that are undertaken by several liberal/neoliberal peacebuilding projects of the UN. Closely allied to the peacebuilding discourse is that of statebuilding, indeed both are significant components of the good governance agenda (particularly for weak or failing states) that is aimed at 'facilitating sustainable development, social peace and the development of democracy and the rule of law' (Chandler 2010: 1).[16] These projects, as in Afghanistan (see Piotukh 2015), do not address issues of structural injustices. Such projects are congenitally flawed as their conceptualization, based on the principles of good governance, assumes that the local population can be mentored into imbibing liberal/neoliberal norms and learning to behave responsibly. But atrocity crimes are not sudden eruptions, plotted by the 'devil'[17]; there is a historical context in which a group (ethnic, religious, or national) becomes vulnerable and is targeted and victimized, a point bluntly made in the very title of Mahmud Mamdani's book *When Victims Become Killers*. The same argument is stated in Ashis Nandy's plainspeaking: 'The pathological form of the Taliban was created. It was not an original sin.'[18] The tragic flaw in liberal peacebuilding is writ large in the example of Afghanistan. A two-decade-long peacebuilding project along with the presence of the American military could not institutionalize democracy or effectively de-Taliban(ize) the country. The exit of the American military from Afghanistan in 2021 saw a swift takeover of the country by the Taliban. Life came full circle for all stakeholders but most tragically for the Afghani people!

[16] Statebuilding has become 'one of the critical all-consuming strategic and moral imperatives of our terrorized time' (Robert I. Rotberg in Chandler 2010: 5).

[17] I borrow the term from Romeo Dallaire's book title *Shaking Hands with the Devil*.

[18] See OP Jindal Distinguished Lecture with Ashis Nandy on Partition Violence, 12 March 2014. https://www.youtube.com/watch?v=4CbUrm74oL0&t=5264s.

Conflict over resources as a cause for violence (and atrocity crimes) between local groups is not because of the 'barbaric' and non-modern traits of a not yet fully 'civilized' people. The non-local actors (e.g., multinational corporations and foreign states) are also parties in the conflict, but their role in generating these violent conflicts is rarely discussed in the R2P or good governance discourse. In this regard, the 'best practices' including that of corporate social responsibility are merely cosmetic measures as the problem is not just the nexus of these corporations with local corrupt and criminal elements of the state (politicians and bureaucracy). Treating the symptom without addressing the cause can at best provide short-term relief from the problem. We need the courage to acknowledge what appears to be a counterintuitive argument in neoliberal times that the problem lies in the very nature of the neoliberal mode of extraction and (non?) distribution of resources (see Galtung 1969, 1971;Kaldor 2012, 2013; Taussig 1984; Watts and Kashi 2008). If the structures and processes that make atrocity crimes possible are not questioned then the promotion of R2P as a panacea for such problems is duplicitous or politely put, naïve. The array of liberal/neoliberal security/development practices that aim at conflict transformation is characterized by the same limitation. After all, how can conflict transformation take place when causal structures and processes remain untransformed?

Addressing these causal concerns takes us to the realm of global justice. There is a rich corpus of writings on the subject from liberal and critical perspectives. Frantz Fanon (1965) had famously described European aid to former colonies as just aid and a form of belated reparation. The upscaling of progressive liberal theories of justice to the global level (Beitz 1999; Held 2004; Rawls 1999a, 1999b; Sen 1999, 2009) is indicative of the normative recognition that interconnectedness between countries must breed an expansive notion of responsibility for both the individuals and states/societies towards their counterparts. From this perspective the idea of justice ceases to be narrow, it moves beyond securing the ICC's verdict of punishment to the killers, and brings in its purview causes that led to the *present* killings and may lead to such acts in the future. Work in this direction must be taken seriously. After all, in the art of government as liberal/neoliberal rationality, security is about securing a particular form of development and 'freedom is nothing but the correlative development of apparatuses of security' (Foucault 2007: 48).Foucault by drawing attention to the historical a priori (1972: 126–131) does not dismiss humanism, freedom, and human rights but only questions their being 'limited to certain frontiers' (in an interview with Rux Martin 1988: 15). Asking the *right* questions including the difficult ones must be, at the least, the responsibility of an intellectual enterprise. Raising the issue of root causes of atrocity crimes may be ambitious but certainly not naïve, I recall here a popular slogan from the 1960s French students' movement: 'Be practical. Do the impossible' (Singh 2006: 962). We need to change the terms of the debate on R2P.

References

Abu-Lughod, Lila. 2013. *Do Muslim Women Need Saving?* Massachusetts: Harvard University Press.

Aneja, Urvashi. 2014. India, R2P and Humanitarian Assistance: A Case of Norm Containment. *Global Responsibility to Protect* 6 (2): 227–245.

Aradau, Claudia, and Tobias Blanke. 2008. Governing Crisis, Securing Circulation: Towards a Reconceptualisation of Security. *Paper prepared for the International Studies Association Annual Convention*, 26–29 March 2008, San Francisco.

Barnett, Michael N., and Martha Finnemore. 2004. *Rules for the World: International Organizations in Global Politics*. Ithaca: Cornell University Press.

Basaran, Halil Rahman. 2014. Identifying the Responsibility to Protect. *The Fletcher Forum of World Affairs* 28 (1): 195–212.

Beitz, Charles. 1999. *Political Theory and International Relations*. Princeton: Princeton University Press.

Bellamy, Alex J. 2014. *Responsibility to Protect: A Defence*. Oxford: Oxford University Press.

Bellamy, Alex J., and Tim Dunne. 2016. *The Oxford Handbook of Responsibility to Protect*. Oxford: OxforSd University Press.

Bellamy, Alex J. 2021. The International Community and Atrocity Crimes: The Responsibility to Protect. In *The Oxford Handbook of Atrocity Crimes*, eds. Barbora Holá, Hollie N. Brehm, and Maartje Weerdesteijn, 441–459. Oxford: Oxford University Press.

Bellamy, Alex J. 2022. Sovereignty Redefined: The Promise and Practice of R2P. In *The Responsibility to Protect Twenty Years On: Rhetoric and Implementation*, ed. Pinar G. Ercan, 13–32. Palgrave McMillan.

Breakey, Hugh. 2012. The Responsibility to Protect: Game Change and Regime Change. In *Norms of Protection: Responsibility to Protect, Protection of Civilians and their Interaction*, eds. Charles Sampford, Angus Francis, and Vesselin Popovski. Geneva: United Nations University.

Cairns, Edmund. 2014. R2P and Humanitarian Action. *Global Responsibility to Protect* 6 (2): 141–161.

Chakrabarty, Dipesh. 2016. Whose Anthropocene?: A Response. In *Whose Anthropocene? Revisiting Dipesh Chakrabarty's 'Four Theses'*, eds. Robert Emmett, and Thomas Lekan, 103–113.

Chandler, David. 2003. Rhetoric without Responsibility: The Attraction of 'Ethical' Foreign Policy. *The British Journal of Politics and International Relations* 5 (3): 295–316.

Chandler, David. 2010. *International Statebuilding: The Rise of Post-Liberal Governance.* New York: Routledge.

Chandler, David. 2015. The R2P Is Dead, Long Live the R2P: The Successful Separation of Military Intervention from the Responsibility to Protect. *International Peacekeeping* 22 (1): 1–5.

Chesterman, Simon. 2021. Responsibility to Protect and Humanitarian Intervention: From Apology to Utopia and Back Again. In *The Oxford Handbook of the International Law of Global Security*, eds. Robin Geib and Nils Melzer, 808–820. Oxford: Oxford University Press.

Chomsky, Noam. 2009. The Responsibility to Protect. *Lecture Delivered at the UNGA*, July 23, 2009.

Collier, Paul, V. L. Elliott, Havard Hegre, Anke Hoeffler, Marta Reynal-Querol, and Nicholas Sambanis, 2003. *Breaking the Conflict Trap: Civil War and Development Policy.* Washington, DC: World Bank & Oxford University Press.

Cooper, Andrew F., and John English. 2005. International Commissions and the Mind of Global Governance. In *International Commissions and the Power of Ideas*, eds. Ramesh Thakur, Andrew F. Cooper, and John English. Tokyo: United Nations University.

Deng, Francis, Sadikiel Kimaro, Terrence Lyons, Donald Rothchild, and William I. Zartman. 1996. *Sovereignty as Responsibility: Conflict Management in Africa.* Washington, DC. Brookings Institute.

Dillon, Michael. 2015. *Biopolitics of Security: A Political Analytic of Finitude.* New York: Routledge.

Duffield, Mark. 2007. *Development, Security and Unending War: Governing the World of Peoples.* Cambridge: Polity Press.

Dunne, Tim, and Nicholas J. Wheeler. 2012. Operationalising Protective Intervention: Alternative Models of Authorisation. In *Routledge Handbook of the Responsibility to Protect*, eds. W. Andy Knight, and Frazer Egerton. London: Routledge.

Engelen, Ewald, Ismail Erturk, Julie Froud, Sukhdev Johal, Adam Leaver, Michael Moran, Adriana Nilsson, and Karel Williams. 2011. *After the Great Complacence: Financial Crisis and the Politics of Reform.* Oxford: Oxford University Press.

Evans, Anthony J. 2015. The Financial Crisis in the United Kingdom: Uncertainty, Calculation, and Error. In *The Oxford Handbook of Austrian Economics*, eds. Peter J. Boettke, and Christopher J. Coyne. Oxford: Oxford University Press.

Falk, Richard A. 2015. *Humanitarian Intervention and Legitimacy Wars: Seeking Peace and Justice in the 21st Century*. New York: Routledge.

Fanon, Frantz. 1965. *Wretched of the Earth*. New York: Grove Press.

Fishel, Stephanie. 2013. Theorizing Violence in the Responsibility to Protect. *Critical Studies on Security* 1 (2): 204–218.

Fiott, Daniel, and Joachim Koops, eds. 2015. *The Responsibility to Protect and the Third Pillar*. London: Palgrave Macmillan.

Focarelli, Carlo. 2015. The Responsibility to Protect in the Global System. In *The Responsibility to Protect (R2P): A New Paradigm of International Law?*, ed. Peter Hilpold, 417–438.

Foucault, Michel. 1972. *The Archaeology of Knowledge and the Discourses of Language*. New York: Pantheon.

Foucault, Michel. 1980. *Power/Knowledge: Selected Interviews and Other Writings 1972–1977*, ed. Colin Gordon. New York: Pantheon Books.

Foucault, Michel. 1990. *The History of Sexuality: An Introduction*, vol. I. New York: Vintage Books.

Foucault, Michel. 1994. *"Confronting Governments: Human Rights." In Essential Works of Foucault 1954-1984*Vol 3: Power. J.D. Faubion ed. London: Penguin.

Foucault, Michel. 1997. *Society Must Be Defended: Lectures at the College de France, 1975–1976*. New York: Picador.

Foucault, Michel. 2007. *Security, Territory, Population: Lectures at the College De France 1977–1978*. New York: Palgrave.

Gallagher, Adrian. et al. 2021. Roundtable: The Responsibility to Protect in a Changing Word Order: Twenty Years since its Inception. *Ethics in International Affairs* 35 (2). (Cambridge)

Galtung, Johan. 1969. Violence, Peace, and Peace Research. *Journal of Peace Research* 6 (3): 167–191.

Galtung, Johan. 1971. A Structural Theory of Imperialism. *Journal of Peace and Research* 8 (2): 81–117.

Glanville, Luke. 2016. Does R2P Matter? Interpreting the Impact of a Norm. *Cooperation and Conflict* 52 (2): 184–199.

Glanville, Luke. 2021. *Sharing Responsibility: The History and Future of protection from Atrocities*. Princeton: Princeton University Press.

Held, David. 2004. *Global Covenant: The Social Democratic Alternative to the Washington Consensus*. Cambridge: Polity.

Hilpold, Peter. 2015. From Humanitarian Intervention to the Responsibility to Protect. In *The Responsibility to Protect (R2P): A New Paradigm of International Law?*, ed. Peter Hilpold, 1–37.

Human Security Unit. 2014. *Strategic Plan 2014–2017.* New York: United Nations. Accessed 21 September.

Hunt, Charles T., and Alex Bellamy. 2010. Mainstreaming the Responsibility to Protect in Peace Operations. *Working Paper No.3. Program on the Protection of Civilians.* St. Lucia: Asia-Pacific Centre for the Responsibility to Protect.

Huntington, Samuel P. 1968. *Political Order in Changing Societies.* New Haven: Yale University Press.

Illingworth, Richard. 2023. *Strengthening the Responsibility to Protect: A Transitional Cosmopolitan Approach.* Routledge.

International Monetary Fund. 2008. The Fund's Engagement in Fragile States and Post-Conflict Countries—A Review of Experience—Issues and Options. *Prepared by the Policy Development and Review Department, in consultation with Other Departments.*

Kaldor, Mary. 2012. *New and Old Wars: Organized Violence in a Global Era.* Cambridge: Polity Press.

Kaldor, Mary. 2013. In Defence of New Wars. *Stability: International Journal of Security and Development* 2 (1): 1–16. http://www.stabilityjournal.org/articles/10.5334/sta.at/. Accessed 16 Sept 2015.

Kassim, Yang Razali. 2014. *The Geopolitics of Intervention: Asia and the Responsibility to Protect.* Singapore: Springer.

Kingsbury, Damien. 2012. *Sri Lanka and the Responsibility to Protect: Politics, Ethnicity and Genocide.* New York: Routledge.

Kolmasova, Sarka. 2023. *Advocacy Networks and the Responsibility to Protect: The Politics of Norm Circulation.* Routledge.

Lee, Kelley. 2021. Pandemics and Borders: How to Manage Travel Restrictions More Effectively. *The President's Faculty Lectures*, Simon Fraser University. https://www.sfu.ca/publicsquare/events/2021/kelley-lee.html.

Leftwich, Adrian. 2004. Thinking Politically: On the Politics of Politics. In *What is Politics?: The Activity and its Study*, ed. Adrian Leftwich. Cambridge: Polity Press.

Lenin, Vladimir Il'ch. 1963. *What is to be done?* trans. and eds. S. V. Utechin, and Patricia Utechin, with an introduction and notes by S.V. Utechin. Oxford. Clarendon Press.

Martin, Rux. 1988. Truth, Power, Self: An Interview with Michel Foucault, October 25, 1982. In *Technologies of the Self: A Seminar with Michel Foucault*, eds. Luther H. Martin, Huck Gutman, and Patrick H. Hutton. Amherst: University of Massachusetts Press.

Marx, Karl. 1843. *A Contribution to the Critique of Hegel's Philosophy of Right*. https://www.marxists.org/archive/marx/works/1843/critique-hpr/intro.htm. Accessed 16 Sept 2015.

Mazur, Jay. 2000. Labor's New Internationalism. *Foreign Affairs* 79 (1): 79–93.

McDougall, Derek. 2014. Responsibility While Protecting. *Global Responsibility to Protect* 6 (1): 64–87.

Milanovic, Branko. 2003. Two Faces of Globalization: Against Globalization as We Know it. *World Development* 31 (4): 667–683.

Myrdal, Gunnar. 1968. *Asian Drama: An Inquiry into the Poverty of Nations*. Middlesex: Penguin Books.

Nandy, Ashis. 2009. *The Intimate Enemy: Loss and Recovery of Self Under Colonialism*. New Delhi: OxfordUniversity Press.

Orford, Anne. 2012. In Praise of Description. *Leiden Journal of International Law* 25: 609–625.

Pape, Robert A. 2015. Response to Roland Paris Article. *International Peacekeeping* 22 (1): 9–10.

Piotukh, Volha. 2015. *Biopolitics, Governmentality and Humanitarianism: Caring for the Population in Afghanistan and Belarus*. New York: Routledge.

Ramsay, Maureen. 1997. *What's Wrong with Liberalism?: A Radical Critique of Liberal Political Philosophy*. New York: Leicester University Press.

Rawls, John. 1999a. *A Theory of Justice*. Cambridge, Mass.: Belknap Press of Harvard University Press.

Rawls, John. 1999b. *The Law of Peoples: With 'The Idea of Public Reason Revisited.'* Cambridge, Mass.: Harvard University Press.

Rittel, Horst W. J., and Melvin M. Webber. 1973. Dilemmas in a General Theory of Planning. *Policy Sciences.* 4: 155–169.

Rostow, Walt Whitman. 1960. *The Stages of Economic Growth: A Non-Communist Manifesto*. Cambridge: Cambridge University Press.

Rostow, Walt Whitman. 1963. *The Economics of Take-Off into Sustained Growth: Proceedings of a Conference Held by the International Economic Association*. London: MacMillan.

Rostow, Walt Whitman. 1971. *Politics and the Stages of Growth*. Cambridge: Cambridge University Press.

Sen, Amartya. 1999. *Development as Freedom*. New York: Knopf.

Sen, Amartya. 2009. *The Idea of Justice*. New York: Allen Lane/Penguin Books.

Serrano, Monica. 2011. The Responsibility to Protect and its Critics: Explaining the Consensus. *Global Responsibility to Protect* 3: 1–13.

Singh, Randhir. 2006. *Crisis of Socialism: Notes in Defence of a Commitment*. Delhi: Ajanta Books International.

Slobidian, Quinn. 2018. *Globalists: The End of Empire and the Birth of Neoliberalism*. Harvard University Press.

Snyder, Timothy. 2015. The Next Genocide. *New York Times*, September 12, 2015. http://www.nytimes.com/2015/09/13/opinion/sunday/the-next-genocide.html?_r=0.

Stewart, Patrick. 2011. Libya and the Future of Humanitarian Intervention. *Foreign Affairs* 88 (4). https://www.foreignaffairs.org/articles/libya/2011-08-26/libya-and-future-humanitarian-intervention. Accessed 16 Sept 2015.

Stiglitz, Joseph. 2002. *Globalization and its Discontents*. New York: W.W. Norton.

Taussig, Michael. 1984. Culture of Terror-Space of Death: Roger Casements's Putumayo Report and the Explanation of Torture. *Comparative Studies in Society and History* 26 (3): 467–497.

Thakur, Ramesh. 2015. The Development and Evolution of R2P as International Policy. *Global Policy* 1–11.https://doi.org/10.1111/1758-5899.12258.

Thakur, Ramesh. 2020. *Reviewing the Responsibility to Protect: Origins*. Implementation and Controversies: Routledge.

Watts, Michael, and Ed. Kashi. 2008. *Curse of the Black Gold: 50 Years of Oil in the Niger Delta*. New York: PowerHouse Books.

Weiss, Thomas G. 2001. Researching Humanitarian Intervention: Some Lessons. *Journal of Peace Research* 38 (4): 419–428.

Weiss, Thomas G., and Monica Serrano, eds. 2014. *The International Politics of Human Rights. Rallying to the R2P Cause?* New York: Routledge.

World Bank. 2011. *World Development Report: Conflict, Security, and Development*. Washington DC: World Bank Publications.

Young, Iris Marion. 2011. *Responsibility for Justice*. New York: Oxford University Press.

References

Africa Research Bulletin: Political, Social and Cultural Series. 2012. Libya-NATO Killings Report. 49 (5): 19290B.

African Union. 2000. *Constitutive Act of the African Union*. Lome, Togo.

African Union. 2004. *Solemn Declaration on a Common African Defence and Security Policy*.

Commonwealth Secretariat. 1990. *Common Index and Glossary to the Brandt, Palme and Brundtland Reports of the Independent Commissions on International Development, Disarmament and Security, and Environment and Development*. London: Commonwealth Secretariat.

European Council. 2008. *Report on the Implementation of the European Security Strategy- Providing Security in a Changing World*. Brussels. S407/08. December 11, 2008.

Fontana, Allesandro, and Mauro Bertani. 2003. Situating the Lectures. In *Society Must Be Defended: Lectures at the College de France, 1975–76*, ed. Michel Foucault. New York: Picador.

Foucault, Michel. 1991. Governmentality. In *Foucault Effect*, ed. Graham Burchell, Colin Gordon, and Peter Miller. Chicago: University of Chicago Press.

Hehir, A. 2019. R2P and the Limits of Norms. In *Hollow Norms and the Responsibility to Protect*, 57–85. Cham: Palgrave Macmillan.

Kennedy, David. 2013. Law and the Political Economy of the World. *Leiden Journal of International Law* 26: 7–48.

Krause, Keith, and Michael C. Williams, eds. 1997. *Critical Security Studies: Concepts and Cases*. Minneapolis, MN: University of Minnesota Press.

R. Kashyap, *The Political Economy of Security/Development in the Neoliberal Age*, International Political Economy Series, https://doi.org/10.1007/978-3-031-37279-7

Lemke, Thomas. 2011. *Biopolitics: An Advanced Introduction*. New York: New York University Press.

Marx, Karl 1919. *Manifesto of the Communist Party*. Vancouver: Whitehead Estate.

Polger, John. 2008. Foucault's Dispositif and the City. *Planning Theory* 7 (1): 51–70.

Price, Richard, and Christian Reus-Smit. 1998. Dangerous Liaisons? Critical International Theory and Constructivism. *European Journal of International Relations* 4 (3): 259–294.

Price, Richard. 1995. A Genealogy of the Chemical Weapons Taboo. *International Organization* 49 (1): 73–103.

Rabinow, Paul, and Nikolas Rose. 2003. Foucault Today. In *The Essential Foucault: Selections from the Essential Works of Foucault 1954–1984*, ed. Paul Rabinow and Nikolas Rose. New York: New Press.

Rashid, Ahmed. 2015. Foreword. In *The Islamic State*, ed. Charles R. Lister. Washington: Brookings Institution Press.

Simons, Jon. 2013. Power Resistance and Freedom. In *A Companion to Foucault*, ed. Christophe Falzon, Timothy O'Leary, and Jana Sawaicki. Blackwell: West Sussex.

Thakur, Ramesh, and William. 2015. Introduction: Theorising the Responsibility to Protect. In *Theorising the Responsibility to Protect*, ed. Ramesh Thakur and William Maley. Cambridge: Cambridge University Press.

United Nations General Assembly. 1974. *Declaration on the Establishment of a New International Economic Order (NIEO)*. UN Doc. A/RES/S-6/3201. 1 May 1974.

United Nations General Assembly. 2011. *Human Rights Council. Report of the Human Rights Council on Its Fifteenth Special Session*. UN. Doc. A/HRC/S-15/1. 25 February 2011.

United Nations General Assembly. 2011. *Human Rights Council. The Current Human Rights Situation in the Syrian Arab Republic in the Context of Recent Events*. UN Doc. A/HRC/RES/S-16/1. 4 May 2011.

United Nations General Assembly. 2011. *Human Rights Council. The Human Rights Situation in the Syrian Arab Republic*. UN Doc. A/HRC/RES/S-18/1. 5 December 2011.

United Nations General Assembly. 2011. *Security Council. Letter Dated 9 November 2011d from the Permanent Representative of Brazil to the United Nations Addressed to the Secretary-General - Responsibility While Protecting: Elements for the Development and Promotion of a Concept*. UN Doc. A/66/551-S/2011d/701. 11 November 2011. (RwP Concept Note).

United Nations General Assembly. 2012. *Human Rights Council. The Deteriorating Situation of Human Rights in the Syrian Arab Republic, and the Recent Killings in El-Houleh*. UN Doc. A/HRC/RES/S-19/1. 4 June 2012.

United Nations General Assembly. 2013. *Human Rights Council. Good Practices in National Criminalization, Investigation, Prosecution and Sentencing for Offences of Torture.* UN Doc. A/HRC/52/30. 13 March 2023.

United Nations General Assembly. 2013. *Human Rights Council. Report of the Special Rapporteur on Torture and Other Cruel, Inhuman or Degrading Treatment or Punishment, Juan E. Méndez.* UN Doc. A/HRC/22/53. 1 February 2013b.

United Nations General Assembly. 2013. *Human Rights Council. Report of the Human Rights Council on its Twenty Third Session.* UN Doc. A/HRC/23/2. 27 August 2013.

United Nations General Assembly. 2021. *The Responsibility to Protect and the Prevention of Genocide, War Crimes, Ethnic Cleansing and Crimes Against Humanity.* UN Doc. A/RES/75/277. 18 May 2021.

United Nations Secretary-General. 1998. *The Causes of Conflict and the Promotion of Durable Peace and Sustainable Development in Africa.* Report of the Secretary-General. UN Doc. A/52/871-S/1998/318. 13 April 1998.

United Nations Secretary-General. 2005. *In Larger Freedom: Towards Development, Security and Human Rights for All.* Report, of the Secretary-General. UN Doc. A/59/2005. 26 May 2005.

United Nations Secretary-General. 2019. *Implementing the Responsibility to Protect: Accountability for Protection.* Report of the Secretary-General. UN Doc. A/71/1016-S/2017/556. 10 August 2017.

United Nations Secretary-General. 2019. *Responsibility to Protect: Lessons Learned for Prevention.* Report of the Secretary-General. UN Doc. A/73/898-S/2019b/463. 10 June 2019.

United Nations Security Council. 2004. UN Doc. S/RES/1547. 11 June 2004.

United Nations. 2005. Addendum 2, Peacebuilding Commission: Explanatory note by the Secretary-General, Background. *In Larger Freedom: Towards Development, Security and Human Rights for All, Report of the Secretary-General,* New York: United Nations. Available at http://www.un.org/larger freedom/add2.htm. Accessed 23 May, 2006.

United Nations. *Charter of the United Nations.* Available at http://www.un.org/en/documents/charter/.

Wendt, Alexander. 1992. Anarchy Is What States Make of It: The Social Construction of Power Politics. *International Organization* 46 (2): 391–425.

World Bank. 1980. *World Development Report.* New York: Oxford University Press.

Index

R. Kashyap, *The Political Economy of Security/Development in the Neoliberal Age*, International Political Economy Series,
https://doi.org/10.1007/978-3-031-37279-7

C

D